KT-213-172

Management Accounting for Financial Decisions

B *contemporary*
H **BUSINESS SERIES**

Series Editor: Professor Andrew Lock
Manchester Polytechnic

The Contemporary Business Series is designed with the needs of business studies undergraduates and MBA students in mind, and each title is written in a straightforward, student friendly style. Though all of the books in the series reflect the individuality of their authors, you will find that you can count on certain key features in each text which maintain high standards of structure and approach:

● excellent coverage of core and option subject
● UK/international examples or case studies throughout
● full references and further reading suggestions
● written in direct, easily accessible style, for ease of use by full, part-time and self-study students

Books in the series include:

Accounting for Business
Peter Atrill, David Harvey and Edward McLaney

Management Accounting for Financial Decisions
Keith Ward, Sri Srikanthan and Richard Neal

Quantitative Approaches to Management
Robert Ball

Management Accounting for Financial Decisions

Keith Ward, Sri Srikanthan and Richard Neal

BUTTERWORTH HEINEMANN

Butterworth-Heinemann Ltd
Linacre House, Jordan Hill, Oxford OX2 8DP

PART OF REED INTERNATIONAL BOOKS

OXFORD   LONDON   BOSTON
MUNICH   NEW DELHI   SINGAPORE   SYDNEY
TOKYO   WELLINGTON

First published 1991
Reprinted 1993

© Keith Ward, Sri Srikanthan and Richard Neal 1991

All rights reserved. No part of this publication
may be reproduced in any material form (including
photocopying or storing in any medium by electronic
means and whether or not transiently or incidentally
to some other use of this publication) without the
written permission of the copyright holder except in
accordance with the provisions of the Copyright,
Designs and Patents Act 1988 or under the term of a
licence issued by the Copyright Licensing Agency Ltd,
90 Tottenham Court Road, London, England W1P 9HE.
Applications for the copyright holder's written permission
to reproduce any part of this publication should be addressed
to the publishers

British Library Cataloguing in Publication Data
Ward, Keith
  Management accounting for financial decisions.
  I. Title   II. Srikanthan, Sri   III. Neal, Richard
  658.15

ISBN 0 7506 0067 5

Typeset by Key Graphics, Aldermaston, Berkshire
Printed in Great Britain by M & A Thomson Litho Ltd, East Kilbride, Scotland.

Contents

Preface

Our main aim in writing this book was to try to present a more readable and practically-based approach to management accounting than we had found currently available in the market. Many traditional texts seem, to us at least, to be intimidating but, more importantly, they explain most of the accounting techniques without placing them within the context of the role of managers.

Thus, this book concentrates on the decision-making function of managers and the important supporting role fulfilled by management accounting systems. In this way we have attempted to achieve a good balance between the purpose and principles of accounting and the techniques used in practice. The importance of good accounting systems to support the wide range of management decisions is stressed throughout the book and the needs of the different types of decisions are considered. Therefore, both short-term targets and strategic goals are dealt with as part of the comprehensive review of the relevant management accounting techniques.

The book contains many illustrative examples and real-life case studies, which are designed to enable readers to gain a good practical appreciation of the ways in which management accounting can contribute significantly to the achievement of the overall objectives of all organizations. At the same time, this book also challenges the performance of management accounting in many businesses today by critically analysing traditional management accounting techniques. More relevant approaches which can add more value in current competitive markets are considered throughout the book but, in particular, the last chapter deals with suggestions for improving the effectiveness of the contribution made by management accounting.

The content and style of this book should make it appropriate for second and third year undergraduates studying business studies, as well as for the core courses in management accounting on an MBA programme. No previous knowledge of the subject has been assumed, and a review of financial accounting has also been included in order to link together the various financial techniques as well as to highlight the differences.

We have tried to produce a readable and interesting text which reflects our own interest in, and enthusiasm for, the subject and encompasses the issues raised by students when we have taught management accounting courses. Only you, the reader, can judge whether we have succeeded.

We would like to express our thanks to the secretarial support who produced the manuscript; namely Sheila Hart, Marjorie Dawe, Dawn Richardson and Chris Williams but most significantly Doris Muncaster, who typed most of the final manuscript single-handedly. We should also mention the support given to us by our close family and friends; in particular Angela, Samantha and Robert Ward, Sita, Sanjayan and Kesavan Srikanthan, and Carol and Peter Neal.

Part One

Introduction and Overview

1
Introduction and overview

A major role of managers is the 'taking of decisions'. Indeed it can be argued that it is primarily this discretionary ability to take decisions which distinguishes managers from other employees in an organization. It also separates different levels of management: more senior managers having the authority to make more important decisions. In most organizations, some decisions are regarded as so important that no single manager can take them alone; these are taken by a committee of senior managers acting as a whole. Under the Companies Acts, some such critical decisions in limited companies are taken by the board of directors or are required to be referred to the shareholders (the owners of the company) at a general meeting to which all shareholders must be invited.

Defining the subject

If decision-making is such an integral part of management, it is logical that management accounting which is, after all, concerned with accounting for management should concentrate on 'accounting for management decisions'. However, accounting is principally restricted to financial issues. As such, it can be regarded as the common business language, enabling apparently completely different resources (such as people, machines, energy and buildings) to be meaningfully compared and contrasted by subscribing to each a financial value. Therefore it is sensible when considering the involvement of accounting to focus our attention on decisions which have a financial dimension; but as will become apparent through this book this really does include a vast range of management decisions.

Thus management accounting for financial decisions is, as is implied by the title, the major emphasis of the book. This somewhat over-simplistic definition of management accounting requires clarification as it can be the subject of several possible interpretations.

Management accounting for financial decisions could refer only to the recording of the financial results of managers' decisions after the decisions have been taken and indeed been implemented; i.e. a historical score-keeping role. Alternatively, it could mean the function of trying to monitor the financial outcome of decisions as they are implemented and thereby to affect the ultimate result by making changes (i.e. subsequent decisions) so as to exercise some degree of control over future events. Unfortunately no-one can exercise control over the past and thus the historic role of accounting is limited to that of explaining what happened and, as far as possible, why!

A third potential interpretation is for a role of providing background financial analysis of the context in which the decision is to be taken (once again a historically based role). Such an analysis enables decision-makers to be better informed prior to taking any decision, and should consequently improve the quality of their decisions.

A more positive development of this role is to use this historical analysis, plus other relevant inputs, to predict the likely financial outcomes of forthcoming decisions. This would highlight the more financially attractive, or less risky, alternative options available to the decision-makers. In this way management accountants are placed, not only very clearly as part of the management team taking the decision, but also in a role with a future time focus through the need to forecast potential decision outcomes prior to their implementation.

It is also possible to expand this third interpretation further so as to include financial analysis of the external business environment as well as the internal resources of the organization. There would be almost universal agreement that the inclusion of some level of external analysis is essential to provide any meaningful assistance to decision-makers, but modern management accounting takes this external review and comparison further. The effectiveness of management's financial decisions can only be properly explained historically against a comparison of the financial results for similar organizations (e.g. competitors) facing a similar external environment. What appears to be a good financial performance in an absolute sense may seem completely different when placed in the appropriate relative context. For example, if a division of a large group increases its profits by 50 per cent over the previous year, this seems at first sight an excellent performance, but it is much less outstanding if the rest of the industry all improved by at least 100 per cent in the same time period.

In the same way, this actual performance must be placed in the context of what was expected, and this expectation (forecast, prediction, budget or financial plan) has to be established against the anticipated external business environment. It is possible to go still further and to try to take into account probable competitor actions and reactions, either to business initiatives started by the organization or in response to significant changes in the business environment, which will affect both organizations but not necessarily equally. This high level of involvement in accounting for external factors and influences is one area of what has become

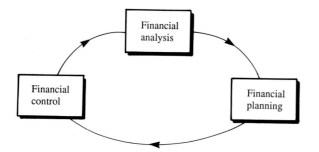

Figure 1.1

known as strategic management accounting, because this area of accounting acknowledges and concentrates on the important influence that external factors have in determining the appropriate business strategies for the organization. This is considered in more detail in Chapter 10 which deals with strategic decision-making.

Not surprisingly, as all these possible interpretations refer to important aspects of managerial decision-making, management accounting is involved in every potential interpretation. In fact these apparently different roles are closely integrated and, as illustrated in Figure 1.1, indicate that management accounting is a continuous process of analysis, planning and control.

The integrated nature of management accounting

Analysis

It is very difficult to take even the very simplest financial decision without some degree of financial analysis. An example of a very simple financial decision illustrates this point: should an organization place its surplus funds on deposit at a bank so as to earn an annual rate of interest of 10 per cent? First, the organization needs financial information to determine what level of surplus funds, if any, it has and what is the time-scale before these funds will be needed by the organization. Second, it needs information as to the attractiveness of the 10 per cent rate of interest being offered by a particular bank relative to alternative forms of investment available. This clearly involves obtaining financial information on the external environment. Third, there should be some analysis of the risk involved in depositing funds at this bank; perhaps it is offering a high rate of interest because it desperately needs to attract funds to avoid impending bankruptcy.

In fact the required financial analysis can be made even more comprehensive, but this very straightforward decision highlights several important aspects of financial analysis. The decision process inevitably means choosing among alternatives; if there are no alternatives there is no need to take a decision and consequently no need to do exhaustive financial analysis! A first priority in any financial decision must be to ensure that all the relevant alternatives are being considered. This can often prove almost impossible but, even if achieved, it can be very difficult to make all the comparisons of these alternatives as meaningful as is practical. Practicality must be taken into consideration as the cost of carrying out the comparisons can become considerable, and the cost can easily outweigh the financial benefit of finding and implementing the best alternative. Thus, cost/benefit analysis is important to ensure that the limited analytical resources available in the management accounting area are focused on those potential decisions where they can make the greatest contribution. It may be possible, after a lot of investigation, to obtain a marginally better rate of return on our surplus funds which were available for investment. If our earlier decision was where to invest £2,000 over the weekend, a difference in interest rate of 0.1 per cent p.a. will make no material impact on the total return and is not worth wasting analytical resources on achieving; in fact the benefit of the higher rate is 1p. However, if the same decision was being taken on behalf of a large cash-rich multinational which had £2 billion available to invest for 1 year, then the same interest rate difference of 0.1 per cent p.a. would have an impact of £2 million on the total interest received over the year; consequently it might be worth expending a considerable amount of effort by the group's treasury management to obtain the best possible interest rate. Thus, even given the same external factors, the internal impact can differ considerably and each decision must be properly evaluated using the specifically relevant costs and benefits, instead of making broad sweeping generalizations such as, 'that's too small to worry about!'

The practical aspects involved in this cost/benefit analysis will be discussed in more detail in Part Four where the design and operation of cost effective financial management information systems are considered, and many of the practical techniques used in the financial analysis process are presented and illustrated in Part Two, and Chapters 6 and 7 of Part Three.

It should by now be clear that good historic financial analysis is essential to establish the starting point for the decisions required and that this involves far more than simply keeping an overall score-card for the business. Most financial decisions only significantly affect specific parts of the organization and even these parts may be affected in different ways and to different extents. Consequently, good financial analysis looks at the relevant parts of the organization and breaks the business into appropriate sub-groups which can help to focus the attention of the decision-maker. These sub-groups may be divisions, departments, products or groups of customers, etc., and different groupings will be relevant to different decisions. In order to carry out the analysis in this segmented way the financial information must be accessible in a suitable format.

Not only is segmented financial analysis necessary but the role of financial analysis is clearly far broader than that of the financial score-keeper or 'bean counter', which is still frequently the description applied to the internal role of the financial manager. Indeed, it is also important that financial analysis is not regarded as the exclusive province of the accountants, as much of the base information needed will not be readily available to them but will be well known to other managers in the organization. Also, accountants may not be aware of all the possible alternatives which are available to the business, nor of all the implications arising from some of these alternatives. This is particularly true where the financial decision is based on or involves technical relationships which is often the case in operations areas of the business, with research and development problems, or in marketing decisions where many external interrelationships may be involved. The importance of the role of financial analysis in these cases is to convert these complex and differently based issues into the common business language of accounting, using financial values as the basis of translation.

Thus this role cannot be done by management accountants alone and it also highlights that financial analysis is not, of itself, a decision-making function. Its role is to establish the starting point and to provide information to aid the actual decision-maker, and this is discussed in detail in Part Two of the book and illustrated in Figure 1.2.

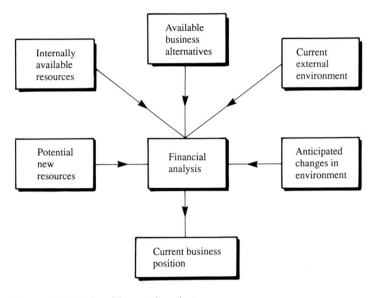

Figure 1.2 *Role of financial analysis*

In too many organizations, this process is not sufficiently clearly understood and financial managers seem to act in the role of absolute decision-maker across most functional areas of the organization whenever a decision has financial implications. This is particularly the case when a decision has cross-functional impact, and the supporting argument put forward is that only they, as financial managers, fully understand the 'common business language'. If these financial managers enjoy the power base that has been established for them there is little personal incentive for them to teach their colleagues in these other functions how to speak this 'common business language', or more especially to explain that the real role of financial analysis, and hence management accounting, is being abused.

However, in most cases, their notable lack of expertise in these other areas of the business normally forces a change; hopefully before the business collapses financially.

Financial planning

Even good financial analysis on its own often adds little value to the business, because the analysis has to be put into the context of the business' objectives if it is to focus correctly the decision-maker's attention. These business objectives show 'where the organization is trying to go, whereas a principal function of financial analysis is to show 'where it is at present'. Obviously decisions should be made to fill 'the gaps' between the present and the desired future positions, as is shown in Figure 1.3, and management accounting has an important role in providing relevant financial information to support these important planning decisions.

Figure 1.3 *Role of financial planning*

This financial planning role is vital but it is an area of management accounting which is not as well developed in many businesses as it could be. Most organizations are now relatively efficient at providing historical financial information, at least for the organization as a whole, but many are not very good at translating this historical financial analysis into meaningful financial plans, which actually assist the business in achieving its objectives.

Financial planning involves developing specific action plans which are designed to achieve the objectives and goals of the business. This presumes that the organization has a well defined set of goals and objectives but, if it does not, the first stage of the strategic planning process has to be to develop them as it is meaningless to plan in a vacuum. It is like trying to plan a journey without knowing the destination: which direction do you take and what mode of transport is appropriate, etc?

This definition of financial planning, which is explored in detail in Part Three, also immediately distinguishes planning from any form of 'wish list' because there must be a structured series of steps which *should*, if successfully implemented, lead to the achievement of the business targets. These targets should also, as far as possible, be measurable, and this implies quantifiable, because otherwise it is very difficult to establish whether they have, in fact, been achieved or not. Thus vague 'motherhood' goals such as 'getting better' or even 'being the best' should be turned into more specific objectives such as 'improving the return on investment to 20 per cent' or 'having the highest return on investment in the industry'.

Clearly this type of financial planning must be based on an understanding of where the business is and what alternatives are available, both in terms of options and resources. Returning to our journey planning question, it is even harder to plan a journey somewhere if you do not know where you are starting from! Hence good financial analysis is a prerequisite, and good in this instance not only means accurate but also up to date and relevant. If this is not true, even the most detailed plans can be rendered useless because they are based on out-of-date and now false assumptions, and this can most easily be made the case by changes in the external business environment.

Even when the financial analysis is the most comprehensive and up-to-date possible, financial planning still involves predicting the outcome of decisions and events in the future. The only 100 per cent certainty is that some of these predictions will be wrong and therefore the financial plans will not be achieved in their entirety. Obviously the type of decisions involved and the degree of volatility in the external environment together with the timescale of the plans will have a great impact on the ability to plan accurately, but all financial plans will contain errors.

If this is unfailingly true, is it still worthwhile investing the time, effort and cost in the financial planning process, particularly in view of the earlier discussion regarding the essential use of cost/benefit analysis? The answer is a resounding yes, because if the process is done well it yields immense benefits to the organization even if the planned results are not fully achieved.

First, the financial planning process shows what the predicted outcomes are of any proposed series of actions and this immediately gives the organization the opportunity to decide if these are acceptable or not. Normally, the range of alternative options is financially evaluated and the choice among these options is often made much clearer once their likely outcomes have been established. Also a good financial planning process will highlight the critical assumptions made in the plan for each major option. The critical assumptions are those that have the greatest financial impact on the outcome for any expected level of change and, as is illustrated in Chapter 9, this is calculated using sensitivity analysis.

However, an even greater benefit is gained if the financial plan can be modified as it unfolds over time and the errors in the assumptions and predictions are revealed and corrected. The actual outcomes of planned decisions will be seen and they may be so significantly different to those originally forecast that the original objectives will not be achieved without a change to the plan. Alternatively, the outcome of the plan may be dramatically affected by a false assumption about the external business environment, and if the actual environment had been forecast in the first place a different financial plan would have been implemented.

These events require new decisions to be taken during the life of the plan and no financial plan should ever be regarded as an immutable tablet of stone which must be adhered to no matter how irrelevant it has become. A financial plan should represent the best efforts of the organization at the time at which it was prepared and given the knowledge possessed at that time. As times change and more relevant knowledge is obtained, the plan must be amended if the best possible results are

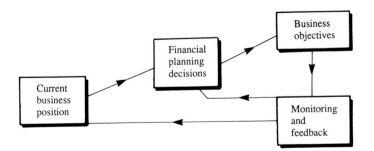

Figure 1.4   *Including feedback in financial planning*

to be achieved. Thus financial planning is a self-updating process and is made much more effective by an appropriate monitoring and feedback process, as is demonstrated in Figure 1.4. This enables future planning decisions to be based on inputs which are the results of previous planning actions, and these new decisions may lead to dramatic changes from the original plan if circumstances should so require.

Financial control

The financial control system, which is needed to implement this updating process, has to monitor the achievement, or lack thereof, of pre-set objectives and highlight where problems and opportunities occur. In some cases the divergence may have been predicted in the original plan as one potential result so that a contingency plan should have been developed, and the control system could simply trigger the implementation of the appropriate contingency plan. In most cases however, the actual specific situation will not have been predicted but the feedback system gives the organization a chance to respond rapidly to events and situations, which were not considered at the time of preparing the original plan. As discussed in Parts Four and Five the developments in computer technology have opened up massive opportunities to improve the financial planning and control systems and greatly to enhance their contributions to business performance.

However, it is important that the primary role of such a financial control system is clearly understood, because in many businesses financial control is seen as apportioning blame to managers who have underperformed or overspent. Financial control becomes much more positive when it is used as a learning process for the business and more particularly the decision-makers and financial planners. It should enhance the ability to plan and make decisions in the future, as well as minimizing the damage caused by the inevitably wrong assumptions and predictions made in the original financial plans.

Thus management accounting is a continuous process of analysis, planning and control because good financial control demands new decisions as the plan is updated and new decisions require more financial analysis to support them. This can be shown diagrammatically, as in Figure 1.5. Clearly the distinctions become blurred as management accounting becomes more integrated into the decision-making process of the organization, but the whole process can and should be regarded as a decision support system. This description has important implications for the design and implementation of effective management accounting systems.

Providing information not data

Managers who take decisions require information not data. This distinction is far more then semantics, because many management accounting systems still provide a lot of data but very little really usable information.

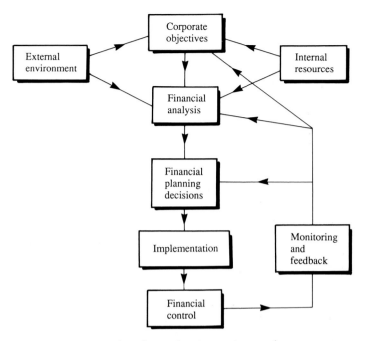

Figure 1.5 *Financial analysis, planning and control process*

Data can be defined as facts, or things assumed to be facts, which can be made the basis of reasoning or calculation. This is particularly true for, and is in no way a criticism of, the ideal system where, as far as possible, the data-base is supplied automatically by the necessary processing of the individual financial transaction. Such a design dramatically reduces the collection costs caused by duplication and significantly improves the integrity of the data automatically collected by removing transcription errors, etc. However, so far the system has provided no information which can be used to support managers' decisions, because the automatic collection process is carried out, of necessity, at the lowest possible level of data aggregation (i.e. the individual transaction).

Thus in the sales area of the organization, sales data are normally captured into a data-base from the individual sales invoices and possibly the sales orders as well. If a manager is interested in sales information on particular products or by specific customer categories, providing a list of all the sales invoices for the relevant period is not very helpful. The data-base must, at the very minimum, tabulate and summarize the raw data so that they become more readable and intelligible.

However, information is more than summarized data as it can be defined as 'the communication of instructive knowledge'. Information is data processed so as to add usable knowledge and it is the usable knowledge which is of real value to decision-makers. Unfortunately, the transformation of data into real information is still a largely unfulfilled role for management accounting because most financial information systems stop at the intermediate stage of readable, summarized tabulated data.

At least the communication of this level of financial information enables the decision-maker to continue the processing and turn the financial input into really valuable decision support material. A major problem here is that many management accounting systems produce reports and other forms of financial output in formats which are designed by accountants for accountants. If the communication process is to be productive and management accounting is to function properly as a decision support system, the financial information must be presented to the decision-makers in a form which they can understand. A large sheet of paper showing forecast sales levels, actual sales levels and the differences between them for separate product groups for this month, the year to date, and this month last year as well as by sales areas, may contain a mass of useful information which could help sales and marketing managers to improve the allocation of their field sales force personnel etc., but it is most unlikely that it will.

There are massive opportunities provided by computer technology to produce financial reports in a multitude of easy-to-read formats, such as graphs, histograms, pie-charts, and without a lot of arduous reprocessing of the base data. Given today's technology decision-makers can, and should, have individually tailored financial reports if it assists in their decision- making process. This area of providing properly designed financial information is considered in detail in Part Four.

Although managers require information to aid the decision-making process, they also require relevant information if they are not to be buried under a deluge of paper, or electronic messages. If all the processed financial data are transmitted to all managers, theoretically the managers who need to know will know because everyone has been told everything. In practice either no-one will have time to make any decisions or they will ignore all the financial inputs and make the decisions on some other basis. Too much information can be worse than too little, as with too much the managers may not make any decision if they are desperately trying to assimilate all the available information. At least with too little the manager has the opportunity properly to consider what little information is available and to exercise judgement when taking the decision.

Obviously the objective is to provide the right level of relevant information, so that managers do not waste time considering a lot of irrelevant material, to the right managers (i.e. the decision-makers) in time for it to be helpful in making the decision (i.e. at the right time). Although somewhat trite, this concept of 'the right information to the right manager at the right time' is crucial to the design of management accounting systems, as is shown in Chapter 11.

An important element in deciding what is the right level of information, what is the right time, and even who is the right manager is the particular type of decision which the organization is facing.

Types of decision

There are a number of factors which are common to nearly all financial decisions, but there are also several very different types of decision for which different financial techniques are appropriate.

As already stated, all decisions require the exercise of choice among alternatives, although for financial decisions the alternatives may not be that obvious, and the best decision is normally the choice which has the highest overall benefit relative to its cost (another application of the cost/benefit concept). If the decision was how to spend a free Saturday afternoon then the list of possible alternatives would be relatively easy to draw up depending on the person's leisure interests or pile of unfinished domestic jobs. The characteristics of the possible alternatives could be defined as occupying an afternoon's time but this may be their only common factor as they could include a round of golf, going to a football match, seeing a film at the local cinema, visiting friends, going to a museum or art gallery, etc. With financial decisions it is not surprising that the only common characteristic tends to be money!

A business may have a wide range of alternative investment projects, ranging through expansion of existing businesses to completely new ventures, but it probably does not have an unlimited supply of funds to enable it to finance all these potential projects. The principal role of the financial decision is to select the most attractive projects and effectively to rank in order of priority all the possible ways of spending money so that if more funds become available, the business would know which project it would do next – unless circumstances, and hence the ranking of the alternatives, change. Decision-making, and hence management accounting, is a dynamic process.

For any commercial organization there is always an alternative use for money; at the very least, surplus funds can be placed on deposit, as discussed earlier, and earn interest. Therefore there is a cost associated with not taking up this alternative opportunity. More accurately speaking, it is a foregone opportunity rather than a cost, and it is therefore known as the opportunity cost. This concept is explained in more detail in Chapters 3 and 6, but it highlights that in financial decisions there is definitely 'no such thing as a free lunch'.

Financial decision-making is concerned with the allocation of scarce resources, one of which is normally funding, and the use of accounting attempts to reduce the complex set of other resources used and the potential benefits created to the common language of money. However, in many decisions some of the results will be conflicting and the decision-maker has to make a choice after considering the conflict. For example an automation process in a factory may reduce processing costs but it may mean that some workers will have to be made redundant. The decision has to balance the efficiency gain against the cost and impact of a redundancy programme. This reinforces the need for a set of business objectives against which these conflicting results can be weighed.

Many other examples of these conflicts in the results from financial decisions are given throughout the book and they are particularly common in the marketing area of the business and in cross-functional decisions, particularly between marketing and operations or manufacturing. It may be more efficient and cheaper to produce a limited range of products, and this may also enable greater automation to be introduced, with further cost savings. However, there may be a strong marketing argument that such a restricted range may reduce total potential sales and require lower selling prices per unit than would be possible with greater variety.

This conflict also regularly surfaces whenever the subject of quality is raised in the business – can the extra cost incurred be recovered in additional selling prices or greater sales volumes (e.g. through higher levels of repeat purchases from satisfied, loyal customers)? Thus it is clear that such financial decisions, which cross over more than one functional area, are normally more complicated in their required analysis than decisions which are concentrated in one discipline. However, the greatest complications tend to be caused by the significantly heightened behavioural problems created by the crossing of functional boundaries. Managers can often look at decisions from their own vested interests and, if there are conflicts among these, it is essential that their managerial performance evaluations push them towards the decision which is in the interests of the business and the achievement of its overall objectives. As previously stated people, i.e. managers, take decisions, not organizations; and thus the behavioural problems of financial decision-making cannot be ignored.

Another clear differentiation in financial decisions can be drawn in terms of value (high value and low value) and this is often used by businesses as their most important method of classifying decisions. Any decision involving over (say) £100,000 is classified as a high value issue and hence is important! As a consequence the financial analysis and subsequent monitoring to which the decision is subjected is greatly enhanced. This concentration purely on value can be a great mistake.

First it is obvious that 'high' value is a relative measure; the large conglomerate would set a different level to the small local shop retailer. More importantly the risk associated with a 'high value' decision may be very small and the range of potential outcomes limited and easily predictable, whereas a smaller value investment decision may have a far greater range of results. Therefore the risk associated with a decision may be a more logical basis on which to dedicate analytical resources.

Financial decisions also differ considerably in their time-scale from a short-term opportunity to build up stock levels prior to the seasonally expected sales increase to a decision to increase substantially the main production capacity of the business or to build a nuclear power station or even a tunnel under the English Channel. Normally as the time-scale involved becomes longer so the degree of uncertainty involved increases as forecasting the future benefits expected to accrue from the investment with any degree of accuracy becomes more difficult. These long-term benefits are also worth less in real terms even if they are eventually received because the business has had to wait for them. If the cash had been received sooner, it could, at the very least, have been earning interest on deposit and this foregone opportunity cost must be included in the financial evaluation. With very short-term decisions this time-value of money is not so important but for long-term decisions it is vital and hence different evaluation techniques are required for different time-scales. Chapters 6 and 7 consider these techniques in detail.

A further important way of differentiating decisions is to separate regular routine decisions from the one-off unique decisions that all businesses face from time to time. The regular decisions, such as reviewing selling prices and negotiating wage increases, are clearly important but the advantage is that because they can be predicted in advance, the organization can develop an information analysis system to provide the decision-maker with a high level of relevant financial decision support. In the case of a surprise problem or opportunity, the business will not normally have the time to set up such a sophisticated system and, in any case, the required base data may not exist or may not be stored in a suitable format. What is worrying is that this type of one-off decision may be needed as a consequence of a fundamental but unexpected change in the external environment or an internal technological breakthrough, etc. If so, the decision may have very far-reaching implications for the strategy of the organization in the future, and it is therefore critical that the best possible decision support is provided and yet the decision may be required instantly or in a very short period of time. The problems involved and some of the ways in which businesses can improve their management accounting systems in this area of strategic decision-making are considered in Chapters 10 and 13.

For many of the regular decisions faced by the business there is a very useful technique for concentrating the attention of the decision-makers on the key areas which they can influence. A lot of the relationships in financial decisions can be depicted by predictable input to output relationships which are physically controlled and do not respond directly to changes in their financial values. It is impossible for decision-makers to exercise control over these unless they fundamentally change the way in which the process is carried out. Consequently the decision-maker should concentrate on either the desired level of input or the required level of outputs and the other variable can be determined by the engineering style relationship – hence this type of cost is called an 'engineering cost'. For example in a car assembly plant, the manager does not normally exercise control over the price of rubber, and hence the price of car tyres. If their price increases substantially, say by 25 per cent, it is not practical for the manager to decide unilaterally to reduce consumption of tyres (by fitting only three to each car, or not including a spare). The required usage is determined by the number of cars to be assembled.

In this area the manager has little discretion and no control over the total costs of the tyres used, and the financial information should reflect this. Criticizing the performance of this manager because the cost of tyres increased would probably be very demotivating. Fortunately companies can avoid this by the use of appropriate control systems, such as the use of standard costing which is explained in Chapter 3 and shown in use in Chapter 12. This useful distinction between discretionary activities, where the manager can exercise control, and the more engineering-type relationships should not be limited to regular decisions and the production environment. It can be very widely applied within the organization. For example, the level of discretion which can be exercised by the sales director of a business with regard to the size of the field sales force is much more limited than it may at first appear. The expenses of the sales force contain a wide range of costs and this may seem to indicate that the sales director can alter any of these items so as to alter the total cost.

A closer examination of this problem, which is made in more detail in Chapter 11, shows that most of these costs are either closely controlled by the external environment (e.g. the industry involved will dictate the salary and commission levels, type of car supplied, etc.) or by the method of operation selected by the company (e.g. car running expenses, accommodation and subsistence, and entertaining will be the result of the physical size of the area covered and the number of customers, frequency of calling, etc.), as is illustrated in Figure 11.5 (p. 259). Therefore managerial discretion can be exercised regarding the number of people employed in the field sales force or in how they are deployed. The rest of the cost structure can be monitored and controlled by a model which reflects the appropriate input to output relationships; as with most financial relationships this engineering model is not static and will need to be kept updated on a regular basis.

Management versus financial accounting

Management accounting has been described already as a continuous process of analysis, planning and control in the context of providing decision support for financial decision-makers. Financial managers in an organization fulfil several other roles and it may be useful to separate management accounting from these other functions and to highlight the differences. The principal sub-divisions are into accounting and financial management. Financial management, or corporate finance as it is increasingly becoming known, is primarily concerned with raiding suitable funds to finance the needs of the organization, and to manage those funds when raised. In other words it is concerned with the appropriate sources of funds to finance the investment decisions evaluated using the management accounting techniques described in this book, as is shown in Figure 1.6. Clearly there needs to be a close interaction between the two roles but a large part of the corporate finance as it is increasingly becoming known, is primarily concerned with raising potential and current providers of funds (e.g. the banks, capital markets, etc.).

Even within the accounting function it is normal to split the roles of management accounting and financial accounting. Financial accounting covers the actual recording of every financial transaction and hence operates in a historical time-frame but it also involves the preparation and publication of the external set of financial statements (discussed in depth in Chapter 2). This set comprises the director's report, profit and loss account, balance sheet and source and application of funds statement, together with the detailed notes thereon and is legally required

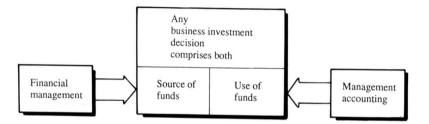

Figure 1.6 *Relationship of management accounting and financial management*

to be produced annually by all limited liability companies. Publicly quoted companies also publish interim results half-way through the year (for USA publicly quoted companies, quarterly figures are required).

As stated, these financial accounts are published externally and in fact have to be filed with the Registrar of Companies, where they are available to anyone who takes the trouble to look at them. Any reports prepared internally to support management decisions can be kept as confidential as the managers see fit and this creates a fundamental difference between financial and management accounting.

The wide availability of published financial statements means that companies will wish to avoid giving away any sensitive information, particularly with respect to future plans. This is critically important as part of the interested 'public' will be competitors, customers and suppliers (as shown in Figure 1.7), all of whom would be keenly interested in knowing what the organization is planning. Therefore externally available sets of financial accounts are focused exclusively on reporting past events, and consequently are restricted to the role of explaining these historic happenings.

The emphasis of management accounts should be almost the reverse as their primary role is to help managers control the future. This desire for control also leads most organizations to produce their management accounts on a relatively frequent basis (normally monthly) and to split up the business into segments which are appropriate to the way in which it is actually controlled. Published financial statements are legally required only annually and are produced for the whole of the legal entity, another indication of their inappropriateness as a control document. Also these externally available documents are subject to an independent objective review by professionals (the auditors) so that external users can place greater reliance on them, but this process increases the time lag between the end of the accounting period and their publication. If the objective is to aid control, any unnecessary delay is unacceptable and management will often agree to including approximations and estimates if it speeds up the production of key financial information.

In fact, because not all financial decisions are made with the same frequency, it is illogical to produce management accounts on a single timetable. Many organizations now prepare some reports on a daily or weekly basis, as appropriate, but only prepare a full set of management reports every three months.

Another significant difference is in the form and style of presentation. Published financial statements are all produced in a standardized manner, because of the legal constraints and the rules laid down by the professional accounting bodies which govern such legally required documents. Due to the keen attentions of competitors and other external parties, the information made available is in summarized form even though it is historically based. Companies are also very concerned to ensure that all interested parties receive the same level of financial information as 'insider trading' may take place if privileged information is given to one group. None of these issues should be relevant to the preparation of restricted access management accounts and every manager can, and should, receive individually tailored financial reports containing the appropriate level of detailed information. Managers should not use this internal information to their personal

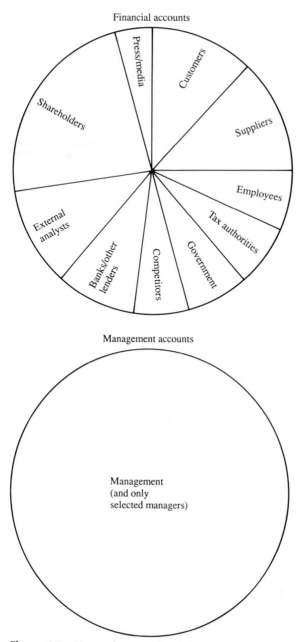

Figure 1.7   *Users of accounting information*

financial advantage as they would to guilty of insider trading, but it is obviously sensible that the departmental manager needs detailed information on individual expense centres, whereas the main board could not cope with such detailed information for the whole business. The design of this segmented and tailored form of management information is considered in Chapter 11.

Management accounts		Financial accounts
Decision support } Provision of management information }	Basic functions	{ Transaction recording { Publication of external financial statements
Confidential	Availability	Publicly available
Present/future	Time focus	Historic
Planning and control	Main emphasis	Explanation
As needed – monthly	Regularity	Annual
Fast but approximate	Speed of preparation	Slow but detailed
Segmented to control units	Form of presentation	Whole of legal entity
Tailored to manager	Style and detail	Standardized summarized

Figure 1.8   *Summary of differences between management and financial accounting*

Future improvements in management accounting

In this introductory chapter, several criticisms have already been made of the way in which management accounting is currently applied in many organizations, and there will be other such examples later in the book. In order to redress this seemingly negative approach, the new opportunities for management accounting to make a greater contribution to the business and the achievement of its objectives will be considered in detail in Chapter 13. Also throughout the book examples of the best practices in management accounting will be given so as to illustrate the positive contributions already being made to the success of many businesses.

Several references have already been made to the tremendous impact which the dramatic advances in information technology (IT) have had on the way in which management accounting is currently put into practice. The ever expanding power and speed of modern computers have enabled financial managers to consider developing much more comprehensive financial information systems than were practical in the past. It should be remembered that the IT revolution has not, of itself, produced new financial decision-making techniques. IT's contribution has been to make the implementation of the best of the existing techniques a practical proposition. Thus much more financial analysis can now be performed in a cost-effective manner and in a time-scale which makes the results of great added value to the relevant decision-makers.

As a consequence, these managers now expect to be provided with valid financial information in support of their forthcoming decisions, no matter how complex the problem or how wide-ranging the number of variables. As mentioned above, satisfying this expectation represents one of the major challenges facing management accounting at present and in the future, and this is discussed in more detail in the final chapter. However, the main objective of this book is to communicate a clear and practical understanding of the management accounting role in and contribution to financial decisions. Within this context, IT represents one mechanism, albeit an important one, for enhancing the contribution made by management accounting.

Therefore, although the impact of IT is considered in detail in the book when considering the design and implementation of financial control systems, the earlier chapters concentrate on the rationale of the relevant techniques. Thus in the illustrative examples and case-studies used throughout the book the numbers have been kept simple so that the underlying logic of the relevant financial decision-support technique is not unduly confused by the added problem of coping with a vast array of alternatives. For example, resource allocation decisions are set in companies apparently producing only three or four products, whereas in reality they may produce hundreds or thousands. The increased volume of options does not change the relevance of the correct analytical technique but makes the manual computation of all the required calculations more time-consuming and less practical. Not surprisingly, there is now a vast range of computer software systems available to help financial managers cope with these processing problems. At one extreme there are very sophisticated computer models which are normally designed to deal with one very specific type of problem in a wide range of companies. Thus, in the case of having to cope with resource allocation decisions with hundreds of products and many different operating constraints, a linear programming computer package would be very beneficial. At the other extreme, there are software packages which really provide the financial manager with building blocks which can be used to process the basic financial data. A good example of this type of package would be spreadsheets because the company can define its own mathematical relationships between two pieces of data and hence develop its own uniquely tailored financial information system. This type of system can be of great value in the area of financial planning, when it is very useful to examine the possible outcome of a wide range of potential situations.

These financial packages enable vast volumes of data to be handled very quickly and the output can also be presented in almost any desired format by using the capabilities of modern graphics and tabular reporting packages. This means that managers do not have to compromise on their individual needs for precise information, presented in their preferred format. The right combination of software packages, customized IT systems and reporting systems should enable decision-makers to be very demanding in the way their required financial decision-support information is now supplied. The technology is already available, but for many companies the reality is still a long way away. As already mentioned, today's management accountants need to be able to satisfy their ever more demanding customers by making the theory come to life.

Summary

Management is concerned with making decisions and a key role for management accounting is acting as a provider of financial information to support these decisions. This can best be done as a continuous, iterative process consisting of three main stages:

- Analysis
- Planning
- Control

Management accounting systems should act as decision support systems providing the right information to the right people at the right time. This involves identifying the type of decision involved because different financial decisions require the application of different financial techniques.

Questions

1 'The role of the management accountant is simply to act as the scorekeeper for the business'. Discuss.
2 Which of the three main areas of management accounting, i.e. analysis, planning and control, is most important and why?
3 'Financial plans are inevitably wrong.' If so, why do businesses invest time, effort and cost in preparing detailed financial plans?
4 How does the concept of opportunity cost link into the statement 'there is no such thing as a free lunch'?
5 What are the key differences which distinguish management accounting from financial accounting and financial management?

Part Two

Analysis

Review of financial statements

Overview

As has been discussed in Chapter 1, the accounting function is split into the roles of management accounting and financial accounting. While the function of management accounting will vary from one organization to another and be dependent on the specific requirements of the organization's decision-makers, financial accounting's function can be more clearly and uniformly defined: it is to record every financial transaction and to prepare and publish, on at least a yearly basis, a set of financial statements which are for external use by shareholders, investors and government authorities. In order to protect the interests of these external parties, certain legal requirements for financial reporting are laid down in the Companies Acts and legal pronouncements. The accountancy profession too has tried to exercise a degree of control over financial reporting, through the design and implementation of fundamental accounting concepts and professionally binding Statements of Standard Accounting Practice.

To make the published financial statements as readable and useful as possible, there are standard methods of presentation of the financial information that these statements contain. These statements must include a profit and loss account, a balance sheet, a statement of source and application of funds, directors' report and auditors' report, as well as detailed notes to explain and expand upon the information presented.

The financial information thus reported should give a 'true and fair' view of the financial performance of the organization during the reporting period, as well as showing its financial position at the end of the period. Using various ratios, the users of the information can analyse performance in an absolute sense, and more importantly, they can make a relative comparison with organizations in the same or other industries, e.g. to compare investments.

Introduction

Throughout this book we argue that much of the information contained in externally used published financial statements and reports is irrelevant to managers in their roles as decision-makers within the organization, because such historical information shows where the business is at present rather than indicating where the organization should be going. However, an understanding of financial accounting and the nature and purpose of financial reporting is nonetheless an essential prerequisite for undertaking the financial analysis role of management accounting. Therefore, before beginning to discuss the specific requirements of management accounting for financial decisions, it is useful to review financial accounting and reporting and the role and content of published financial statements.

Financial accounting and reporting

The function of financial accounting is to record clearly every financial transaction that the business is involved in and then to classify and summarize these facts and figures for presentation in the form of periodic financial reports and statements. These statements are made available for use by a wide range of external users (shareholders, banks and other lenders, government, tax authorities) and it is therefore important that they should give a 'true and fair' representation, both of the business' financial performance during the year and of its financial position at the end of the year. All of this information is of course available for use internally by the managers of the company but, because it is historic and summarized, its usefulness on making decisions about the future is very limited.

The preparers of these financial statements are required to exercise considerable judgement as to exactly what they report and how the data are presented. However, many accounting rules and conventions have been developed to restrict this wide range of possible choices and to limit the selection to a few generally acceptable bases, so that financial statements are comparable among different companies and over time. Some of these rules have been made into legal requirements, but essentially the law, through the Companies Acts, guides companies on the disclosure and publication of financial information, while accounting standards, which are established by the professional accounting bodies, deal with the detailed presentation of that information.

Limited liability companies are legally required to submit a copy of their annual accounts to the Registrar of Companies (Companies Act 1985, s. 241). Section 221 requires that limited liability companies keep accounting records that are sufficient to show and explain the company's transactions and are capable also of disclosing reasonably accurately the financial position of the company at any point in time. The directors of the company are given responsibility for managing the funds supplied by shareholders, bankers and other creditors. Financial accounting systems are partly designed to produce reports to show how effectively the directors are undertaking this responsibility; this is often referred to as financial 'stewardship'. Shareholders are given protection under the Companies Act 1985 and the Company Directors Disqualification Act 1986 against the directors' failure to perform their stewardship role in a reasonable manner. In such circumstances, directors may be liable to pay damages. The rights of creditors are dealt with in the Insolvency Act 1986, and although it is the company which is in contract with the creditors, and therefore liable if it fails to repay amounts owing, directors may still be personally liable for not exercising their duties in the best interests of the company. The set of accounts which have to be produced for external registration must comprise a profit and loss account, a balance sheet, the directors' report and the auditors' report and, where appropriate, group accounts (s. 239).

Each of these documents discloses different information on the company and is considered in detail later in this chapter. However, before considering how these financial statements are prepared, it is important to understand how this set of accounts fit together. The profit and loss account shows the trading activity of the business during the period (i.e. for legally required financial statements, the period is a year) and consequently reflects the level of sales made by the company. In order to determine whether the company made a profit on these sales, it is necessary to deduct the expenses incurred in achieving this level of sales. Consequently, profit for the period is defined as sales revenue less expenses.

These sales and expenses are included in the profit and loss account based on the physical activity having taken place, rather than money having been paid to or from the company. However, these flows of money (or funds as they are now normally described) are obviously also critical to understanding the financial position of the business. Therefore, although not legally required under the Companies Acts, it is an accounting standard requirement that companies produce a source and application of funds statement for the same accounting period. This shows where the money came from (i.e. the sources) and how it was used by the company (i.e. the applications); so that readers of the financial statements can assess whether adequate funds are available for the company's needs and how effectively these funds are being deployed.

There are fundamental differences between the bases of preparing these two documents which can result in significant timing differences between the movement of funds and the recognition of the sale or the expense in the profit and loss account. As a result, it is useful to prepare a third document which reconciles these timing differences and also shows the financial position of the business at a point in time: remember that both the profit and loss account and the statement of source and application of funds are prepared for the period, not at a point of time therein. This role is fulfilled by the balance sheet which is prepared as at the last day of the accounting period.

Accounting concepts

As well as the legal requirements, which now also include European Directives issued by the EC, financial reporting within the UK is also under the influence of the Accounting Standards Board (formerly the Accounting Standards Committee) which, since 1971, has issued a series of Statements of Standard Accounting Practice (SSAP). Each of the major developed countries has its own version of these accounting standards; e.g. in the USA they are known as FASBs (because they are issued by the Financial Accounting Standards Board), and there is also an International Accounting Standards body. These bodies lay down minimum standards of disclosure which are supposed to be mandatory. Underpinning these accounting standards are four fundamental accounting concepts as discussed in SSAP 2: *Disclosure of accounting policies* (1971). The four concepts are 'consistency', 'going concern, 'accruals' or 'matching', and 'prudence'.

The 'consistency' concept says that the interpretation and presentation of like things should be treated consistently within each accounting period and from one period to the next so that the financial performance during the year just ended can be validly compared by analysts, shareholders and potential investors with the previous year's performance. This concept of consistency is of importance in management accounting too. When meeting the information requirements of individual decision-makers there is likely to be a plethora of financial reports being produced on different timetables and possibly using different source documents. Under these circumstances it is important to prepare the reports for each of these individual managers on a consistent basis in terms of regularity and the information given, although consistency between different independent areas of management is not necessary: it is a fallacy that all internal accounts and reports should be consolidated for the sake of neatness to give overall totals if these totals are irrelevant to the needs of individual managers.

The 'going concern' concept assumes that the enterprise will continue in the same business for the foreseeable future. It is an important concept in financial reporting as some expenditure is capitalized in the balance sheet as an asset only because it is expected to generate a financial benefit at some point in the future. As far as managers are concerned this concept allows them to reflect their plans for the future in the published financial statements. The company invests funds now to get a return which may be received over many years in the future.

It is worth remembering at this point that financial accounting does not attempt to reflect at all times the value of a business to a potential buyer. The accounting view of the business is that it is a financial system for adding value to the resources it uses. Its financial success is measured by comparing the value of its output with the cost of its input resources; this is a measure of operational efficiency. This issue will be returned to later in this chapter.

The 'accruals' or 'matching' concept states that the costs incurred in the current accounting period may be carried forward in the balance sheet to be matched with consequent sales revenue earned in future periods provided that there is a logical relationship between the two items, which can be reasonably justified. The relationship should be causal, in that the expenditure incurred now has helped to create the future sales revenue. This concept encourages capital investment by enabling the company to spread the cost of an asset over its economic life. This is achieved by deducting the total cost from the sales revenue produced as the resource is used rather than when it is purchased.

The fourth concept (which overrides the matching concept whenever a conflict between them occurs) is the concept of 'prudence'. It states that *future* sales revenues, and hence profits, are not anticipated unless they are reasonably certain. If uncertain, the current costs cannot be carried forward and so they must be written off against any sales revenues in the period in which they are incurred, thus affecting current profits rather than being offset against future revenues and profits, as they would under the matching concept. However, immediate provision is made for all known future liabilities and losses, so that these future costs are brought forward into the current period of trading. In circumstances where there is any doubt as to whether these future sales revenues will be realized, it is prudent to write off the associated costs in the current year.

Prudence is an invaluable concept in external financial reporting as it should help to protect shareholders and creditors by preventing the overstatement of earnings in the current accounting period. This enhances the ability to pay creditors as they fall due because the company cannot pay excessive dividends to its shareholders out of falsely overstated profits. The concept can however be wholly inappropriate in management accounting and particularly in the area of planning and control. An overly prudent system of management accounting could lead to a result where resources are not efficiently allocated, leading to sub-optimal decision-making. Financial resources should be allocated to parts of the business on the basis of opportunity cost; i.e. what is the cost of the next best alternative which must be foregone in order to undertake the decision being considered? It is important in financial decision-making to make a comparison of alternative courses of action to ensure that resources are allocated in the way which will be of greatest benefit to the organization. The concept of opportunity cost is explained more fully in Chapter 3.

These problems of over-prudence are particularly evident in the accounting treatment of marketing expenditure. It is argued by prudent accountants that when dealing with marketing expenditure there is no great certainty if and when sales revenues will be generated by any particular marketing activity. Thus under the prudence concept all marketing expenditure, including major activities associated with new product launches, has traditionally been written off against profits in the current accounting period. This conservative treatment of marketing expenditure for external financial reporting purposes does not preclude managers from properly evaluating these major marketing investment decisions over the long term (marketing does after all frequently involve long-term investment decisions, and is not merely a question of allocating expenditure within the current year; thus marketing expenditure today could easily generate sales revenue over a number of subsequent accounting periods). However, the influence of the fundamental financial accounting principles has been strong enough on internal accounting for management decisions for many organizations to operate both accounting systems under the same principles, to the detriment of long-term marketing investment and its proper financial evaluation.

Accounting conventions in the UK and the USA provide many opportunities for managers to indulge in non-value creating exercises which can help to meet short-term profit and return on investment targets. This can be achieved by reducing expenditure on areas which, under the prudence convention, will be written off against this year's sales revenues, but where the real impact will not be felt until subsequent periods of trading. As a result, short-term operating performance appears to be improved, even though the long-term prospects for the company have been reduced. A clear example of this would be the reduction of expenditure on long-term research, which is normally written off as it is incurred because any resulting future sales revenue can hardly be regarded as certain. It is often argued that the widespread ownership of many UK and USA publicly quoted companies and the openness of these countries' capital markets increases the pressure for continuous short-term improvements in financial results, particularly when compared to the position in other countries, such as Japan and Germany.

Such short-term accounting needs can distract the manager from making decisions which are in the best interests of the long-term health of the company. Career progression of managers is often so rapid that there is not enough time to evaluate the real effectiveness of the long-term decisions that a manager makes. Therefore, to some extent managerial performance is inevitably judged over the shorter term. However, this must not be allowed to prevent decisions being taken which are in the best long-term interests of the company. Reconciling these short- and long-term performance measures should not be an unsolvable problem, provided the correct internal short-term performance measures are used, which fit into the long-term investment strategy. This is discussed in detail in Chapters 7 and 8.

The profit and loss account

The profit and loss account, or income statement, shows the impact of the trading activity of the firm and the consequent net income generated by this sales activity in any given accounting period. For management purposes, the firms profitability may be analysed into four separate sections. This can be illustrated by reference to an example of a computing company which assembles and distributes units bought in from overseas. The cost of assembling the units is shown in the manufacturing and assembly account, which takes into account changes in the stocks of raw materials and work-in-progress during the year and is shown in Figure 2.1. The differentiation is made between the prime costs of assembly and manufacturing, which are the direct labour costs, direct material costs and direct expenses, and the indirect factory overheads. The classification of direct and indirect costs is, as will be seen in the subsequent chapters of Part Two of this book, a vital step in the process of analysing financial information for making decisions about different segments of the business.

The figure of direct plus indirect costs is transferred to the trading account and adjusted for changes in finished goods stock to give the total cost of sales. Deducting this cost of goods sold from sales revenue for the period gives the gross profit or loss figure, as highlighted in Figure 2.2.

From this gross profit figure of £100,093,000, the other operating expenses (such as research and development, marketing, selling and distribution costs, administrative expenses) are deducted to give the operating profit of £20,232,000, as illustrated in the profit and loss account in Figure 2.3. This operating figure is adjusted to allow for net interest payable or receivable and the profit both before and after taxation is shown.

The profit after taxation is transferred to the profit and loss appropriation account which shows how much of the profit is paid out to shareholders in the

Manufacturing and assembly account for year ended 31 December 1990

		£000s
Raw materials (components and part-assembled units)		
Opening stock		25,950
Purchases		152,397
		178,347
Less closing stock		15,009
Costs of materials consumed		163,338
Assembly and production wages		87,238
Prime cost of assembly and production		250,576
Factory overhead:		
Non-assembly wages	7,496	
Rates	389	
Insurance	520	
Gas, water, electricity	3,616	
Non-assembly material (e.g. packaging)	12,822	
Factory salaries	18,517	
Depreciation	11,481	54,841
		305,417
Less increase in work-in-progress		1,071
Factory costs of assembly and production		304,346
Less stock of finished goods in factory		3,000
Cost of goods sent to warehouse in trading account		301,346
*WIP Opening stock	289	
WIP Closing stock	1,360	
Increase in WIP	1,071	

Assumption: Stock is valued as for financial reporting purposes, i.e. using absorption costing method.

Figure 2.1

Trading account for year ended 31 December 1990

	£000s	£000s
	£	£
Sales revenue		406,907
Finished goods in warehouse		
Opening stock	18,564	
Factory production transferred	301,346	
	319,910	
L ess closing stock	13,096	
		306,814
Gross profit to profit and loss account		100,093

Figure 2.2

form of dividends. As can be seen in Figure 2.4 an interim dividend of five pence per share was paid during the period as well as the proposed final dividend of ten pence per share. The remainder of the net profit can then be either transferred to revenue reserves, for investing in the future growth of the business, or carried forward to the next year's account as the balance on the profit and loss account. The profit that is retained within the business is an important source of capital for financing future growth, and it is essential that senior managers strike the right balance between satisfying any short-term needs of shareholders to receive an income stream from their investment and ensuring the future success of the business through reinvestment of current profits.

An abbreviated format for the profit and loss account is used for external financial reporting under the Companies Acts. It may also provide much of the historic financial information needed by certain managers within the organization. An example for the computing company is given in Figure 2.5.

It can be seen that the profit and loss account format used for financial reporting does not contain as much detail as the internal report shown in Figure 2.3; e.g. the breakdown of the selling and distribution costs and administrative expenses is of little real value to external users, although obviously of great use to the managers who must control this expenditure.

It can also be seen that there is a difference in operating profit between the two formats. This arises because in the internal reporting format interest has been split into that which is payable on short-term loans (i.e. bank interest) and is

Profit and loss account for the year ended 31 December 1990

	£	£	£000s £
Gross profit from trading account			100,093
Selling and distribution costs			
Carriage outwards	6,928		
Salesmen's expenses	3,601		
Salesmen's salaries	16,684		
Sales office salaries	4,263	31,476	
Advertising		5,000	
Servicing costs		20,492	
Administration expenses:			
Office salaries	6,380		
Directors' salaries	9,500		
Depreciation (office premises,			
fixtures and fittings)	1,790		
Provision for bad debts	2,393		
Audit fees	209	20,272	
Bank interest		2,621	
			(79,861)
Operating profit			20,232
Investment income			368
Profit before interest and taxation			20,600
Less loan interest			(1,311)
Profit before taxation			19,289
Taxation			(7,343)
Net profit for year to appropriation account			11,946

Figure 2.3

regarded as an operating expense, and that which is payable on more long-term loans. Under the external reporting format the two types of interest are usually combined to show the total interest payable by the business on all its debt, both short-term and long-term, so that a direct comparison can be made with the interest receivable on investments by the business.

Profit and loss appropriation account for the year ended 31 December 1990

	£000s	£000s
Balance brought forward from previous year		8,172
Net profit for year		11,946
		20,118
Available for appropriation		
Interim dividend 5 pence per share	3,873	
Proposed final dividend 10 pence		
per share	7,747	11,620
Balance carried forward to next year		8,498

Figure 2.4

To the operating profit figure of £22,853,000, shown in the external reporting format, is added 'interest receivable' by the company from investments in stocks and shares and other capital interests, and shares of profits of related companies. Interest payable on loans, etc. also needs to be subtracted at this stage.

This gives a figure of profit on ordinary activities before taxation. Taxation is then deducted to give profit on ordinary activities after taxation. The company may well have an interest in an associated company, income from this would be included under 'minority interests'. Income which arises from items not expected to recur in the future, e.g. the closure of a significant part of the business, is included under 'extraordinary items'. The total of all income ordinarily and extraordinarily generated is then divided into that which is to be distributed to shareholders in the form of dividend payments and that which is to be retained by the business for reinvestment.

Accounting for inflation

The problem of trying to show a true and fair view of a business financial performance during times of high inflation is one that gave rise to a long drawn out and often heated debate within the accountancy profession during the 1970s. It was never resolved (SSAP 16: *Current cost accounting*, issued in 1980, was made non-mandatory in 1985 after popular disapproval), but during the early 1980s

**Profit and loss account for the year ended 31 December 1990
(abbreviated format used for external financial reporting)**

	£000s
Turnover	406,907
Cost of sales	(306,814)
Gross profit	100,093
Advertising maintenance expenditure	(5,000)
Distribution and servicing costs	(51,968)
Administrative expenses	(20,272)
Operating profit	22,853
Interest receivable	368
Interest payable	(3,932)
Shares of profits of related companies	—
Profit on ordinary activities before taxation	19,289
Taxation on profit on ordinary activities	(7,343)
Profit on ordinary activities after taxation	11,946
Minority interests	—
Extraordinary items	—
Profit attributable to shareholders	11,946
Dividends	(11,620)
Retained profit for the financial year	326

Figure 2.5

when inflation returned to an acceptable, low level there became little apparent need for the debate to continue. However, as we enter the 1990s with inflation again reasonably high, the impact on profit measurement is once more an issue that must concern managers and accountants, and so is relevant for discussion in the context of accounting for management decisions.

The accountants' method of measuring profitability by reference to return on investment, as discussed later in this chapter, involves placing the profit achieved in the period in the context of the net assets employed during the period in order to measure the relative return that management has earned on the employment of these assets. If no allowance is made for inflation in this calculation (i.e. historical cost accounting is used, under which assets are shown at the cost when purchased, less accumulated depreciation resulting from usage), profit will normally be overstated in times of rising prices. This is because the cost of a resource (e.g. raw material) input at the start of the accounting period is matched with sales revenues made at a higher relative money level at a later date within this accounting period. There will also be an understatement of the real value of the assets employed if these assets are shown at their historical cost on the balance sheet. To redress this impact of inflation, managers need to adjust the level of depreciation and the charges made for stocks and work-in-progress used in the period which are included in the profit and loss account. Also the fixed assets and net working capital (especially stocks and work-in-progress) need to be adjusted in the balance sheet.

The overall issue of stock valuation can be a major problem area in financial analysis and so it will be discussed in depth separately in Chapter 5.

Depreciation

When a business purchases a long-term capital item, e.g. a piece of machinery, it should represent this expenditure as a fixed asset on the balance sheet, so as to match the cost of this asset to its use over its economic life. This defines an asset as a resource which is employed in the business, but has not yet been totally used up in the trading activities during the current period; i.e. it has value to the business for the future beyond the current accounting period. Such items of machinery and other fixed assets are not fully charged to the profit and loss account in their year of purchase because their useful economic lives are assumed not to expire within the current accounting period. However, as the asset ages its remaining value to the business will diminish year by year and so the remaining cost which is included on the balance sheet must also be reduced. The cost of using the assets each year should also be matched against the sales which are generated as a result and thus a charge for depreciation of that asset is taken against profit each year. For example, if an item of machinery bought for £1,000 is deemed to have a useful economic life of ten years, depreciation can be charged to the profit and loss account on a straight line basis at the rate of £100 each year. By the end of the asset's life its value will be nil, assuming it has no residual value; i.e. the cost is spread over the life of the asset. The £100 charge is in effect the cost to the business of utilizing the resource during each accounting period. If the asset is expected to have a residual value at the end of its useful life, the total cost which has to be written off is the reduction in value, i.e. the original purchase cost less the residual value.

In situations where the fixed asset is not retained for its full expected life but is sold earlier, the actual proceeds received from disposal may be lower than the net book value of the asset which remains on the balance sheet if straight line depreciation has been used. This will result in the company suffering a 'loss on disposal' and this will have an adverse impact upon the profit and loss account in the period of disposal. To overcome this the company can use a more accelerated method of depreciation, where relatively more depreciation expense is charged to the profit and loss account in the early periods of use. Thus the net book value should represent more accurately the potential disposal proceeds of the fixed asset and no significant loss or gain on any early disposal will arise. The most commonly used method of accelerated depreciation is the 'reducing balance' method, where a constant annual percentage rate of depreciation is applied to the reducing balance (i.e. the remaining net book value) of the fixed asset.

It should be realized that the depreciation process is part of the matching process of accounting and does not by itself ensure that funds are available to replace the asset at the end of its life. However, the depreciation expense does reduce the profit available in each period for distribution to shareholders and so the company should retain the resources within the business to replace fixed assets, even though these resources may not be in the form of cash.

Readers should also familiarize themselves with the term amortization. Amortization is the generic name given to all accounting processes by which the book value of a fixed asset is progressively reduced from its original cost to its scrap or resale price and the difference is charged to the profit and loss account. Depreciation is one such process, and it is normally used when referring to an asset, such as a piece of machinery, with an indeterminate economic life, the length of which is limited by its own technology or by physical deterioration.

Example 1: Straight line depreciation

A company purchases ten new cars for its salesforce for £10,000 each. The cars will be kept for three years before being replaced with new cars. It is estimated that, due to the high mileage which the salesforce will drive during the three years, the cars will have residual (trade-in) values of £4,000 at the end of year 3.

The cost to the company of using the cars will be equal to the drop in value (cost less residual value) of £6,000 per car over the three years. The simplest method of matching this cost involves proportioning the £6,000 per car equally over the three years which gives a depreciation expense of £20,000 per year in total for the ten cars (as shown in the profit and loss account of Figure 2.6).

As is the case with all forecasts, particularly those made for three years ahead, there is a high probability of this residual value estimate being inaccurate so that the cars will actually realize a different value to that forecast on their eventual sale by the company. This sale will therefore generate a gain or loss on disposal which must be recorded in the accounting statements appropriately, being classified as a non-trading item.

The reduction in value of the asset must be reflected in the balance sheet as the future value of the asset is being consumed by the business, and assets must not

Balance sheets as at the end of each year

	Year 1	Year 2	Year 3	Year 4*
	£	£	£	£
Fixed assets:				
Motor vehicles at cost	100,000	100,000	100,000	—
less Accumulated depreciation	20,000	40,000	60,000	—
Net book value	80,000	60,000	40,000	—

* Asset sold at beginning of year 4

Profit and loss accounts for each year

	Year 1	Year 2	Year 3	Year 4
	£	£	£	£
Depreciation expense	20,000	20,000	20,000	—

Figure 2.6 *Extracts from balance sheets and profit and loss accounts*

be stated in the balance sheet at more than their future value to the business. It is normal accounting practice to show the original cost of the fixed assets, less the cumulative amount of depreciation expense, on the face of the balance sheet, or in the supporting detailed notes, so that both the scale of the original investment is easily identifiable throughout the asset life and the proportion of the asset which has been used up is revealed.

Example 2: Comparing straight line depreciation with reducing balance depreciation

A computer company decides to depreciate its computers over five years; but, to allow for the relatively high risk of their being scrapped after only two or three years due to technological obsolescence, the company chooses to use an accelerated method of depreciation. The cost of the asset is £200,000 and under the straight-line method the depreciation expense would be a constant £40,000 per year.

However, under the reducing balance method the annual depreciation expense reduces over the economic life of the asset. In order to write-off the £200,000 cost over the five-year expected life at a constant annual percentage of the remaining balance, an annual percentage rate of considerably greater than 20 per cent used under the straight line depreciation method is required. The actual constant percentage required in this example is about 65 per cent. (*Note*: It is mathematically impossible to reduce a value to exactly zero using a constant pecentage of a reducing balance, but for accounting purposes a sufficiently accurate approximation can be obtained.)

As can be seen in Figure 2.7 the year 1 depreciation expense is significantly greater under the reducing balance method, thereby minimizing the effect of a write-off should the asset's life turn out to be less than the anticipated five years.

Under both methods the total cost of £200,000 will be depreciated over the economic life of 5 years, but the different timing of the depreciation expenses in the annual profit and loss accounts will have a significant impact on the reported profits of the company. It is worth noting that there is no effect on the cash flow of the business as a result of this type of change in depreciation policy, as the cash flow impact has already been felt when the asset was originally purchased.

Statement of source and application of funds

The statement of source and application of funds or funds flow statement, which is really a form of cash flow statement (in fact it was recently recommended that cash flow statements should replace the statement of source and application of funds because cash flow as a concept is easier to understand and also more relevant

	Straight line depreciation £		*Reducing balance depreciation* £
Cost of asset	200,000		200,000
Year 1 depreciation (@ 20% on cost)	40,000	((@ 65% on reducing balance)	130,000
Net book value at end year 1	160,000		70,000
Year 2 depreciation	40,000		45,500
Net book value at end year 2	120,000		24,500
Year 3 depreciation	40,000		15,925
Net book value at end year 3	80,000		8,575
Year 4 depreciation	40,000		5,575
Net book value at end year 4	40,000		3,000
Year 5 depreciation	40,000		3,000
Net book value at end year 5	£ –		£ –

Figure 2.7 *Comparison of straight line and reducing balance methods of depreciation*

to management, as will be discussed later in this chapter), is prepared to reflect the physical movements of funds of the business and changes in working capital (stocks, debtors, creditors, cash) over the same accounting periods for which the profit and loss account shows the financial results of the trading activity. Because of the complementary nature of these two documents, it is vital that they are prepared for the same time period. They can illustrate different aspects of the company's financial position, and reconciliation of the timing differences between the two is only possible if the basis of presentation is common. The statement of source and application of funds for our computer company is given as Figure 2.8.

While the profit and loss account shows the amount of profit made during a period, the funds flow statement illustrates the movements of funds in and out of the business, and describes how these funds were applied and from which sources they came. A distinction can also be made between applications resulting from changes in working capital, which are often short-term planning decisions, and from purchases of new fixed assets (long-term planning decisions). It is therefore an invaluable tool for financial planning.

It also attempts to analyse whether the business is financing its activities in a manner that is appropriate to the uses to which the funds are put. Businesses actually fail, not because they report accounting losses but, because they run out of money. It is therefore important to ensure that the business is soundly financed.

Potential sources of finance can be divided between external sources and those internally generated by the company. Internal sources are the most readily available and the main one should be the cash generated from operations (i.e. net profit or loss for the period after adjustments for items that do not result in a physical movement of funds, e.g. depreciation). Other internal sources include the disposal of fixed assets and any reduction in funds tied up in net working capital. Issuing more shares in the company would generate external funds, but can also change the ownership of the company.

Borrowing extra money in the form of bank debt or loan capital can produce new funds without changing ownership, although the company takes on additional liabilities, i.e. to repay the money borrowed. Further analysis of the movement of funds is required to ascertain how the financial requirements of the business have changed during the accounting period. The uses of funds should be analysed between investment in new fixed assets and changes in working capital and the causes of each investment – is the increased investment caused by expansion of the scale of operations (new plant and machinery) or higher sales volumes, or because the company is trading less efficiently (e.g. it needs more working capital invested because it is holding higher relative stock levels or taking longer to collect cash from customers in terms of days sales outstanding as debtors)?

Another key question to be answered through the funds flow statement is whether these increased funds are invested in the business on a short-term or long-term basis. This should decide the most appropriate source of finance. It is beneficial to match the time-scale of cash requirements by raising the funds on a similar time-scale, as it is not appropriate to raise long-term finance to cope with, for example, a seasonal peak in stock requirement levels.

Examples of the applications of funds which are not directly the result of changes

Statement of source and application of funds for the year ended 31 December 1990

	£000s	£000s
Source of funds		
Profit on ordinary activities before taxation		19,289
Adjustment for items not involving the movement of funds:		
Depreciation	13,271	
Repayments from finance leases	7,197	20,468
Total generated from operations		39,757
Share issues		305
Net increase in non-current liabilities and loans		6,504
Proceeds from sale of fixed assets		860
		47,426
Application of funds		
Dividends paid	23,074	
Taxation paid	10,136	
Investment in finance leases	12,409	
Purchase of fixed assets	35,417	
Loan repayments	11,541	(92,577)
		(45,151)
(Decrease)/increase in working capital		
Stocks	4,675	
Debtors	21,276	
Creditors	(25,720)	
		231
Movement in net liquid funds		
Cash at bank and in hand	(29,522)	
Loans and overdrafts	(15,860)	
		(45,382)
		(45,151)

Figure 2.8

in the scale of operations are the payment of dividends, the payment of taxation and the redemption of loan or share capital.

While the funds flow statement can show how the working capital composition of the business has changed over the accounting period, it does not give a clear indication of the cash flow position. Indeed it may actually obscure movements that are relevant to the liquidity of the enterprise; e.g., a shortage of cash may be lost in a working capital increase if stock or debtors increase. Also, because it is an historical statement and only represents a picture of the business at the year end its usefulness in management decision-making is limited.

Profit versus cash

Profit is assessed on the basis of trading activity, but cash flow relates to the physical movement of funds. A business can be profitable but still be insolvent and vice versa. This is because of timing differences. The profit figure is adjusted for accruals and prepayments which reflect respectively the later or earlier payment of expenses, as well as depreciation. No such adjustment is made to cash flow. Cash flow therefore provides a more factual impression of the current state of the business; e.g. are there enough short-term funds either in the business or available to the business to pay creditors or wages to employees?

The use of cash flow also allows rates of return on the investment in assets by the firm to be calculated on a discounted cash flow (DCF) basis. DCF techniques are discussed in detail in Chapter 7 and are a realistic measurement for evaluating long-term investment decisions because they take a longer-term perspective. They do not differentiate between the accounting treatments of capital and revenue items and they do not have to rely upon unrealistic balance sheet representations of the net book value of fixed assets.

When measuring accounting income, profit is shown as it is earned rather than when cash is received from customers or paid out by the company to suppliers. All of these timing differences in physical receipts and payments are normally included separately in the funds flow statement by analysing changes in outstanding debtors etc. at the end of the period compared to those outstanding at the beginning. Thus, if customers owe more cash at the end of the period than they did at the beginning, it is evident that the business has increased the amount invested in financing debtors.

There is one such timing difference that cannot be included in the funds flow statement other than by adjusting profit, and this is depreciation. The cash generated from trading will be greater than the profit reported in the profit and loss account by the level of any depreciation included therein. The source of funds from operations can therefore be shown as profit plus depreciation, provided the other timing differences in working capital are included separately in the cash flow statement. Current depreciation expenses do not represent an actual cash outflow and therefore require adjustment in the cash flow statement, but the actual funds used to purchase new or replacement fixed assets must be included in the statement as a cash outflow from the business or an application of funds.

Cash outflows can be separated into current expenses and capital expenses. When calculating profit, current expenses are deductible in the period in which they are spent but capital expenses are spread over a number of years and the periodic depreciation is deducted from each period's profits. So profit is calculated after deducting some cash flows but not others, and after depreciation expense which is not a cash flow at all.

When analysing financial plans and budgets it is desirable to differentiate between specific 'development' activities (e.g. the purchase of a new machine to expand or improve existing operations, or marketing investment in the launch of a new product) and expenditure designed to maintain existing levels of activity. This helps to avoid the business reallocating expenditure from one category to the other in order to achieve a short-term profit target at the expense of being able to achieve the longer-term growth target; this is considered in detail in Chapters 7 and 11.

The balance sheet

The differences between the profit and loss account and cash flow statement are reconciled in the balance sheet. The balance sheet shows the financial position of the business at a particular point in time, which for financial reporting purposes is the last day of the accounting period.

The balance sheet is a statement of the assets (or resources) and the liabilities (or obligations) and the share capital and reserves of the company, as at the date on which it is prepared. It can therefore be regarded as a cumulative statement of the funds flow position of the company from the day it was founded.

Finance is raised from various sources to invest in the resources which the business operates. These assets are likely to include fixed assets, such as buildings, plant and machinery, current assets (or working capital), such as stocks, debtors, cash and other investments. One source of finance is the capital invested in the company by shareholders. This is shown on the balance sheet as share capital and reserves, and includes ordinary share capital, preference share capital reserves and revenue reserves. Capital reserves may include revaluations of assets or the contribution of capital by shareholders over and above the nominal value of their shares (share premium account). Capital reserves cannot be distributed to share-holders, except in the event of the company's liquidation. Transfers from the profit and loss account for reinvestment in the business are included in the revenue reserve. Revenue reserves are free for distribution.

Alternative sources of finance are long-term loans and debentures, short-term finance from banks and credit from suppliers. These are the company's liabilities.

Each of these sources of finance has a cost to the company for its use; i.e. interest is paid on outstanding loans and debentures and dividends may be paid to shareholders, who may also expect to receive a capital gain as the share value increases. This cost can be expressed as an annual rate of return. How much finance should be acquired, and of which type, is determined by the relative return demanded by lenders or investors depending upon their perception of the risk

Balance sheet as at 31 December 1990

	£000s	£000s
Fixed assets		
Tangible assets		67,223
Intangible marketing assets		20,000
		87,223
Current assets		
Stocks	32,465	
Debtors	95,745	
Marketable securities	—	
Cash at bank and in hand	4,012	
	132,222	
Creditors: amounts falling due within one year	(153,092)	
Net current (liabilities)/assets		(20,780)
Total assets less current		66,353
Creditors: amounts falling due after more than one year		(7,852)
Provisions for liabilities and charges		(11,270)
		47,231
Capital and reserves		
Called up share capital (77466 50 pence shares)		38,733
Profit and loss account		8,498
		47,231

Figure 2.9

associated with the particular investment. The managers of the business can assess the best mix of funding by calculating the company's optimum overall cost of capital based on the weighted average of the costs of debt and equity capital. Debt capital requires a lower rate of return than equity capital because it has a prior call on profits and assets, thus reducing the lender's risk level, and because the interest payable on it is chargeable against profits as a cost for tax purposes. It is therefore to the equity shareholders' benefit if the company has some gearing in its balance sheet, as this can boost the return on their equity investment. Within the long-term financial process, it is a role of the financial managers to determine the future financing arrangements and, on the basis of the proportion of the various forms of funding to be employed, to compute the weighted average cost of capital for the firm.

An asset is normally entered in the accounting records at the price paid to acquire that asset. This cost forms the basis of accounting for this asset. Accounting does not therefore normally reflect the value of assets to the business. As mentioned earlier, this concept may make it difficult during times of high inflation to measure how efficiently the management has carried out its stewardship function. Consequently, where appropriate, assets may be revalued to their current value, such as is required by current cost accounting.

What is the *value* of an asset to the business? A good rule of thumb is to consider how the business might suffer if it were deprived of the use of the asset. Bearing this in mind, there are three possible bases for valuation, and normally the lowest of the three is used:

1   How much would the business get if the asset is sold (net realizable value)?
2   What will it cost to replace the asset (replacement cost)?
3   What are its expected future earnings worth today (present value)?

If a company does not purchase a fixed asset but develops it internally in the normal course of business, this item will frequently not appear in the accounting records as an asset; particularly if the item is intangible, such as technical knowledge, expertise and brand names. Because published financial statements do not reflect the value of a company's intangible assets, significant differences can arise between all these various values (i.e. the book value of a company's assets, their break-up value, the value of the company if sold as a going concern) and the market value of its shares.

The role of the balance sheet in financial reporting has been a major issue of debate since the late 1980s, and at the time of writing there is still great uncertainty as to the future role and format. During the 1980s there has been a number of mergers and takeovers among firms with valuable intangible assets, such as food and beverage brands and newspaper publishing titles, where the difference between the book value of the acquired company's assets (which does not include intangible assets) and the market value of its shares has been significant. It has been argued that if companies were allowed to put market values on all their assets, both tangible and intangible, this would represent a more true and fair view of the value of the company and would make them less susceptible to predators. (Indeed some companies have already gone down this road; e.g. Ranks Hovis McDougall plc has put values on acquired and internally developed brands, Grand Metropolitan plc has valued some of its recently acquired brands, and News International plc and Reed International plc include the values of their newspaper titles as assets on the balance sheet.)

However, to use the balance sheet as a valuation statement would require casting aside the prudence concept and trying to estimate the value of the assets of a business as the net present value of the future cash flows from the business (i.e. including future profit streams) or the realizable value of these assets if the business were broken up. The counter argument is that it is impossible to put accurately a value on all the company's assets, and that anyway this would not automatically put the company out of the reach of predators. As well as going against the concept of representing assets at cost, this automatically brings into the debate the treatment of depreciation. If assets are valued above cost, does the associated depreciation also increase, thereby reducing profits?

To put the brand accounting debate into its correct context, the central issue was how to account for goodwill arising out of an acquisition. Acquisitive companies like Grand Metropolitan found that, if they carried out a programme of investments in other companies, the goodwill (i.e. the excess of the consideration over the book value of the assets acquired) which arose and which had to be written off against reserves had a serious distorting effect on their balance sheet, by reducing shareholders' funds. The latest advice from the accounting profession is for companies to capitalize those elements of the goodwill which can be specifically identified (i.e. brand names, trademarks, etc.) as Grand Metropolitan and the like had begun to do, but to amortize those assets over a given period, say 20 years. This amortization expense would reduce profits each year, a situation considered by many of the companies involved to be just as bad as reporting dwindling shareholders' funds on their balance sheets. Amortization of these intangible assets is argued against on two fundamental counts: first, if their value does not in reality decrease over the 20-year period, there is no need for amortization; and second, these assets are being maintained through (in the case of a brand) marketing activity which is already written off against current year profits, so why take a double hit in their externally reported financial accounts.

The debate about the balance sheet and the valuation of assets, although principally concerned with financial reporting, should have important implications for management accounting. The practice of financially evaluating any investment in assets by discounting the cash flows generated from the use of that asset over its life is an important discipline for management in their planning and control roles. This will be discussed further in Parts Three and Four.

Directors' report

This was initially a short, formal document with little additional information to the profit and loss account, but since the 1967 Companies Act it has become an important supplement to the more detailed accounting documents. The contents should include:

- A report containing a fair view of the development of the business of the company
- Details of dividends to be paid
- Names and interests of the directors for the year
- The principal activities of the company
- Details of any significant changes in fixed assets
- Details of political or charitable donations
- Details of share capital and any changes in the year
- Details of employee policies and development.

Auditors' report

All companies are legally required to have their accounts audited by suitably qualified independent persons. The auditors must make a report to the shareholders on the financial accounts that they examine and which are laid before the company in general meeting (s. 236[1]). This report forms part of the published accounts. It states whether in the auditors' opinion the company's balance sheet and profit and loss account (and where applicable the group accounts) have been properly prepared in accordance with the Companies Acts and show a true and fair view of the company's affairs at the end of the financial year and of the company's profit or loss for the year.

The auditors must also judge whether the information contained in the directors' report is consistent with the accounts. If they believe there is an inconsistency they should state the fact in their report.

Stock Exchange requirements: admission of securities to Listing

There are a number of additional requirements to the information disclosed in published financial statements which have to be met before a company is given a full Listing on the London International Stock Exchange:

- Additional information, if the published accounts do not give a true and fair view
- Reasons for significant departure from standard accounting practices, where appropriate
- A geographical analysis of turnover and of contribution of trading operations carried on outside the UK and Republic of Ireland
- Particulars of significant contracts between the company and substantial corporate shareholders
- Particulars of any shareholders's authority for the purchase by the company of its own shares.

Measuring historical performance of the business: return on investment (ROI)

ROI is a measure of investment centre performance which makes use of the historic information contained in the financial statements (specifically the profit and loss account and the balance sheet) that have been discussed above. In its simplest format ROI is calculated thus:

$$\text{Return on investment (ROI)} = \frac{(\text{Sales revenue} - \text{expenses})}{\text{Net investment}} \times 100\%$$

However, as will be seen, there are several variations on this format, which can make ROI an unsuitable measure of performance.

ROI was first put to use by giant US corporations Du Pont and General Motors in the 1920s and 1930s. It was used by senior managers to help them allocate capital among the wide range of operating units on a regular basis and to measure how efficiently this capital had been put to use. It was also still considered appropriate to look at performance over the life of the investment in the project. This was because many businesses were in cyclical industries (heavy engineering, shipbuilding, automobiles) with long economic lives of assets where years of slack demand were expected. Unimpressive performance during these years would not cause investors to panic provided there were expectations of customer demand and hence sales revenue and profits picking up again.

This method of judging financial performance is widely used today for both total companies and their separate operating units, but similar caveats must be observed. Thus shareholders should judge the performance of their investment in a company over quite a long time-scale. However, because of the different competitive environment (shorter life-cycles and more competitors) and different investor expectations (business ownership is more widespread and the small investor often wants short-term indicators of future performance), there is much greater pressure for good financial performance in the short-term. Unfortunately ROI is still used as a financial indicator by the majority of companies, because it is easily calculated using the information that is readily available in the published accounts. It is also easy to manipulate!

There are several ways of reading a figure which purports to represent investment performance, but essentially it is some measure of net profit expressed as a percentage of the capital employed in the business.

At the divisional level of the company, the use of ROI has to be very carefully applied. In order for ROI to be an effective measure of divisional managerial performance, net profit should be adjusted for depreciation and inflation, which are both estimates made by accountants with their varying interpretations. Also, interest payments should be excluded if the managers concerned have no control over the source of funding supplied to their division. Factors, over which the managers whose performances are being assessed have no control, may also be included in the normal accounting measurement of capital; e.g. loans may be negotiated at the corporate level and then allocated to each division or cost centre. Thus if the interest expense is excluded from the profit measurement, the corresponding debt should not be deducted in the capital calculation.

Discussion about ROI automatically reintroduces the complicated issue of the timing of profits and when to include particular items in financial accounts. (This is why it is considered that the use of cash flow in performance measurement is preferable wherever possible. This will be discussed on several occasions later in the book.)

For calculating financial performance of long-term projects, some method of averaging must be used to calculate an annual return, as profits may vary in each year of the life of the project. There are obvious problems involved in using averages as the basis for making decisions, and managers should be looking at the changes in performance from year to year so they can monitor and control performance of the business properly. The only way of trying to overcome the problem of averages is to calculate a rate of return for each year using some measure of net book value of assets. However, in order to calculate a return for the project as a whole, this still involves some process of aggregating and averaging these annual rates of return.

Further problems are encountered when dealing with marketing expenditure, which is prudently written off in the current year. If this expenditure was treated as a long-term investment, it would increase profit in the first year but would also raise the level of investment involved in the business. This would give a more realistic interpretation of the financial performance by a new product development project, which under normal financial accounting presentations appears to generate large accounting losses in its early development years, before apparently producing huge profits out of virtually no investment base.

Although it is an overall corporate objective to earn profit, this profit needs to be put in the context of the investment required. This also enables the financial performance of each division to be compared against objectives which are consistent with the corporate objectives. In order to use the concept of the investment centre, which is considered in Chapter 11, divisional managers should not only be able to control their level of profit but also to decide on the level of investment which should be employed within their division to achieve the agreed objectives. Thus the division is given responsibility for controlling its own level of profitability, i.e. the rate of profit per £ of investment, rather than concentrating on the absolute level of profit. For this reason investment centres are often run as self-contained, fairly autonomous entities, although the operating divisions are never entirely independent of the centre of the group which exercises control over all the investment centres by providing the necessary investment funding.

Funds should be allocated to the divisions according to the financial return which can be achieved. This too is commonly measured using ROI, although for forward-looking investment decisions a cash flow based measure such as internal rate of return (IRR) is more relevant, and this is discussed in detail in Chapter 7.

The financial control system will compare the actual performance of each division against expected levels shown in the financial plans and budgets. This relative comparison against expectations does help to alleviate some of the measurement problems which exist in the absolute ROI evaluations, as long as the two measurements are made on a consistent basis. However, it also highlights the need for coordination in the objective setting and control processes, so that the interests of any one division are not put before the overall interests of the group.

The financial control process can be made easier by breaking down the investment centre into profit, revenue or cost centres; i.e. recognizing that there is a hierarchy of managerial discretion. In cost centres managers can only affect costs, whereas in revenue centres changes in sales revenues and some costs can be brought about by management action. At the profit centre level, discretion is exercised over all sales revenue and costs and in an investment centre there is the additional discretion over the level of investment made. However, it is important that the business does not concentrate just on the performance of subdivisions because success is determined by the overall performance in the market place, and the control system must therefore also provide relevant financial information on product, customer and market performance.

Different levels of calculating ROI relevant to different types of analysis

Return on shareholders' funds or equity (ROE)

If the analysis is taking place from the point of view of the shareholders in the company, they will be interested in the profit that is earned on their collective investments. This profit may partly be distributed to them in the form of dividends, or it may be held back for possible distribution in future years by being ploughed back into the business by being invested in an increase in the assets employed, so as to help the company grow.

However, it should be remembered that the balance sheet is not a valuation statement of the business and so shareholders' equity used does not represent a market value of the shareholders' investment. Thus the return on equity calculated cannot be compared directly to investing cash in other forms of investment. ROE is calculated thus:

$$\text{Return on shareholders' equity} = \frac{\text{Net profit after tax}}{(\text{Share capital} + \text{reserves})} \times 100\%$$

The objective of the shareholders should be to earn a return over time which adequately compensates for the risks that they run in investing in the company. Also, in an inflationary period investors require a return which is sufficient to take into account that their funds will lose effective purchasing power as consumption is delayed by holding their investment in the company.

Any new investor in a company is buying the prospect of future profits, but the position of the company in their life-cycle can affect this. Thus, a very high current return on shareholders' funds may not be sustained in the future if the major products are near the end of their life-cycles. In order to avoid dramatic changes in the levels of return provided to shareholders, companies often build diversified portfolios of products to balance future profit streams and cash flows and offset the associated risks of fluctuations from year to year.

Return on capital employed (ROCE)

Return on equity takes into account the impact of the way in which the company is financed. A financial measure is needed which reflects the overall operating performance of the company and separates it from the impact of the use of debt funding in the business. ROCE is a good indicator of such overall performance.

$$ROCE = \text{Return on net assets}$$

$$= \frac{\text{Profit before interest and tax}}{\text{net assets*}} \text{(PBIT)} \times 100\%$$

* where net assets = fixed assets + current assets − current liabilities.

If debt is deducted from the denominator of the calculation then an adjustment should also be made to the numerator to take account of the cost of that debt which has been charged against profit.

Accounting rate of return

This is a method for evaluating long-term projects and, as such, is considered in Chapter 8. The rate of return is calculated by dividing the average annual profits expected to be earned by the project by the investment required. The main argument in favour of this rate of return is that it is similar to the criterion used to judge the performance of an existing business (i.e. ROCE). However, there are again the problems involved in the timing of profits and averaging these profits to arrive at an annual measure.

Effects of taxation

Although tax planning is an important part of financial planning, it is common practice to calculate some overall return measures, particularly for internal divisions of a company, on a 'before-tax' basis the particular level of tax charged in any year may not bear any direct relationship to the financial performance of the business. With a government fiscal policy which reduced the nominal rate of corporate tax progressively over four years from 52 per cent to 35 per cent, it may appear that the after-tax profit of the company has improved each year, even if the before-tax profit levels of each of the years are unchanged.

Analysing investment returns

Analysts both inside and outside a company, having calculated a return on capital employed, will wish to compare this with other companies in the same industry; while 15 per cent may be good return for a certain type of retailer, the industry average for a high technology manufacturing company may be nearer 30 per cent. The computing company being used as the example in the Appendix to this chapter appears to have quite a healthy return on its investment, but it would have to be compared with other companies in its industry in order to make a more meaningful analysis.

The overall ROCE ratio can also be broken up into two parts to enable further comparative analysis to take place. Since capital employed is equal in value to net assets (as shown in the balance sheet), net assets and capital employed are interchangeable in the ROCE ratio. By simple arithmetic, ROCE or return on net assets (RONA) can be broken down into:

$$RONA = \frac{PBIT}{Sales\ revenue} \times \frac{Sales\ revenue}{Net\ assets} \times 100\%$$

i.e. RONA = Profit margin × Net asset turnover × 100%

Therefore it can be seen that RONA or ROCE can be improved by increasing the profit margin or improving the net asset turnover ratio. Thus a company can employ many alternative strategies to achieve its required ROCE. For example, the high value of fixed assets on the manufacturing of complex products, as opposed to virtually no such investment for some service industries, need not greatly reduce the net asset turnover ratio because unit sales may be correspondingly high (as in the car industry).

Other areas for financial analysis

Financial status ratios

The ability of the business to pay cash when it is due is of paramount importance to lenders. Financial status ratios are designed to indicate whether or not this is likely to happen. They consider both the short-term ability to pay and the longer-term funding status of the business.

Solvency ratios

Solvency ratios consider how the company is being financed in the longer term. They compare the amount of borrowed funds used in the business with the level of shareholders' fund and are commonly expressed in one of the two ways shown below:

$$\text{Gearing ratio} = \frac{\text{Long-term debt}}{\text{Shareholders' equity} + \text{long-term debt}} \times 100\%$$

$$\text{Debt to equity ratio} = \frac{\text{Long-term debt}}{\text{Shareholders' equity}}$$

Thus a gearing ratio of 50 per cent is equivalent to a debt:equity ratio of 1:1. The debt:equity ratio shows the value of shareholders' funds per £ of debt in the company; whereas the gearing ratio highlights the proportion of the long-term funding which is provided by debt.

Borrowed funds typically receive a rate of interest which is fixed regardless of the profitability of the business. Thus, the proportion of funds that can be borrowed will depend on the lender's perception of the risk of non-repayment, which is closely linked to the volatility of cash flows from the business. This can also be expressed by reference to the proportion of profits which are used to pay interest on the borrowed funds. If the proportion of debt financing used is high, interest costs will absorb a great proportion of profit before interest. Thus a downturn in profitability could leave the lender at risk. This risk is shown by calculating the interest cover ratio which indicates the amount by which operating profits can fall before the interest costs put the company into a loss-making position.

$$\text{Interest cover} = \frac{\text{Profit before tax} + \text{interest payable}}{\text{Interest payable}}$$

Interest cover will logically fall as the level of gearing rises (assuming constant profits). Therefore, when doing financial analysis the two relationships must be considered together.

Liquidity ratios

The short-term financial position needs to be sensibly managed as well, if the company is to avoid a liquidity crisis. The objective of *liquidity ratios* is to indicate the relationship between the levels of current assets and current liabilities for the operation of the business and to show the trend over time rather than the absolute value at one particular moment.

$$\text{Current ratio} = \frac{\text{Current assets}}{\text{Current liabilities}}$$

The current ratio will be affected by the way the business is operated. A decrease in the current ratio may indicate potential liquidity problems, but a more reliable indicator is the acid test ratio. This excludes stocks and work-in-progress from its calculation, as it is not very easy to turn them into cash in a liquidity crisis.

$$\text{Acid test ratio} = \frac{\text{Debtors} + \text{cash} + \text{marketable securities}}{\text{Current liabilities}}$$

Valuation ratios

Financial status ratios are of interest to anyone considering investing in a company, but the main determinant will be the prospects for future profits and returns from the investment. A shareholder can obtain a return by receiving a dividend or, if the profits are retained by the company to make the business grow, from an increase in the value of the shares held, as the prospects for future profits are improved.

The main basis of share valuation should ignore the question of dividends and concentrate on the profits earned by the company, whether paid out or retained. Anyone owning a share in a company is entitled to a proportionate share in the profits after tax based on the number of shares in the company. This measure of profit per share gives a good indication of financial performance over time, provided that it is adjusted for inflation, as it removes any distortion caused by changes in the number of shares in existence. The relationship is normally described as earrnings per share.

$$\text{Earnings per share} = \frac{\text{Profit after tax}}{\text{Number of shares issued}}$$

This analysis only indicates past profit performance and the investor is really buying profits which will be earned in the future. Hence the analysis should compare performance both over time and with similar companies so that the prospects for the future can be assessed. This is done through the price/earnings multiple, which indicates the level of future growth expected in the profits of the company. The market price for any share is found by multiplying the present earnings per share figure by the price/earnings ratio, although the relationship is most commonly depicted as:

$$\text{Price/earnings multiple} = \frac{\text{Market price per share}}{\text{Earnings per share}}$$

For shareholders who like to receive regular income from their investments, the level of dividends paid influences the attractiveness of the shares. The normal way to calculate dividend income is to express it as a yield on the market price of the shares so that it is comparable to the income received from alternative forms of investment.

$$\text{Dividend yield} = \frac{\text{Net dividends paid per share}}{\text{Market price per share}} \times 100\%$$

All of the ratios explained above have been calculated using the information contained in the financial statements of the computing company referred to throughout this chapter. The calculations, with analysis, are contained in the Appendix at the end of this chapter.

Statement of value added

The financial statements so far discussed provide a clear picture of recent performance and financial status of the business, but further analysis is still needed to compare companies even if they are in the same industry as these companies may follow different strategies which have significantly different impacts on financial statements.

The concept of 'adding value' differentiates between the processes carried out on the resources input by the company from the externally purchased goods and services. Out of the value added the company pays for all its internally created costs; e.g. wages, depreciation of machinery, etc. The balance left over is profit.

The value added statement can focus attention on the proportion of internal activity which is available to the business as profit. This can be a useful way of comparing the relative success of different strategies. Our computer company adds value by assembling and distributing part-assembled units. Another company may manufacture many of the components itself and then assemble them, but it perhaps does not put as much of its resources into selling and distribution.

Information requirements for making management decisions

We have repeatedly mentioned the limited usefulness of the historic published financial statements in management decision-making; but what are the information requirements for making management decisions?

The first crucial requirement is the separation of management accounting from the financial reporting system and its concepts and conventions. It should be recognized that all managers require information to make their decisions, whether they be in research and development, production, sales, marketing, or distribution. So the financial information system must be adapted in each case to meet their needs; i.e. to add value to the resources that they input into their department.

The essential nature of management accounting is: first, controlling the efficiency by which the value chain converts input resources into output; and second, facilitating the attainment of pre-set strategic objectives (broken down into divisional, business and specific functional objectives) by the effective deployment of scarce resources.

The importance of the value chain and of measuring input/output relationships has long formed the basis of the management accounting system. However, unfortunately it has not adapted itself to the move away from manufacturing as the key value creator to other areas of the business, such as marketing or logistics. This is discussed further in Chapter 13.

The basis of the management decision-making process is choosing among alternatives to see which is likely to be most effective in reaching pre-set objectives. Managers therefore require information to be able to evaluate the opportunity cost of foregoing one or more alternatives to choose the best available alternative.

In the next three chapters the key analytical concepts, including opportunity cost, will be addressed fully.

Appendix: ratio analysis (All values in £000s)

Return on investment (ROI)

Return on shareholders' equity (ROE)

$$= \frac{\text{Net profit after tax}}{\text{Share capital and reserves}} \times 100\%$$

$$= \frac{11946}{47231} \times 100\%$$

$$= 25.3\%$$

This informs shareholders of the profit that is earned on their collective investments in the company.

The 25 per cent return calculated here would need to be compared with alternative investments available to the shareholders to see whether this is a satisfactory performance, given their perception of the risk involved.

Return on capital employed (ROCE)

or

Return on net assets (RONA)

$$= \frac{\text{Profit before interest and tax}}{\text{Sales revenue}} \times \frac{\text{Sales revenue}}{\text{Net assets}} \times 100\%$$

i.e. RONA = Profit margin × Net asset turnover × 100%

$$= \frac{22853}{406907} \times \frac{406907}{66353} \times 100\%$$

$$= \frac{22853}{66353} \times 100\%$$

$$= 34.4\%$$

RONA or ROCE can be improved by increasing the profit margin and/or improving the net asset turnover ratio. It is an indicator of how well the management are putting to use the capital invested in the business. The figure of 34 per cent would appear to be a good return on investment; but to make a realistic assessment of performance, the return made should be compared with similar companies in the same industry.

Solvency ratios

$$\text{Gearing ratio} = \frac{\text{Long-term debt}}{\text{Shareholders' equity} + \text{long-term debt}} \times 100\%$$

$$= \frac{7852}{47231 + 7852} \times 100\%$$

$$= 14.3\%$$

The gearing ratio here shows that 14.3 per cent of the firm's long-term funding is provided by debt. Thus there is only a low risk of not being able to cover the interest payments on debt capital out of profits.

Debt to equity ratio

$$= \frac{\text{Long-term debt}}{\text{Shareholders' equity}}$$

$$= \frac{7852}{47231} = 0.17$$

$$\text{Interest cover} = \frac{\text{Profit before taxation} + \text{interest payable}}{\text{Interest payable}}$$

$$= \frac{26785 + 3932}{3932}$$

$$= 7.8 \text{ times}$$

This low level of risk is further expressed in the interest cover ratio, which indicates how much operating profits can fall before the interest costs put the company into a loss-making position.

Liquidity ratios

$$\text{Current ratio} = \frac{\text{Current assets}}{\text{Current liabilities}}$$

$$= \frac{132222}{153092}$$

$$= 0.86$$

The current ratio shows that current assets are not sufficient to pay for all current liabilities in a liquidity crisis. When stocks are excluded from the calculation (as in the acid test ratio), the resultant ratio of 0.65 may give concern to management who may need to act, to reduce creditors for example.

Acid test ratio

$$= \frac{\text{Debtors} + \text{cash} + \text{marketable securities}}{\text{Current liabilities}}$$

$$= \frac{99757}{153092}$$

$$= 0.65$$

Valuation ratios

Earnings per share $= \dfrac{\text{Profit after tax}}{\text{No. of shares issued}}$ $= \dfrac{11946}{77466}$

$= 15.4\text{p per share}$

The earnings per share gives an indication of past profit performance on a per share basis. However, as the investor is buying profits which will be earned in the future, he needs further analysis. The

Price/earnings multiple $= \dfrac{\text{Market price per share}^*}{\text{Earnings prer share}}$ $= \dfrac{110}{15.4}$

$= 7.14$

* Assume market price is 110p per share

price/earnings multiple shows the level of future growth expected in the profits of the company. It is the reciprocal, multiplied by 100, of the earnings yield; i.e. the p/e multiple of 7.14 corresponds to an earnings yield of 14 per cent p.a.

Dividend yield

$= \dfrac{\text{Net dividends paid per share}}{\text{Market price per share}} \times 100\%$ $= \dfrac{15}{110} \times 100\%$

$= 13.6\%$

Dividend income, when expressed as a yield on the market price of the shares, can be compared to income received from alternative forms of investment, e.g. in a building society.

3

Practical techniques used in the financial analysis process

Overview

The analytical role of the management accountant involves the collection and processing of cost and other financial information. This vital information will provide reference points indicating to management the existing state of the business and the external environment. Once the information has been gathered it needs to be analysed to establish what resources are currently available, how they have been utilized and what will be needed in the future to achieve the organization's objectives. Analysis of the external environment will identify the opportunities that exist for effectively deploying these resources to achieve some competitive advantage: a cost advantage perhaps, or a differentiated product (i.e. good or service). Within this external analysis there should be a comparison of the business against its competitors. There is, however, the problem of obtaining financial information on other companies, the primary source of this financial information being the set of published financial statements which are, of course, publicly available. Unfortunately, if, as we continually state, published financial information is of little value to decision-makers *within* the organization, it is certainly going to be of little help to decision-makers in competing organizations. Thus, wherever possible, the analysing organization needs to use other sources of information. A comparison of financial performance within the context of the whole industry, or in relation to the general business and economic environment, or against the financial performance of supplying industries and, where relevant, customers might provide meaningful information. The timescales involved should also be appreciated in the financial analysis, as losses relative to the industry as a whole might be due to, for example, the launch of a new product, when losses should be expected anyway.

The most detailed aspect of financial analysis must therefore be the internal assessment of the business. There is likely to be a mass of data available internally in any organization (including the individual recording of each financial transaction, as reported in summary in the published financial statements). Thus, the rationale for carrying out the financial analysis must be carefully highlighted. A prime objective is to identify where existing resources are being allocated and what level of financial return is being achieved from these resources. This should indicate where constraints exist which are diverting resources away from the targeted areas of the business. Every organization will have a few 'key constraints' or 'limiting factors' (so called because they limit the ability of the business to achieve more financial success) which the financial analysis must identify so that their effective utilization is maximized.

Analysis over time will also show how these limiting factors change, which means that the organization must review the balance of its resources on a regular basis; e.g. the lack of distribution channels may be redressed by the company through increased marketing effort, which means that, as this marketing activity takes effect, the business is no longer constrained by poor access to customers. Constraints are by their very nature a short-term problem; in the long term the resources which are currently tied up will be released and be available elsewhere in the organization, thereby creating a new set of short-term constraints.

The availability of funds to finance the growth of the business may be another critical resource constraint. Financial analysis must therefore differentiate between the profit generated from the performance of the business and the financial strength of the business, which is dependent upon its present cash levels and readily available access to funds.

The cash flow analysis needs to consider the different time periods in which the company needs available finance. In the short term, the business needs cash to buy stock, pay wages and operating expenses. A shortage of cash could seriously affect the company's ability to trade effectively. Overcoming a short-term cash flow problem may involve not replacing stock, and this could lower sales and hence reduce profitability. If cash is required to finance growth over the long term, the existing level of trading should be producing a steady new level of cash inflows which can be reinvested in the business to finance the growth. The rate of cash generation could be the key constraint to this growth. A cash injection (e.g. by borrowing funds from an external source, such as a bank) might accelerate this growth, but the company must be able to support this additional finance by earning a sufficient return to pay the interest on these borrowed funds *and* still sustain the rate of growth of the business. The effects of inflation on cash in terms of reducing its purchasing power also need to be considered in this analysis.

Chapters 4 and 5 show how financial analysis is used in planning, but first this chapter identifies some of the common analytical techniques which form the basis of the management accountant's role in analysis for financial decisions.

Committed and discretionary costs

As has already been mentioned, there are fewer constraints imposed on long-term planning than on short-term decisions. Managers are thus given greater scope to make the decisions that they see as appropriate and consistent with the strategy of the business and their own specific objectives. This raises other important issues regarding management accounting for financial decisions. In the short term (e.g. for a period of up to one year) most costs are committed and many costs are also fixed or static regardless of what is happening to the level of activity. A committed cost is a cost where the management, by taking a previous decision, has already committed itself to spend the funds involved (even if payment has not been made);

e.g. a contract to lease computing equipment for a three-year period represents a committed cost for years 1, 2 and 3. The amount of the committed cost is pre-determined and can be altered only by another major decision to reverse or amend the earlier commitment. Such a decision will normally involve the business in incurring a further cost, such as a cancellation fee. Planning and control of a committed cost can only therefore be undertaken at the point in time just before the commitment is made. Such a long-term committed cost should be evaluated using proper capital expenditure evaluation techniques (e.g. discounted cash flow) and it is normally controlled within the capital expenditure budget, which is discussed in Chapters 7 and 8.

Long-term planning is the key to managing effectively committed fixed costs because once a commitment has been made the fixed costs are difficult to influence by short run actions. If funds have not yet been committed the management can exercise its discretion through the current decision whether or not to spend. As decisions are based on assessing future costs and benefits, these discretionary costs are more relevant and so it is important to differentiate them from committed costs.

In many businesses, a large proportion of non-operating or non-manufacturing costs can be regarded as discretionary; e.g. research and development, marketing, employees training and development. They are not pre-determined by some previous commitment. Management is therefore able to vary the level of investment in these areas as it feels necessary. This can however create difficulty in controlling these costs because there is no established method for determining the appropriate amount to be spent in any one period, whereas for most direct operating costs there is a more definable relationship between the level of activity and the required cost level.

One way of addressing the problem of controlling discretionary items is to make a comparison with the level of expense incurred in past periods for the same item. However, past periods are a weak basis for comparison because they may represent excessive or deficient budget allocations in the past. More importantly, the financial evaluation should be carried out in the context of the business' *current* internal and external environment which may have altered significantly, thus making the comparison with the past irrelevant and misleading.

Some organizations fix the amount of discretionary expenditure according to some percentage of sales turnover. This can be dangerous. Future sales are very often determined by discretionary items such as research and development and marketing investment. However, if current sales revenues declined, the budgeted expenditure for future research and development and marketing would be proportionately reduced when it may be more logical to increase it in order to stimulate future sales. The normal reason for choosing sales revenue as a basis for determining discretionary budgets is not because of any possible causal relationship between sales revenues and discretionary expenditure, but simply because sales revenue is felt to be an indicator of what the company can afford to spend.

Control of discretionary costs, because of their very nature, cannot be a structured discipline. There is no mathematically derived optimum relationship between inputs (as measured by costs) and outputs (as measured by sales revenues) for discretionary costs. Therefore the control function must focus on measuring the effectiveness of the expenditure rather than the efficiency of the input to output relationship. The expenditure needs to be fully justified against the identified objectives for the project so that the potential performance can be financially evaluated. The use of non-financial control parameters (e.g. physical milestones) may also be necessary where the financial outcome of any expenditure is difficult to establish.

Opportunity cost

The aim of financial analysis is to allow managers to concentrate their efforts on those areas of business where using their judgement, or discretion, will have the most significant impact. This should give them the opportunity to carry out effectively the chosen strategy that they believe is most appropriate to the organization's objectives, available resources and external environment. The analysis will have highlighted any areas where the business may be constrained or where resources are not being effectively utilized.

As will be shown in Part Three, a major part of the planning exercise is to reallocate resources so that they are better used within the business and to acquire any additional resources which can be financially justified. There are financial decision-making techniques which are very helpful in this area because they force managers to quantify the benefits obtained by using resources in any particular way. One such technique involves considering what alternative financial benefit must be given up in order to use a particular business resource in a specific way. If there is an opportunity which gives a better financial return, then the business can be made better off by reallocating this resource.

The general term for this analytical technique is the 'opportunity cost', which is the benefit which would be obtained from the foregone alternative; i.e. the next best available opportunity, which would have been realized had there been sufficient resources. For example, part of the opportunity cost to Ford of investing in the development of the new Escort was the lost profit that was given up (foregone) by replacing the existing Escort. It is important to note that the financial information relevant to any decision relates to *future* costs and benefits; any past costs are irrelevant to the future decision. The concept of opportunity cost as used in planning and decision-making is discussed further in Chapter 6.

Classifying costs into fixed and variable

As time scales increase fewer and fewer costs can be regarded as fixed because the business can vary almost all costs to suit the activity level that is forecast. Indeed one of the more useless economics sayings is 'in the very long run all costs are variable, whereas in the very, very short run all costs are fixed'. Classifying costs into fixed and variable is very important in practical financial decision-making, because if a cost is generally fixed and will not change as a result of the decision being considered it can be ignored in the financial analysis. This distinction is vitally important in short-term planning, where many costs will be fixed and the few variable ones need to be identified in order to be able to monitor and predict the short-term changes caused by variations in the level of activity. To do this, the relevant range for each cost must be identified. For a relevant range, fixed costs remain constant while variable costs alter in proportion to the movement up or down the range. The relevant range can be determined in terms of sales value or sales volume, time or some other variable. It may be limited in one or both directions as costs may increase with activity but not reduce in the same way; rental costs being a good example. In some companies material costs are the only truly variable costs in the short-term as others, including labour, are becoming increasingly fixed in relation to short run changes in activity. The control of material costs and particularly the control of stocks of raw materials has therefore become an important management discipline.

Cost–volume–profit analysis

Variable costs have been differentiated from fixed costs: a fixed cost remains unchanged for the specified relevant range, whereas a variable cost will vary proportionately with a change in the level of activity. For long-range planning most costs will change over the period of the plan. However, when considering budgets with a much shorter timescale, many more costs will be fixed. This allows analysis in the short term to focus just on the variable costs. It is possible to classify all the expenses of the business as either fixed or variable costs. However, some business costs are difficult to categorize at first glance because part of the cost is fixed while the other part increases in direct proportion to changes in activity. Although it is possible to classify these costs into a third category, as semi-fixed or semi-variable costs, this is unnecessary and confusing, as each of these costs can, and should, be split into its fixed and variable components.

Once costs have been analysed into fixed and variable elements, they can be graphically represented to show the profit position of the business for any particular set of circumstances within the short-term timescale. This is the period in which the output of the firm is restricted to that available from the current operating capacity. The operating capacity cannot be adjusted in the short term because of the committed costs of existing labour and the time it takes to re-set capacity through installing new machinery or hiring and training more employees.

By analysing the relationship between cost, volume and profit, decision-makers can choose among alternative operating levels which differ in total sales volume and in the composition of that volume. Although the technique does have its limitations, which will be discussed later in this chapter, it is a powerful tool for short-term decision-making.

The objective of cost–volume–profit (CVP) analysis is to see what will happen in financial terms if a specified level of activity or volume fluctuates in the short term. In the analysis the critical output levels can be identified; e.g. at what level will profit be maximized or at what point does the business break even? This is vital information for short-term decision-making as one of the most important variables influencing total sales revenue, total costs and profits is sales output or volume.

Profit is calculated by subtracting expenses from revenue;and expenses are the sum of fixed costs and variable costs (given that all expenses have been classified as either fixed or variable):

Profit = Revenue − expenses

Profit = Revenue − (fixed costs + variable costs)

Thus a business will begin to make profit beyond the level of activity where revenue equals expenses (where the business 'breaks even'). In Figure 3.1 break-even occurs at point B. Beyond B, as volume increases so too does profit, as sales revenue exceeds total cost (within the given relevant range).

This break-even chart is only valid for the particular set of assumptions on which it is based and therefore, if any of the cost relationships change, the chart must be redrawn.

The assumptions of CVP analysis

1   Only one selling price and a constant variable cost per unit is applicable to the whole range of the chart, hence sales revenue and variable costs are drawn

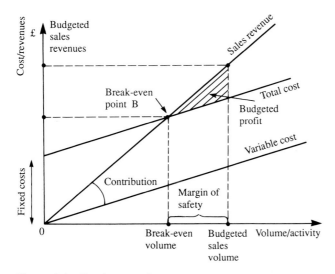

Figure 3.1   *Break-even chart*

as straight lines. Each chart has a restricted range of activity for the fixed costs to remain fixed: any volume outside this range and the chart must be redrawn with new assumptions. CVP analysis also assumes one sales mix for the products covered by the chart and if this mix changes the slope of the sales revenue line will need to be redrawn.

2 Fixed costs are treated as a constant. Thus the total cost line is drawn parallel to the variable cost line.

> Total costs = Fixed costs + variable costs

3 It is assumed that finished goods stocks are constant and that production equals sales; i.e. that movements in stock levels at varying costs do not distort the profit analysis.

4 The chart is only applicable to the relevant range. This is usually the output range within which the firm expects to be operating in the near future; i.e. normal capacity. Within this range it is assumed that the variable cost per unit is the same throughout the entire range of output. Thus the total cost line is linear (fixed costs are fixed).

What information do the charts show?

1 The point of break-even is shown where the total cost line crosses the sales revenue line; i.e. at the point where neither a profit nor a loss is made.

2 If budgeted sales levels are also plotted on the chart their relationship to the break-even point can be examined. In Figure 3.1 our budgeted sales revenues are above the level needed to break even and so we are budgeting for a profit. The shaded area of the chart indicates the level of budgeted profit. There is a 'margin of safety' available to the business which is the degree to which the sales levels can fall before the business fails to make a profit. This margin of safety can also be expressed as a percentage of break-even sales volumes by using the formula:

$$\frac{\text{Budgeted sales} - \text{sales at break even}}{\text{Sales at break even}} \times 100\%$$

The break-even position is also commonly expressed as a percentage of the total operating capacity of the business. This indicates the scale of the risk that the business will be trading at a loss. Where break even represents a high percentage of total capacity, there is a high risk that sales volumes may be below this level and the company would, in the short term, be unable to reduce its costs to avoid making a loss. It also shows that limited opportunities exist for the company to make large profits even when sales volumes are above break even if the break-even volume is close to capacity.

3   The angle between the sales revenue line and the variable cost line indicates the contribution rate. This shows the rate at which the business covers its fixed costs by sales activity and then makes a contribution to profit.

Contribution = Sales revenue – variable costs

Profit = Sales revenue – variable costs – fixed costs

Therefore: Profit = Contribution – fixed costs

Thus contribution first covers fixed costs and then makes profit.

Contribution analysis

The concept of contribution is one of the most useful concepts in financial decision-making. As the volumes applied to sales and variable costs are the same, contribution per unit (contribution per unit = sales revenue per unit – variable cost per unit) can be used to enable a useful relationship to be derived for the break-even volume.

Profit = Revenue – expenses

and   Revenue = Selling price per unit × volume

and   Expenses = Fixed costs + variable cost per unit × volume

but   Break-even is where Profit = 0

therefore   Revenue = Expenses

therefore   Selling price per unit × volume = Fixed costs + (variable cost per unit × volume)

therefore   Volume (selling price per unit – variable cost per unit) = Fixed costs

therefore   Break-even volume $= \dfrac{\text{Fixed costs}}{\text{Contribution per unit}}$

Thus it can be seen that the break-even point is dictated by the level of fixed costs incurred by the business and the rate at which these fixed costs are covered by making a contribution on each unit of sales.

In Figure 3.2 there is an illustrative example of break-even analysis.

The relationship between sales volumes and profits can also be graphed directly, by combining the relationships shown on the break-even chart into one line, as shown in Figure 3.3. This gives a simple indication of the profit or loss made for any given level of activity. In the shaded area A, fixed costs exceed contribution and therefore a loss is made. In the shaded area B, enough contribution is made

(a)

NSW Ltd

Forecast annual volume (assume 100% capacity utilization)	36,000 units
Annual sales revenue (assuming no changes in level of stocks held)	£360,000
Fixed costs	£120,000
Variable costs per unit	£6

$$\text{Selling price per unit} = \frac{\text{Sales revenue}}{\text{Sales volume}} = \frac{£360{,}000}{36{,}000} = £10$$

1   *Calculate the break-even volume*

$$\text{Break-even volume} = \frac{\text{Fixed costs}}{\text{Contribution per unit}}$$

$$= \frac{£120{,}000}{£10 - £6}$$

$$= 30{,}000 \text{ units}$$

2   *Calculate the break-even capacity*

$$\text{Break-even capacity} = \frac{\text{Break-even volume}}{\text{Volume at full capacity}}$$

$$= \frac{30{,}000}{36{,}000}$$

$$= 83.3\%$$

3   *Calculate margin of safety*

$$\text{Margin of safety} = \frac{\text{Budgeted sales} - \text{Break-even volume}}{\text{Break-even volume}}$$

$$= \frac{36{,}000 - 30{,}000}{30{,}000} = 20\%$$

Figures 3.2   *Break-even analysis example*

4   *Calculate profit forecast*

	£000
Sales	360
Variable costs	216
Total contribution	144
Fixed costs	120
Profit	24

Break-even volume and sales can be shown graphically as in Figure 3.2b

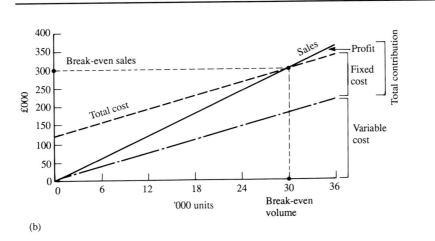

(b)

Figure 3.2   *(continued)*

to cover fixed costs and to make a profit. The point where neither a profit nor a loss is made is the break-even level of acitivity.

For any given set of assumptions these break-even and profit/volume charts can have some very useful applications. They can display the impact of many potential changes in the business and its environment. Specific targets for profit can be incorporated, either as a fixed target profit (when it is treated as if it were an additional fixed cost) or as a percentage of sales (when it is treated like an additional variable cost); and of course by redrawing the chart one can see the impact of changes in fixed costs, selling prices or variable costs. The way in which profit targets can be incorporated into break-even charts is illustrated in Figures 3.4 and 3.5.

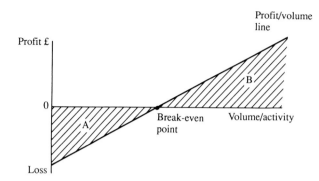

Figure 3.3   *Profit/volume line*

Of greatest value to decision-makers, however, is being able to compare the relative cost structures of different strategies and businesses, and the consequent risks associated with each. A business with a high level of fixed costs and low variable costs needs to achieve a high contribution per unit or a very high volume if those fixed costs are to be recovered and a profit is to be made. If this can be achieved, once the fixed costs are recovered and the break even point is passed, the business will quickly earn large profits due to the high contribution rate. However, should the level of activity fall below the break-even level, substantial losses will be made as the fixed costs will still be incurred. This situation is illustrated

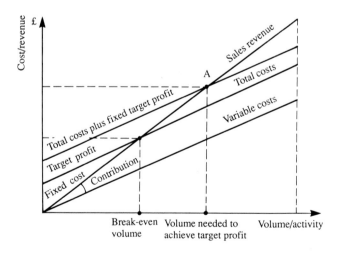

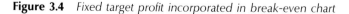

1   The fixed target profit can be added as a fixed element to the fixed costs
    and therefore generates another line parallel to the variable cost line,
    being total costs plus target profit
2   Where this line crosses the sales revenue line the company achieves its
    fixed target profit (that is, at point A on the chart)

Figure 3.4   *Fixed target profit incorporated in break-even chart*

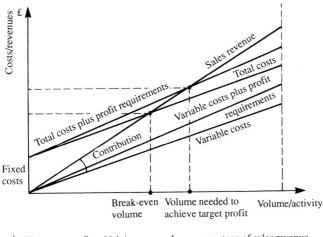

1 The target profit, which is expressed as a percentage of sales revenue
   can be added to the variable cost line increasing the
   gradient and producing a new line – variable cost plus profit requirement
2 This produces a net excess profit contribution towards fixed costs and
   where the new total cost and profit requirement line crosses the sales
   revenue line, the company achieves its objectives

Figure 3.5 *Target profit as a fixed percentage of sales revenue incorporated in break-even chart*

in Figure 3.6, which shows how a small movement in the level of activity can have a dramatic effect on the profits of the business.

If a business has a higher proportion of variable costs then its risk profile is reduced, as can be seen in Figure 3.7, because potential losses would automatically be minimized as most of the costs would decrease with falling sales volumes,

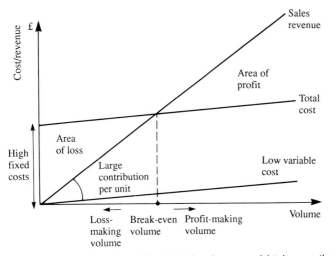

Figure 3.6 *High risk profile: high fixed cost and high contribution*

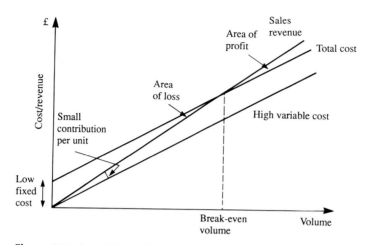

Figure 3.7 *Low risk profile: low fixed cost/low contribution*

although of course profit potential from increased activity is also reduced. A reduction in the risk involved leads to a reduction in the potential return.

Businesses within the same industry can have significantly different cost structures. For example, a computing company that manufacture all its own components may incur very high fixed costs of capital equipment and labour. It therefore needs to achieve a high level of contribution per unit to recover these fixed costs. However, a business that buys in finished products and acts as a marketing and distribution specialist will have a much higher proportion of variable costs.

Standard costing

A standard cost is the level of cost which should be incurred for any given level of activity, normally as determined by some measureable input–output relationship, under specified conditions. If the input–output relationship is predictable, it is possible to build up an 'expected' or 'standard' level of cost for any given level of activity. This can be any repetitive task where the resources needed can be predicted with reasonable accuracy and the cost of those resources identified. Therefore, despite the reference to engineering-type relationships, standard costing need not be restricted to the production environment.

The type of relationships analysed in break-even and contribution analysis form the starting point for short-term budgeting and forecasting. Once the organization is broken down into separate, controllable businesses (or responsibility centres), the major role of the budget is to ensure that the internal resources of the organization are adequately allocated to the businesses and that the plans of each area are mutually compatible with each other and with the overall corporate plan.

The budget should be analysed into its controllable elements so that specific but coordinated objectives can be agreed for each area of the business.

As will be seen in Part Three, these objectives should include non-financial as well as financial objectives: it is important that the financial aspects of the budget are integrated with the tasks and activities of each separate area and are not simply monetary values representing sales revenues or expenditure levels to be achieved. In order to do this, the total costs and revenues need to be broken down into the specific relationships that can be derived and used to predict the level of costs that will be incurred in the future. Such a cost relationship can be defined as an 'engineered' cost if it is possible to calculate the level of output expected from a given level of input.

Standard costing can be used to set the level of resources needed by such a responsibility centre. It is very useful in budgeting as it greatly assists in setting a reference base against which to compare actual outcomes. The level at which companies set 'standards' can vary because it is possible to set standards which establish a very tight target to aim at or which are what the manager actually hopes to achieve.

Using a production environment as an illustration (because the use of standard costing is most common there) standards can be defined at three alternative levels:

1 *'Ideal' standards*. This means that a machine is running at its rated capacity. These standards can only be achieved under exceptional circumstances and then for only short periods of time. Thus normal performance will always fall short of this 'ideal'.
2 *'Expected' standards*. These are the best estimates of what is expected to happen over the budget period. Management recognizes that these standards are unlikely to be met all the time – the business expects to beat the standard as often as it fails to achieve it and over the year the gains and losses should balance out.
3 *'Target' standards*. These tend to be based on previous performance but with an allowance built in for improved future productivity. This assumes that a learning process is in action which makes the operation more efficient. This gain in efficiency is included in the forecast standard cost.

None of these approaches to standard setting is the 'right' approach. However, it is important that the managers with responsibility for monitoring and controlling budgets understand how the standards are set because this will influence how these managers react to their actual achievements against the established standards.

The normal control process involves calculating what costs should have been incurred according to the standard costs and to compare these against the actual costs. This is known as 'variance analysis' but is the calculation of simple differences rather than the statistically based 'variances'. If the actual cost incurred is lower than the standard cost the variance is described as 'favourable'; while if actual cost exceeds the standard the variance is 'unfavourable' or 'adverse'. Unfortunately, these terms and the normal method of presentation, whereby adverse variances are shown in brackets or as negatives, tend to prejudice management reaction to the financial analysis. Thus all adverse variances are bad news while all favourable variances indicate a good performance. This over-generalization can be very dangerous.

If the standards set are properly understood by the managers, then for standards set at the 'ideal' level the company must expect to incur regular adverse variances. If 'expected' standards have been established, both favourable and adverse variances would be recorded during the year and the company would expect the overall net variance to be zero.

Standards are most commonly set at some sort of 'target' level and because achieving a 'target' is normally considered a good performance, it is most likely that some level of adverse variances will be recorded during the year when the actual costs are compared to standards.

Some budgeting systems which use standard costing also include a budgeted (i.e. expected) level of variance to allow for the non-achievement of 'ideal' or 'target' standards.

Standard costs are always composed of two elements – some physical units consumed in some way multiplied by a cost price per unit to generate the financial standard costs:

Standard cost = Standard physical units × standard price per unit.

Variances for each responsibility centre can be identified by each element of cost and analysed according to the price and quantity content. However, the input–output relationship in most cases is determined by the physical aspects of the standard and not by the price; e.g. one can derive a physical standard for the amount of microchips on a computer circuitboard which will be constant over a period of time and does not change just because the price of microchips changes at a point in time.

The financial analysis highlights where the variances have arisen; the managers responsible should then identify the reasons for the variance and take appropriate action. If it is found that the variance is due to a permanent change in the standard, the standard should be altered as it is no longer relevant as a guide to the future.

As well as helping to monitor and control the performance of each business, standards play an important role in motivating managers and assessing their performance. The performance of all managers should be evaluated against measures over which they have a high degree of control and where the successful achievement of managers' objectives is important to the overall success of the business. The setting of a standard or expected level of performance for each manager will allow the efficiency of his or her performance to be assessed. Efficiency is defined as achieving a very high level of output for any given level of inputs; hence with the use of standards the efficiency of actual performance can be assessed against this relative standard.

Some would argue that the comparison of actual performance with standard performance is pointless as comparison can only be made after the event. However, if managers are aware beforehand that their financial performance is going to be judged by using the standards, they are likely to act differently from the way they might if they realized that their performance was not going to be evaluated. Variance analysis can therefore be a good motivator, if used properly. The more important reason for carrying out detailed variance analysis, comparing the actual performance against the standard costs previously established, is to understand which costs are changing and to predict the impact of these changes in the future. Thus movements in cost levels may indicate the need to review selling prices sooner than expected or, if expected cost increases are not being experienced, planned price increases can be deferred or a possible reduction in selling prices may be a sensible strategy. Variance analysis should therefore be viewed as an aid to making financial decisions rather than as an historic reconciliation of actual to standard costs. If used in this positive way, the type of variance analyisis which is required can be tailored to the specific decisions facing a business.

Types of variances

There are essentially three ways of analysing total cost variances:

1   Direct material and operating costs variances
2   Direct labour variances
3   Overhead variances.

Each of these can be further analysed (see Figure 3.8). The formulae for calculating the variances are shown in the Appendix at the end of this chapter, and a detailed practical example of variance analysis is given in Chapter 12.

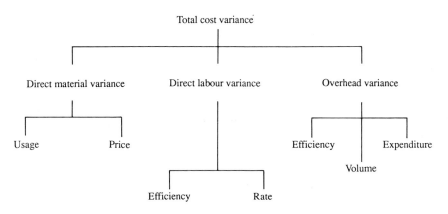

Figure 3.8 *Principal cost variances*

1   Direct material cost variances

A material cost variance may be analysed into:

- a material usage variance
- a material price variance.

An unfavourable material cost variance may have arisen because the amount of material used exceeded the standard quantity specified and/or the price paid for the material used was higher than the standard price per unit. Once the causes have been identified the separate variances can be dealt with by the people responsible for them; e.g. a departmental supervisor may be responsible for a usage variance and a buyer for a price variance.

The usage variance is traditionally calculated using the standard price per unit and not the actual price paid. This difference in price is only accounted for through the material price variance. This is done because otherwise the usage variance could be affected by the buying efficiency of the people purchasing the resources, and this might distort the perception of the performance of the operational managers. This is discussed in more detail in Chapter 12.

The cause of a price variance may be due to the buying department not choosing the most advantageous source of supply. However, the cause may very well be beyond the control of the manager concerned; e.g. there may be a change in market conditions which causes a general price increase for the type of materials used. However, the standard must still be altered if the adverse market conditions prevail for any length of time.

2   Direct labour variances

In a similar way to material cost variance, direct labour variance may be analysed into:

- a labour efficiency variance
- a labour rate variance.

A labour efficiency variance may arise because of the use of poor quality materials or poorly maintained machinery; or the introduction of new equipment, in which case some temporary fall-off in efficiency may be expected and allowed for in the budget, while the workforce becomes acquainted with the new equipment.

An adverse labour rate variance is very often due to a negotiated increase in labour rates which is not yet reflected in the standard labour rate, and is therefore an uncontrollable variance from the point of view of the production manager, who controls the labour concerned.

3 Overhead variances

Overheads include both fixed costs and variable costs. In order to control overheads actual costs should be compared with the budgeted costs for the actual level of activity for each cost centre. This budgeted cost can be derived from either a fixed or flexible budget.

A fixed overhead budget is developed for a specific estimated level of production and specific operating conditions. It is used unchanged throughout the budget period, irrespective of the level of activity. Thus changes in the level of activity will give rise to variances in overhead expenses. However, in most companies, where operating conditions and the level of activity vary from month to month, the flexible budget is more widely used. A flexible budget is a series of budgets established for various forecast levels of activity. By recognizing the difference between fixed and variable overhead costs, it is designed to change in relation to the level of activity attained, so that the actual level of activity can be properly represented in the final 'flexed' budget.

Overhead variances can be analysed into three elements:

- *Overhead efficiency variance.* This is the variance of actual hours or other usage item from the standard usage specified for the actual activity level (i.e. it is similar to a labour efficiency variance).
- *Overhead volume variance.* This is the variance caused by changes in the level of activity from the budget whether fixed or flexible. Where a flexible budget is in use, it is the difference between the standard cost and the flexible budget for the actual activity, which is taken into account by flexing the budget.
- *Overhead expenditure variance.* This is the variance of actual overhead incurred from overhead budgeted for the actual activity and is therefore similar to a price or value variance. The overhead budgeted for the actual capacity may be determined from a flexible budget.

Criticisms of standard costing variance analysis

The comparison of actual performance with the standard will inevitably cause problems if the system for setting the standards is weak. Variances that result from poorly set standards will not have the same significance to managers as variances from tighter standards, which accurately reflect the cost levels that should be incurred. To measure properly managerial performance, like must be compared with like; i.e. the actual costs incurred should be compared against standards based on the conditions under which managers actually operated during the period. Therefore the standards must be constantly under review, especially during inflationary periods if the forecast of inflation proves to be inaccurate.

The standard should be attainable if it is to have a positive motivational impact on managers and other employees. Thus an ideal standard will probably not motivate employees to improve their performance, particularly if the regular adverse variances are large. An expected standard which it is anticipated can be attained during a future specific period is more appropriate for evaluating managerial performance because it takes into account human rates of work, normal machine breakdowns and other unavoidable disruptions.

Provided that the standards are not too loose and that the variances reported to responsibility centres are controllable (financial analysis should make it possible to determine where the variance occurred, who was responsible, and why it happened), standard costs can provide a sound basis for budgetary control and indeed can be made an integral part of the budgetary control system. This will be discussed at greater length in Part Three and Part Four.

It is important to understand that standard costing and variance analysis enables managers to measure the level of efficiency of the operation (i.e. the units of output relative to the units of input) and not its effectiveness (i.e. how well the objectives have been achieved). Efficiency is a measure of technical success/failure in the input–output relationship, but does not guarantee the financial success of the business. Efficiency versus effectiveness is discussed in Chapter 11.

Questions

1 Due to rising energy prices, NSW Ltd anticipates that its costs will be higher than those originally forecast and shown in Figure 3.2 on page 68. Its variable cost per unit will increase to £7 per unit and its fixed costs will rise by between 15 and 20 per cent.

 Given that demand for NSW's product is not expected to change, what will be the impact of these rising costs on the contribution level?

2 Within what range would the company have to set the price for its product if it is to maintain its original forecast level of profit?

3 Give a graphical representation of these possible scenarios.

4 What impact will these revised forecasts have on the break-even capacity of the business?

5 Stancos Ltd manufactures one standard product and operates a system of variance cost accounting using a fixed budget. Below is the budgeted and standard cost data for the first quarter of the year.

Budgeted sales and production:	50,000 units
Standard cost for each unit of output:	
direct materials:	20 kgs @ £3.50 per kg
direct labour:	6 hours @ £4 per hour
Fixed production overheads:	£900,000
Budgeted sales price per unit:	£150

The actual cost data for the period is as follows:

Production: 45,000 units sold at a price 10 per cent higher than budgeted
Direct materials: 970,000 kgs @ £3.80 per kg
Direct labour: 325,000 hours @ £3.75 per hour
Fixed production overheads: £860,000

You are required to:

1. Calculate the budgeted and actual profit.
2. Calculate and analyse the key variances.

Appendix: variance formulae

1 Direct material cost variances

(a) Material usage variance = (standard quantity of materials for actual activity − actual quantity used) × standard price per unit.
(b) Material price variance = (standard price per unit of material − actual price) × quantity of materials purchased.

2 Direct labour variances

(a) Labour efficiency variance = (standard quantity of labour hours for actual activity − actual labour hours worked) × standard labour rate per hour.
(b) Labour rate variance = (standard labour rate per hour − actual labour rate) × actual labour hours worked.

3 Overhead variances

(a) Overhead efficiency variance = (standard quantity of input usage for actual activity − actual input usage) × overhead rate.
(b) Overhead volume variance = (actual activity − budgeted activity) × standard overhead rate.
(c) Overhead expenditure variance = budgeted overheads for actual activity − actual overhead cost.

4

Analysis for management planning

Overview

Chapter 3 dealt with some of the fundamental cost classifications and introduced techniques for helping managers to analyse the basic relationship between costs, revenues and profit. However, for the purposes of sound financial decision-making the basics are not enough. In this chapter we consider other more specific ways of classifying and analysing cost information which enable managers to make decisions about the profitability or contribution of individual products, customers or market segments.

If financial analysis is to be of use for management planning and control, it should match the way in which the activities of the organization are carried out and how the organization is structured. Thus, the financial analysis should not just be restricted to assessing the performance of the organization as a whole, but should include a breakdown into individual divisions, businesses, product and customer segments. How the organization is broken down will depend on the critical factors facing the business in each area.

The group may be split into divisions, organized by particular common factors in their markets (e.g. channels of distribution, size or type of customer) or by an underlying technology or process involved in the product. For some areas of the business a more focused breakdown may be required to analyse the performance of specific products or customers, or both.

Thus, in this chapter we identify the costs that are relevant to making decisions about specific business segments, or that affect the group as a whole. The importance of basing financial decisions on future differential financial costs and benefits is stressed; i.e. those costs and benefits which arise as a result of the decision. To enable segmented analysis to take place, finance managers need to differentiate between costs that are directly incurred in generating income from those segments and costs which are indirect. In certain circumstances, the manager may only need to focus on the direct costs if these are the only differential costs which have been incurred.

The need to report financial performance, for the purposes of management planning and control, on a periodic basis is re-evaluated; instead of automatically producing financial reports for a month or a year, the technique of product life-cycle costing is advocated. The stages of the product's life (embryonic, growth, maturity and ageing) are used to identify the most appropriate financial control parameters.

The financial analysis process should indicate the current allocation of resources and judge their relative effectiveness. Chapter 3 introduced the technique of contribution analysis. In this chapter it is applied so as to identify the optimum allocation of resources within the business by calculating the contribution that is made for each 'limiting factor' or 'key resource' constraint. Thus a base can be developed from which to set budgets for each responsibility centre, as determined by which manager has control over which resource.

Direct versus indirect costs

To work out and analyse the profitability of individual products or business segments, the costs incurred in generating the product sales revenues must be identified. It is important for the analysis to highlight the key differences among the various segments. Breaking the business into sections or segments is the first stage in enabling financial analysis to provide information for future planning. If managers are in a planning role, they need to focus on the allocation of resources required to achieve their objectives, which are normally described by reference to specific products and markets. A good system of financial analysis should indicate the current allocation of resources and their relative success. Therefore, financial performance needs to be analysed into product and customer segments, and into appropriate sub-groups such as channels of distribution, sales territories, etc.

Although *Nielsen Market Information Manual* and *Mintel Market Intelligence*, among others, provide published information on market size and share etc. for many products, it is difficult to obtain explicit financial information on the profitability of competitors' products and customers. Hence detailed internal analysis is required to enable the differences from competitors to be highlighted. If this analysis is well done, a very good approximation of the relative competitive financial positions can be built up, using some logical deductions from the available published information. As many areas of the business as can help in providing the required inputs, plus those who need the information which should be generated as a result of the analysis, should be involved in this very important analytical process.

In analysing cost information to work out product profitability, some costs will be directly attributable to the product and therefore easily identified; i.e. the cost is solely incurred on behalf of this product. The sum of direct materials, direct labour and direct expenses is normally referred to as the 'prime costs'. However, many costs are not directly incurred in producing any single product line. These costs are known as indirect costs. Costs can be classified as direct or indirect by reference to any type of cost object. A cost object is any segment of the business, including products, market segments and cost centres, which needs financial analysis for the purposes of management planning and control. A cost centre is a segment of the business which incurs costs but does not itself generate sales revenues which can offset these costs; these classifications are discussed in more detail in Chapter 11.

When a system of budgetary planning and control is in operation, cost centres can be used for judging the performance of those who are responsible for the running of these cost centres. The overall plan is analysed into specific tasks which can be allocated to the operational areas of the business. Managers are then given responsibility for undertaking these tasks. It is the objective of the financial control system to provide the right information to these managers at the right time. To facilitate this, the appropriate cost centres must be identified.

The costs incurred by a cost centre are analysed by using a yardstick of activity, or cost unit, to measure efficiency. A cost unit is a unit of product, service or time (or a combination of these) in relation to which costs may be identified or expressed. There are two approaches to this identification process: absorption costing and marginal costing. In an absorption costing system all cost centre costs are ultimately absorbed by cost units. In a marginal costing system only the variable costs are related to cost units; the differences between the two approaches to costing are discussed in more detail later in this chapter and in Chapter 5.

These costs are further classified into cost elements (e.g. material cost, labour cost, overhead expenses), and then into direct costs and indirect costs. A direct cost is one which can be allocated directly to a cost centre or cost unit because of its direct association with the production of a cost unit or with the activity of a cost centre. Although indirect costs cannot be directly associated with the production of a single cost unit or with the activity of a cost centre, they should, where appropriate, still be apportioned to the relevant cost centres or be absorbed by the cost units on a suitable basis.

When viewing the company as a whole, all costs are direct but more costs become indirect as the cost objects within the company become smaller, and hence more specific, segments of the business. By definition, all costs are direct at some level of cost object, but this may not be the level at which the particular financial decision is being taken. Where a cost is indirect but it is clear that part of this cost is incurred by the product, customer, or cost object, some system of apportionment can be used to share out the total cost across all the relevant cost centres, products, etc., on the basis of the relative estimated benefit received. Although any system of apportionment of indirect costs can give only an approximate total cost for a customer, product or other cost object, it does provide useful information to management on achieving the most profitable product mix. Some common bases of apportionment are shown in Figure 4.1.

In many cases the basis of apportionment is obvious as it is the main determinant of the size of the indirect cost; e.g. rent and rates will normally be shared out on the basis of the area occupied. However, for some indirect costs there will seem to be no obvious or sensible method of apportionment: e.g. corporate advertising. Some companies might use an arbitrary method such as sales revenue, while others would not try to apportion these costs at all. Instead they would leave them at the centre of the company as a general indirect expense. It is worth noting that there are inherent dangers in trying to apportion smoothly all costs across the organization (the 'peanut butter' effect). If all costs are apportioned, there is a danger that managers may not realize that these costs are not necessarily all direct or variable, and make decisions based on the information supplied including the apportioned costs. The following example from a large multinational organization will clarify this. The overall group consists of three divisions and a head office.

Cost	Basis of apportionment
Rent and rates	Square feet of floor space
Heating and lighting	Square feet of floor space, or cubic volume where appropriate
Depreciation of plant and machinery	Value of items of plant and machinery or Machine time used
Maintenance	Value of items of plant and machinery
Distribution	Freight weights

Figure 4.1 *Some common bases of apportionment*

The divisions generate all the sales revenue, and head office costs (computing, accounting, public relations, senior corporate management, and other support services) are apportioned out to the divisions on the basis of turnover in an attempt to assess the profitability of each division. The overall group financial performance seems quite satisfactory, each division making a profit before head office costs are apportioned and with a projected group net profit of £1 million:

	Division			Total
	A	*B*	*C*	
	£	£	£	£
Sales revenue	20m	40m	30m	90m
Variable costs	10m	28m	17m	55m
Contribution	10m	12m	13m	35m
Divisional fixed costs	8m	10m	7m	25m
Divisional profit before head office costs	2m	2m	6m	10m
Group head office costs				9m
				£ 1m

The finance manager then decides to restate the budget after apportioning head office costs so that these could be used by head office management to assess divisional performance in greater detail. Figure 4.2 shows the result of this analysis, using sales revenue as the basis of apportionment.

Restated budgeted profit and loss accounts

	A	B	C	Total
	£	£	£	£
Sales revenue	20m	40m	30m	90m
Divisional profit before head office costs	2m	2m	6m	10m
Shared head office costs *	(2m)	(4m)	(3m)	(9m)
Net profit	£0m	£(2m)	£3m	£1m

* £9m/£90m or 10% of sales revenue is the basis of apportionment.

Figure 4.2

This now suggests that division B, in spite of generating nearly half of the group's sales revenue and one-third of total contribution, is actually making a net loss for the group of £2 million. The finance manager thought that, in the best interests of the group as a whole, division B would have to be closed down. The analysis of the groups performance that would result from closing division B is shown in Figure 4.3, with the assumption that head office costs are not reduced as a consequence of closing one division.

Restated profit and loss accounts after closing division B

	A	B	C	Total
	£	£	£	£
Sales revenue	20m	—	30m	50m
Divisional profit	2m	—	6m	8m
Original apportionment of head office costs	(2m)	(4m)	(3m)	(9m)
Reallocate B's share of head office cost	(1.6m)	4m	(2.4m)	—
Net profit	£(1.6m)	£ —	£0.6m	£(1m)

Figure 4.3

Rather than improving the situation, it is getting worse; the overall group is making a loss, due now, it would seem, to the poor performance of division A. The finance manager now begins to wonder what the effect would be if this division was to be closed down as well. The not too surprising result is shown in Figure 4.4.

There is clearly something wrong with the finance manager's analytical approach. Prior to apportioning the head office costs the group profit was projected to be £1 million; after the apparent profit improvement decisions, the projection is now a £3 million loss. The problem is that these financial decisions have not been based on things which *really* change as a result of the decision. The head office costs of £9 million have still been included in the financial analysis after divisions A and B have been closed down. This treatment is wrong because their inclusion before and after the changes means that these costs are not affected by the closure decisions and so should be excluded from the analysis.

A more logical approach is to compare what must be given up and what will be gained from the decision. Thus, the decision is based on an evaluation of the differential costs only, which are considered in more detail in Chapter 6. Differential costs are those costs which change as a result of the decision; i.e. those items which are common to both the pre-and post-decision situations can be ignored. The first decision, to close division B because it appeared to be making a loss of £2 million, would have resulted in the loss of £12 million of divisional contribution. Therefore, unless as a result of closing division B more that £12 million can be saved, the group would be worse off if it decides to implement the decision.

It is apparent then that financial managers need to be careful how they apportion indirect costs, but failure to spread indirect costs to those areas of the business

Restated budgeted profit and loss account after closing divisions B and A

	A	B	C	Total
	£	£	£	£
Sales revenue	—	—	30m	30m
Divisional profit	—	—	6m	6m
Apportioned head office costs	(3.6)	—	(5.4m)	(9m)
Reallocate A's share of head office costs	3.6m	—	(3.6m)	—
Net profit	£ —	£ —	£(3m)	£(3m)

Figure 4.4

which benefit from the expenditure may also cause problems. As the basis of apportionment of these shared indirect costs becomes more complex (and thus more arbitrary), it is tempting to abandon the process and concentrate on direct costs only. However, indirect costs are incurred for the benefit of all the cost objects on which they have an impact. Consequently, there is a danger that the relative effectiveness of profitability of any specific cost object could be misconstrued if indirect costs are completely ignored in the financial analysis. This could result in incorrect decisions being taken regarding the future allocation of resources, if these decisions are based on such an incomplete financial evaluation.

If a business has use of group resources but is not required to 'pay' for the use through a cost apportionment system, it is highly likely that the business will not utilize them in the same way that it would if it was charged for their use. Thus 'free' indirect resources, if used uneconomically, could lead to an increase in the total costs of the business. Therefore, a system of pricing for the indirect resource is required that will allow managers to make sensible judgements as to whether 'to buy' the resources or not. This internal system of pricing is known as 'transfer pricing, and this is dealt with again in Chapter 11.

Some of the problems caused by not apportioning indirect costs can be seen in the following example.

Example of cost apportionment

Although it was stated earlier that apportioning rent on the basis of the floor area occupied was one of the more obvious bases, in certain circumstances this can still create complications. A large financial services group occupies a six-storey building in central London. The building served as the group's head office but there was some space occupied by some of the operating divisions as well. Central services, including rent, were charged out to those divisions using these services. Thus rent for the available parts of the head office building was charged to those divisions occupying the spare space and initially divisions L, M and N occupied one floor each. With total occupancy costs for the building budgeted at £1.71 million for the coming year, a charge of £285,000 was to be made to each division. However, competitive pressures faced by division L meant that it was keen to make savings wherever possible. The division therefore decided to move out of the head office and rent cheaper accommodation in outer London at a total annual cost of £170,000, a saving against budget of £115,000. The group could not argue with such a decision, but nobody else wanted to occupy the now vacated floor in the head office building, so the budgeting system recalculated the occupancy cost per floor by dividing the total cost of £1.71 million by the five floors now occupied. This resulted in a charge of £342,000 each to divisions M and N (and apparently an even greater saving for division L).

Division M now decided to move out as well and it found rentable space nearby for £200,000 per year, thus showing a saving of £142,000 against the revised budget. Before division N could also move out, head office was able to find outside tenants for the two vacant floors, to whom it would charge a rental figure of £155,000 per year per floor. Head office recalculated the budgeted charge to division N as shown below at £350,000:

Total occupancy costs (6 floors)	£1,710,000
less Rent received for 2 floors	£310,000
Net cost to group for 4 floors	£1,400,000
Therefore new cost per floor	£350,000

What has been the actual impact on the group of these decisions? By looking at the differential costs it will be seen how much costs have increased. In cash flow terms divisions L and M are now paying out a total of £370,000 in rent which is additional cash leaving the group. However, head office is only receiving £310,000 in additional cash from the outside tenants. Therefore costs have increased by £60,000 in cash terms. This is contradictory to the divisional accounts of L and M which will show an improvement against the budgeted levels based on apportioned costs. An analysis of the opportunity costs available should have enabled head office to agree a rent with its divisions which reflected the cash cost of these division renting alternative space, or the potential rent achievable from an outside party.

Similar problems with the apportionment of indirect costs commonly arise in the valuation of stocks and work-in-progress, particularly for published financial statements. Stocks and work-in-progress have to be valued at cost in published financial statements, but that cost has to include all the relevant costs incurred in bringing the stock to its present condition and location. Indirect costs are likely to form a significant proportion of these costs for most companies; but these can only be attributed to the stock items by a process of apportionment. For a computer software company, for example, the assessment of the cost of contract work still in progress should include the cost of computer development resources used on the project, and this cost will include an apportionment of the depreciation and running costs of the computer. This system of costing is known as 'full costing' or 'absorption costing' because of the absorbing effect of cost apportionment across all relevant cost objects.

Thus:

Direct costs + indirect costs = Full cost

The process of apportionment introduces a substantial degree of management estimation and degree of approximation into the final full cost, and so these costs should not be regarded as precise or accurate in any absolute sense. The degree of accuracy of any such cost classification and apportionment system will to some extent depend on the level of investment and running costs which management is willing to commit to producing this analytical information. There is also a trade-off between speed and accuracy: if the information is needed promptly then accuracy may be sacrificed and more general approximations could be included. Alternatively, managers may be able to delay making a decision until more information or information of greater acccuracy can be made available. As always, managers need to compare the costs incurred in improving the financial information systems with the potential benefits from the better decisions which may result. It is now possible to argue that, with the processing power of modern computers, the trade-off between speed and accuracy should be minimal, and the main problem lies with the inability of financial managers to define precisely the information required.

Product versus period costs

When reporting the profit performance of a business to shareholders at the end of an accounting period it is normal, as discussed in Chapter 2, to determine the sales revenue generated during the period and to deduct all relevant costs incurred in achieving those sales in order to judge the relative success of the trading of the business. Therefore the costs incurred should be 'matched' with the related sales revenue in the accounting period in which the revenue is generated. This involves differentiating between unexpired costs (assets) and expired costs (expenses) for the purposes of stock valuation and profit measurement. Unexpired costs are resources which have been acquired but have not yet been used up by the business, and which are expected to contribute to achieving or supporting future revenue. They are shown as assets in the balance sheet. Stocks of finished goods waiting to be sold or work-in-progress waiting to have more value added to it are prime examples of this type of asset. When the resources have been consumed in the generation of sales revenue they are said to have expired and are then shown as expenses in the profit and loss account.

SSAP 9: *Stocks and work-in-progress* (1975) states that, for stock valuation purposes, only manufacturing indirect costs should be added to the direct costs which are included in the calculation of total product costs. Accountants therefore normally separate costs into product costs and period costs, with non-manufacturing costs being treated as period costs for financial accounting purposes. Product costs are identified with goods purchased or produced for resale. These costs are attached to the product and are included in stock valuations until the products are sold (i.e. it is an unexpired cost). Period costs are not included in stock valuations and as a result they are treated as expenses in the period in which they are incurred. Both product and period costs are eventually classified as expenses. The accounting difference between them is the timing of their classification as expenses in the profit and loss account.

However, this discussion has dealt with the accounting treatment in published financial statements and out concern is with management accounting for financial decisions. Is the distinction between product and period costs relevant to decision-making, and can period costs be ignored in the same way that fixed costs can, if they really are fixed?

Differentiating between the financial decision aspects of short-term and long-term planning is vital as it dictates where most managerial effort should be allocated. It is a pointless task to allocate effort to an area which cannot be changed within the relevant time-frame of the plan. Thus, short-term planning concentrates on those areas that can be changed and where managerial judgement is important.

In the short term many costs are committed and a lot of cost levels are fixed or static irrespective of what happens to the level of activity. Costs of distribution, for example, are likely to be constant in the short term, even allowing for (small) changes in the size of each order, as the same number of deliveries has to be made to the same customers. As the planning time-scale increases different modes of delivery could be adopted, so that, if order sizes stayed lower than before, the total distribution costs would be reduced.

Thus for the short-term decisions there will be certain costs that can be ignored in the financial analysis because they are constant, or fixed, within the relevant range. This range will normally be determined by the short time period, and during this period there will be costs, such as rent and rates or certain marketing activities, which are very difficult to associate with particular sales revenues because they are related more to the specific time period. These period costs are therefore often treated as an expense in the specific *accounting* period to which they relate.

If it is accepted as a general truism that products generate sales revenues, not accounting periods, managers require cost and revenue information about the product in order to make effective decisions. This can best be done by concentrating on assessing the product's performance over its economic life, rather than trying to identify and evaluate individual periodic related performance. Thus, financial managers need to identify the stages of the product's life, and then to set objectives, strategies and budgeting controls accordingly, and identify the cost and revenues for each stage.

It is traditionally recognized that there are four stages to a product's life: embryonic, growth, maturity and ageing. Market share and sales revenues increase rapidly from the embryonic stage through growth and peak as the product moves to maturity. Relative cost will be high during the embryonic stage (due to high expenditures on development and launch) and maintained at quite a high level during growth due to the need to increase capacity and to spend heavily on marketing to increase the product's relative market share. Disinvestment will start to occur once the product has matured; so management should be trying to maximize cash flows and profits at this stage. Hence, we can see that management must make different types of financial decisions in each of the stages of the product life-cycle.

Attempts to use a financial control measure which is universally applicable in each stage of the product life-cycle can be dangerous as accounting measures such as return on investment (ROI) can provide misleading information to managers. ROI is subject to varying interpretations, as discussed in Chapter 2. It is also an historical measure, which for the purposes of making decisions about the future, is of limited use. The third major fault with ROI is its over-emphasis on short run performance. It is appropriate to use ROI as a performance measure only at the mature stage of the product's life when the emphasis on control should shift to enhancing profits and cash flows in the shorter term as the attractiveness of longer-term investment decreases. However, at the earlier stages other measures are more appropriate. It is therefore a vital part of the analytical process to differentiate between the stages of the product life-cycle and their appropriate financial control parameters.

In the embryonic stage the company has to invest in the technological development of the product, in market research, to see if the product is marketable, and in launching the product. The long-term nature of this initial investment makes ROI an inappropriate measure; indeed we believe that at the very early stage of the product's life no soundly based financial control measure can be found. The common use of cost centres to control this expenditure is falsely based as the objective of the business is not to spend up to the budgeted expenditure limits, but rather to achieve specific, measurable milestones which may not be meaningfully quantifiable in a financial sense. Thus, the embryonic stage can be most sensibly controlled by reference to the achievement or otherwise of those indentified milestones.

As the product is successfully launched and the market begins to grow, the financial measures become more clearly defined. Marketing is a key investment at this stage and as this expenditure is of a long-term nature any concentration on short-term issues such as improving ROI will damage these longer-term prospects. These investments should therefore be evaluated using long-term decision criteria, such as discounted cash flow (DCF) techniques. In DCF analysis future net cash flows are discounted back into present value terms to enable comparison of alternative projects.

Life-cycle costing allows management to assess fully the long-term implications of investment decisions in a way not possible if one attempts to measure costs by accounting period. Thus, management is able to make proper financial judgements about strategically important decisions by analysing and weighing up the costs and benefits at each of the investment's stages of development. This does not eradicate the need for financial analysis over a shorter time scale (e.g. for the purposes of financial reporting), but this analysis should always be carried out in the context of the longer-term analysis. Product life-cycle costing is discussed in greater detail in Parts Three and Four and is illustrated in Figure 4.5.

Profit versus cash flow

In Chapter 2 a differentiation was made between profit and cash flow and it was stated that financial decisions are better made after analysing the cash flows which result from the decision (i.e. future cash flows) rather than relying on the annual forecast profit and loss account. These forecast cash flows are not subject to the same management judgments regarding the timing of the revenue or expense. (Note: over the full lifetime of any decision all timing differences should net themselves out, and the same result should be obtained by either evaluation.)

Major strategic decisions, e.g. the launch of a new product, have impacts across several accounting periods and thus can complicate the interpretation of published

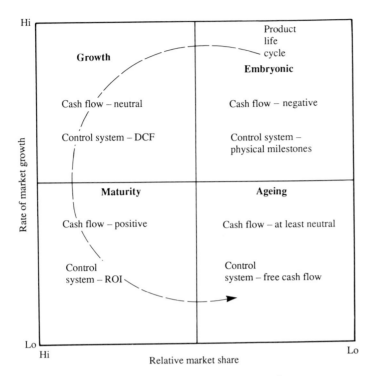

Figure 4.5 *Product life-cycle and financial control parameters*

financial results. They therefore must be evaluated by reference to all relevant costs and benefits, and not simply to those included in any arbitrary accounting period. Hence we employ life-cycle costing and DCF techniques.

The analytical process involved in deciding whether to launch a new product involves estimating its economic life so that annual depreciation can be charged in each year's profit and loss account. It must also be decided how much of the costs go into fixed assets on the balance sheet to be depreciated and how much are expensed immediately as being of no future value, which means that they cannot be treated as assets. This decision will affect the timing of profit in the financial statements, but will not affect the cash spent by the business nor the benefit received from the expenditure, and should not therefore have any impact on the decision.

Financial decisions are based on future financial costs and benefits, and these are better expressed in terms of future cash flows rather than the more judgemental profit figures. When any particular decision is being considered, many of the costs of the business will not change as a result of the decision; e.g. the fixed costs will remain fixed as long as the decision does not move outside the relevant range of the fixed cost. Thus, these costs which remain unaffected by the decision can be ignored in the financial analysis of the future cash flows. It would be feasible to base the decision on a complete review of the cash flows for the business before the decision and compare this with another full cash flow forecast after the decision; but this would be a waste of time as the unaffected costs would be included in both the cash flow forecasts and would therefore net each other out. The decision can be reached much more quickly and simply by assessing the differences between the alternatives; i.e. evaluate the differential future cash flows. Chapter 6 will include a more lengthy discussion on the relevant costs for decision-making, together with examples; but below is an example to illustrate the importance of identifying the differential future cash flows.

Example of differential future cash flows

Product X is not performing well in its market; 68,000 units of Product X are currently being sold annually at a price of £1.95 per unit. The variable cost per unit is £1 and the direct fixed costs for Product X are £20,000.

It is estimated that a price reduction to £1.45 per unit would stimulate demand to 84,000 units. This increase in volume would not affect the variable cost per unit or the direct fixed costs. The differential figures resulting from this price reduction would therefore be as follows:

Cash inflow from sales revenues		
16,000 units @ £1.45	£23,200	
Less 68,000 units @ 50p	(£34,000)	(£10,800)
Less cash outflow		
Variable costs		(£16,000)
Fixed costs		–
		(£26,800)

It can be seen then that some of the costs of this particular product (and market) are not affected by the pricing decision. Changing the price level will alter the sales volumes and hence the sales revenues; and as sales volumes vary, so will those costs which are directly variable with volume. However, some costs will be incurred on a period basis rather then being variable with volume and these costs (e.g. rent, rates, marketing expenditure and other indirect costs) are not likely to be affected unless the volume change is great enough to move them outside the relevant range for which they are a fixed cost.

Marginal costing

As has been shown in Chapter 3, break-even analysis can be a useful tool for considering profit–volume relationships over a limited range of output. However, its value to management is limited when it comes to examining product profitability in a multi-product, multi-market business because of its essential underlying assumptions (constant fixed and per unit variable costs, constant level of stocks and only one average selling price for a stable sales mix in the relevant range). A more useful technique for studying the effects of changes in volume and sales mix is marginal costing.

'Marginal cost' is another term for describing the direct variable costs associated with any decision. It is mainly used for providing information to managers so that they can make short run decisions about sales volume and outputs. Marginal costing can easily be incorporated into the system of recording and collecting costs, where stocks are valued at variable cost, and fixed costs are treated as period costs in profit statements.

The economist's definition of marginal cost is the additional or incremental cost arising from a change in the volume of output by one marginal unit. This incremental cost is often the sum of the prime costs (direct materials, labour and expenses) and variable overheads (indirect costs) resulting from the production of one unit of output. Under normal circumstances the marginal cost will equal the directly variable costs (i.e. indirect costs remain constant). However, if the activity level is moved outside the particular relevant range by the decision the indirect costs are likely to alter as well and then the marginal cost is equal to the differential cost.

As has already been discussed fixed costs stay fixed for a specified relevant range and time span. When they change they usually become fixed again for another relevant range. Therefore many fixed costs increase in steps and can be graphed as shown in Figure 4.6.

If fixed costs do increase in large steps it becomes important to know whether, as a result of a particular decision, a fixed cost will move outside its relevant range and hence increase. For example, deciding to hire additional office secretarial staff would not necessarily increase occupancy costs (rent, rates, heating and lighting, etc.) unless there was no spare office space available and a new building had to be rented. If space were not available then the differential cost of hiring this additional small group of people might be very high. However, if this new higher fixed cost

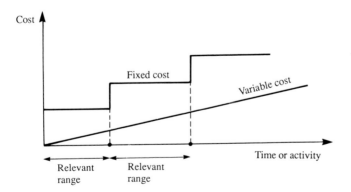

Figure 4.6 *Plateaux of fixed costs*

was taken on, there might well be new spare office space available, which would mean that more people could be hired in the future at no additional rent cost. Thus, it can be seen that differential costs are not uniform but are specific to the particular decision being considered.

Differential versus average costs

Average costs by contrast are much more uniform and are the normal costs obtainable from published financial statements. Average costs are simply the total costs divided by the relevant volume measure. For example, to calculate the average cost per mile of running a company car, the total annual costs are divided by the number of miles travelled per year. A particular model of company car incurs fixed costs of £500 per year to tax and insure, £800 for maintainance (which is planned by time and not mileage) and £1,500 annual depreciation expense. The cost of petrol and oil is 15 pence per mile. If the current mileage is 12,000 per year, then the average cost (shown below) is:

$$\text{Average cost per mile} = \frac{\text{Fixed cost}}{\text{Mileage}} + \text{variable cost per mile}$$

$$= \frac{£2,800}{12,000} + 15\text{p}$$

$$= 38.3\text{p per mile}$$

The financial director considers that this average cost is too high and so he advises the sales director to increase the mileage travelled by each of his rep's cars. Thus if the mileage were to increase, say to 18,000 per year, then the average cost would be reduced to 30.6p per mile:

$$\frac{£2,800}{18,000} + 15\text{p} = 30.6\text{p per mile}$$

Obviously this decision has actually incurred a differential cost increase of 6,000 miles at 15p per mile or £900 (assuming that the fixed cost actually remain fixed given the increased level of activity). If extra maintenance cost had to be incurred, then the differential costs would be even higher. Hence it can be seen that differential cost is far more relevant to decision-making than the more readily available average cost. Because this type of costing technique concentrates on the differences in costs resulting from a decision and does not differentiate between fixed and variable costing, it is most logically described as 'differential costing'.

We will continue to use the more common phrase, 'marginal costing', but readers should also be aware of the meaning of differential costing.

Marginal cost and contribution

As was discussed in Chapter 3, the difference between the marginal cost and the selling price of a product is the contribution that each product makes towards period costs and profit. Thus, assuming there is idle capacity and there will be no increase in period costs, to determine the effect of short run changes in volume on the profit of a company the additional sales of each product are multiplied by the contribution per unit to arrive at the additional operating profit or reduced operating loss that will result from the increase in volume. For example a company receives the following order:

Product	Units	Price per unit
		£
X	500	0.50
Y	200	0.80
Z	600	0.10

Given the marginal cost per unit for each product and available spare capacity, the additional profit can be calculated thus:

Product	Selling price per unit	Marginal cost per unit	Contribution per unit	Incremental Units	Profit
	£	£	£		£
X	0.50	0.30	0.20	500	100
Y	0.80	0.70	0.10	200	20
Z	0.10	0.05	0.05	600	30
					£150

If other costs did increase as a result of accepting the order, this increase would be deducted from the incremental profit to find out the true net effect.

It has been seen how spreading indirect costs can cause problems when trying to make decisions. Concentration on marginal costs can help managers focus on the relevant decision costs. If fixed costs are truly fixed and indirect costs remain constant, then the marginal costs are equal to the directly variable costs (i.e. the decision does not take us outside the relevant range). Therefore if a decision affects the level of sales, the decision requires the use of contribution analysis as it allows decision-makers to focus on variable costs. Those costs which do not change as a result of any particular decision can be ignored for the purposes of that particular decision. Contribution analysis can also be applied to identifying the optimum allocation of resources within a business or a segment of the business. This is very useful when the manager faces resource restraints. These restraints are particularly common in short-term budgeting timescales which are also when the separation of fixed and variable costs is most appropriate. However, for longer-term planning, contribution analysis is not at all useful as few costs remain fixed with changes in activity, and thus contribution rates are not constant and many constraints on resources can be removed by specific management actions.

In order to maximize the performance of the business it is crucial to use these scarce resources in the optional way. The key to the process is the identification of the limiting factor or key constraint for each segment of the business and then the selection of the appropriate strategy that will optimize the contribution per unit of this limiting factor. Achievement of this will ensure that the total contribution for the segment is maximized. However, as the limiting factor may change over time, and for different parts of the business, the evaluation of contributions should be done for customer groupings and channels of distribution as well as for products. Understanding the different profit contributions generated from these segments is the first step in reallocating resources to maximize the overall return.

In many businesses a range of goods and services are sold which share common resources, e.g. sales and marketing resources. To maximize the performance of the business it is important to use these resources in the optimal way. A prime objective of financial analysis is to identify where existing resources are being allocated, i.e. where the effort is being directed, and to judge how effective the business is in this effort, in terms of the level of financial return being achieved from these resources. This analysis should highlight any bottle-necks and constraints which are dissipating resources away from the areas of the business where they should be directed. It should also indicate whether there is a balanced allocation of resources throughout the operation. If a huge effort is being put into stimulating demand for a new product (e.g. via investment in advertising), but the resources that have been employed to ensure that this demand can be satisfied are inadequate, most of the investment will be wasted.

Most companies have relatively few constraints but those that do exist should be identified as they limit the ability of the business to achieve more financial success. Analysis over time will also reveal that these limiting factors change, which means that the business must review the balance of resources regularly.

Where demand for a companys products exceeds its present productive capacity, the company must decide how best to employ its limited capacity. If the short-term objective of the company is to make maximum profit then it should produce the combination of products which result in the highest possible contribution towards fixed costs and profit. The calculation of the contribution that each product makes in relation to the limiting factor will enable the products to be ranked in the order in which they should be manufactured. An example is shown in Figure 4.7.

Analysing the budget

Segmented contribution analysis can be useful if the budget is broken down into the controllable elements of the business; i.e. those over which managers can exercise

NSW Ltd's output is limited by machine hours. The company manufactures four products, all of which are made by the same machine which is already running for 24 hours per day, seven days per week. The purchase of additional machines is not a viable option at this stage.

The machine usage data and the contribution per unit for each of the four products is as follows:

Product	Contribution per unit	Limiting factor usage (machine hours)	Contribution per hour of machine usage	Rank
	£		£	
A	24	6	4	3
B	12	2	6	1
C	20	4	5	2
D	12	4	3	4

It can be seen that, although Product A makes the most contribution on a per unit basis, NSW Ltd should concentrate on meeting demand for Product B as this makes the most contribution in relation to the limiting factor.

The full effective utilization of the machine is 700 hours per month (i.e. maintenance and set-up times occupy 20 hours per month) and the following monthly demand exists for the four products:

Product	Units	Total hours required
A	40	240
B	50	100
C	60	240
D	55	220
		800

Because monthly demand exceeds machine capacity by the equivalent of 100 machine hours the company should limit production according to the following schedule:

Product	Machine hours per unit	Units	Total machine hours	Contribution per machine hour	Total
				£	£
B	2	50	100	6	600
C	4	60	240	5	1,200
A	6	40	240	4	960
D	4	30*	120	3	360
			700	Total contribution	3,120
				Less period costs	1,000
					£2,120

* Assumption: It is feasible to market 30 units of Product D when the market demand is 55 units.

Figure 4.7 *Contribution per unit of limiting factor*

genuine control through their decisions. There must therefore be coordination between how the organization is structured and the way in which managerial performance is judged. Thus, sales and variable costs will be split by products and markets, but it should also be possible to group products or customers together in different ways if this will help decisions on the allocation of resources; e.g. if the key limiting factor is a particular aspect of distribution, this form of analysis may be more relevant to a resource allocation decision.

It is also important that the objectives stated in the budget are broken down into a form compatible with the contribution analysis. This applies to non-financial objectives as well which may be 'task' related. The overall objectives and strategies should be analysed down to the specific tactical level where contribution analysis and differential costs can be used.

These techniques are ideal for comparing alternative tactics, which is part of the planning process. The relative risk of these alternatives must be taken into account (e.g. different cost structures–higher fixed costs indicate increased risk) and critical success factors for any business plan identified. Thus, the attention of managers is focused on those controllable areas which are crucial to the success of the business. The controllability of costs depends upon the level and scope of management authority and the time scale involved; this is discussed below and again, in more detail, in Part Four.

Economic decisions versus assessment of managerial performance

Management accounting information systems have a key role to play in the control and motivation of the management team. The basis upon which managerial performance is judged should be consistent with the objectives of the business as defined in the strategic plan and in the short-term budgets.

Although managers must be motivated to achieve the corporate objectives, goal congruence is not easy to achieve in practice. The simplistic approach is to measure the manager's performance by how well the company meets its objectives, but no one manager, not even the chief executive, can be regarded as having complete control over the achievement of the business objectives. This is because the company is susceptible to uncontrollable, external, environmental factors, such as rising interest rates. However, these factors should not be ignored, and changes from assumptions made in the plan can significantly affect the economic performance of the business.

The financial control system should distinguish those areas for which managers can be held accountable from those where no accountability can be attached. The analysis of both categories can contribute to the learning process, by explaining any variances, and it may enable better forecasts to be made in the future. Therefore, it is vital to separate issues relating to managerial performance measurement from the external environment's impact on the economic results of the company, while still trying to maintain the link in motivating managers to achieve corporate goals.

If managers are primarily evaluated against measures where they have a high level of control over their performance, this can be achieved. The analysed budget can be very useful for managerial performance evaluation if properly broken down into objectives, strategies, etc. for the various areas of the business which are consistent with those for the whole business. However, problems can arise both within the business and from the impact of the external non-controllable factors which can differ from their planned levels. If key tasks or activities within the specific budget area can be identified, managerial performance can be evaluated by monitoring whether these tasks or activities have been successfully completed and the specified objectives achieved. As far as possible the tasks/activities should be selected which are independent of other influences, so that managerial performance can be judged primarily on the performance of these specific, independent items rather than on the overall business performance. The logic is that if all managers achieve their own objectives, the company as a whole should achieve its goal provided the individual objectives have been properly set.

The use of specific individual objectives for managerial evaluation is crucial in focusing management attention on those areas where managers exercise greatest personal control, which are also the parts of the business where their decisions will have greatest effect. However, its use by the management team as an apportionment of blame approach to the financial control system, rather than as a business support system, must be avoided. One way in which this can be done is by subdividing the total business into smaller business areas with more closely focused management teams, because the smaller areas will have more closely identifiable aims and objectives which the managers can associate with as a team.

Zero base budgeting

Once a budgeting system has been operating for some years there is a tendency for next year's budget to be justified by reference to the actual, or budgeted, levels being achieved at present. This, the most common approach to budgeting, is known as incremental budgeting. The current budget is taken as the base, and then adjusted for changes which are expected to occur during the new budget period. However, using such a base, with its historical comparisons and existing level of constraints on resources, can inhibit innovative changes, as well as perpetuating any past inefficiencies in the budgeting system. This can develop into a major problem. The budget should be seen as the first year of the long range plan. Therefore if changes are not stated in the budget it is difficult for the business to make progress towards achieving long-term goals.

A way to break out of this cyclical planning dilemma is to go back to basics and to develop a budget from the assumption of no existing resources (i.e. zero base), as if all expenditure programmes are being launched for the first time. This means that all resources have to be justified and opportunity costs used to compare alternative ways of achieving specified objectives. Each proposed programme is evaluated on a cost/benefit basis and ranked according to its 'value for money' contribution to the organization. The problem is that this process takes time. One solution is to do the zero base budgeting on a rolling basis; i.e. look at one area of the business in depth each year.

Zero base budgeting is of particular use in planning and controlling discretionary items of expenditure, such as research and development and marketing investment, which are not dependent upon past, committed costs.

Budgeting techniques and the evaluation and control of managerial and business performance are further discussed in Chapters 9, 11 and 12.

Questions

1 The monthly rental costs of a factory are £800,000. Within the factory there are three productive centres. Centre A occupies 60 per cent of a total floor space of 1 million square feet, while the rest is divided equally between centres B and C. The factory manufactures four products. Given the data below on the number of labour hours each centre spends on each of the products, how much of the rental overheads should be absorbed by each product?

| Productive | | Product | | |
Centre	*1*	*2*	*3*	*4*
		Labour hours		
A	300	400	260	180
B	300	280	50	—
C	115	75	—	40

2 Draw & Lean, which manufactures household blinds, has budgeted the following service costs in its factory:

Cost Centre	Budgeted costs £
Personnel and training	39,000
Factory administration	25,000
Machine maintenance	30,000
Stores	16,000
	£125,000

The factory has four production centres. Given the following data, apportion the service costs of each centre between the four production centres using the most appropriate bases.

	Machining	Assembly	Painting	Packaging
Machine hours	1,200	400	100	100
Number of employees	200	275	30	50
Labour hours	12,000	16,000	4,000	2,000
Number of material requisitions	800	1,000	300	500

3 Due to progression along the learning curve NSW Ltd now produces its four products more efficiently (see Figure 4.7 on page 97). Less wastage has led to a reduction in variable costs and limiting factor usage has declined as well, as shown below:

Product	Contribution per unit	Limiting factor usage (machine hours)
A	£25	5
B	£14	2
C	£24	3
D	£12	4

Also, as a result of successful marketing and improved product quality, demand has increased for each of the products:

Product	Units
A	45
B	70
C	65
D	65

The full effective utilization of the machine is unchanged at 700 hours per month. Draw up a new production schedule for NSW Ltd and calculate the expected profit for the period (you can assume that period costs are unchanged).

4 A liquid chemicals company, Pea and Leek, is enjoying a busy period for its industry. It has increased its output and sales from 19,350 litres in Quarter 1 to 25,950 litres in Quarter 2 but, though demand is still rising, the company cannot increase its output more than another 5 per cent from its existing labour force which is now operating at its maximum capacity.

Output, cost and price data in Quarter 2 for its four products were as follows:

	W	X	Y	Z
Output (litres)	6,840	10,440	5,220	3,450
			£ per litre	
Selling price	24.30	17.46	14.88	20.52
Costs:				
Direct labour (at £9 per hour)	2.94	1.95	1.49	2.55
Direct materials	11.04	8.46	6.99	9.18
Fixed production overhead	5.88	3.90	2.97	5.10

J Riddle has offered to supply 3,000 litres of X at a delivered price of 85 per cent of Pea and Leek's selling price. Pea and Leek will then be able to produce extra product W in its place up to the plant's total capacity.
(a) Should the company accept J Riddle's offer?
(b) What would be the most profitable combination of sub-contracting 3,000 litres of one product at a price of 85 per cent of its selling price and producing extra quantitles of another product up to the plant's total capacity? Assume that the market can absorb the extra output.

5

Selecting the right analytical techniques for the right decision

Overview

In the first three chapters of Part Two we have discussed the management accountant's role in carrying out the internal analysis of the business and an external analysis of the markets in which the business competes. The internal analysis should establish what resources are currently available and how these resources can be deployed in the future to achieve some competitive advantage. To facilitate this analysis the business is segmented into products, markets or customers. Once segmentation has taken place, and direct and indirect costs and the limiting factors of each segment have been identified, financial decisions should be based on the future differential costs which arise as a result of the decision.

It was shown in Chapter 4 that trying to allocate indirect costs to business segments (the absorption costing approach) can cause problems when trying to make decisions. The alternative approach is marginal costing where only direct manufacturing costs are allocated to products; the indirect costs are treated as period costs. The marginal versus absorption costing debate is the central theme of this chapter and we compare the requirements for financial reporting (where the absorption costing method is used) with the needs of financial managers for more relevant decision costs, i.e. marginal costs. There can be significant differences in profit calculations between the two approaches, particularly when dealing with the valuation of stock. The second half of the chapter addresses the manager's financial information requirements for managing stock; and we draw on some ideas employed by the Japanese which illustrate that some of the traditional approaches used in the West (e.g. economic order quantity models) are focusing managers minds on the wrong areas for analysis.

Marginal versus absorption costing

Accountants in the UK have been slow to develop the use of marginal costing techniques for providing management with information for decision-making and control. This was because of the profession's objection to the use of marginal costing for external reporting. Although today many companies do use marginal costing for internal management purposes, absorption costing is still required for financial reporting (as recommended in SSAP 9).

With a marginal costing system, stocks are valued only at their direct variable cost. All indirect variable and fixed costs are written off in the profit and loss account as period expenses. Traditionally accountants have prepared accounts using the absorption cost basis and have included a proportion of manufacturing overheads in their valuation of opening and closing work-in-progress and finished stocks.

Absorption costing (sometimes referred to as full costing) involves allocating all manufacturing costs to products and valuing unsold stocks at their total cost of manufacture. Non-manufacturing costs (e.g. marketing expenditure, computing and accounting costs), under both the marginal costing and absorption costing methods, are allocated not to the products but are charged directly to the profit and loss account of the period. Hence they are excluded from the stock valuation; in other words, they are treated as period costs.

The choice between marginal costing and absorption costing depends on whether the company believes that its manufacturing overheads are costs which relate to the specific products made in the period or to the period in which they are incurred. Under the absorption costing approach overheads are treated as a product cost and should be assigned to the relevant product rather than the period. This is justified because it is the product which generates the sales revenue when it is sold, and the period is therefore an arbitrary method of accumulating sales transactions. Sales revenue derives from the sale of products and therefore all production costs should be matched with actual revenue in the period of sale. Under the marginal costing approach overheads are assumed to expire with the passage of time regardless of production activity. These costs are incurred to provide a benefit for the operations of the business during a given period of time, and this benefit is felt to be unchanged by the actual level of operations which take place during the period.

The proponents of both absorption costing and marginal costing systems are in agreement that non-manufacturing costs should be treated as period expenses in the period when they are incurred. Disagreement only arises over the matter of whether or not manufacturing overheads should be regarded as period costs or product costs.

Although the absorption costing method of stock valuation is required for external reporting, the marginal costing versus absorption costing debate is still of relevance to management decision-making. Management needs information about the profit performance of its products/segments of the business. It also needs information to evaluate the performance of its managers. Management must therefore decide whether marginal costing or absorption costing provides the more relevant information in assessing the economic and managerial performance of the business.

Impact on profit

The particular accounting technique used cannot alter the total profit made from any specific project or product. However, it can change the period in which profits are reported and this can have a significant impact on the perceived performance of the business. This effect on profit reporting can be seen in the following example.

A company is considering a three-year exclusive contract to supply a component to a computer manufacturer. At the end of the contract there will be no surplus stock. Below are the sales and production forecasts for the three years:

	Year 1	Year 2	Year 3	Total
Forecast sales (units)	10,000	18,000	22,000	50,000
Forecast production (units)	18,000	18,000	14,000	50,000
	£000	£000	£000	£000
Selling price £40 per unit:				
Sales revenues	400	720	880	2,000
Direct variable production				
costs @ £20 per unit	360	360	280	1,000
Indirect expenses	300	150	110	560

Over the three-year period the plan looks profitable and it should generate the following profit:

	£000
Sales revenue	2,000
less direct variable costs	1,000
less indirect expenses	560
	£440

But how will this profit be reported in the profit and loss account for each of the three years?

Under the marginal costing approach any stock carried forward to the following year will be valued at the direct variable production cost only. Hence the indirect costs will be written off as expenses in the year in which they are incurred.

Figure 5.1 shows the profit and loss account for each of the three years using the marginal costing approach. It can be seen that by writing off all the indirect expenses (which include the high initial development and marketing expenses) in year 1, a loss will be reported in that year; whereas in years 2 and 3 sizeable profits will be reported as a result of the relatively low indirect expenses in that period.

For published financial statements (which require the use of absorption costing) at least some of these expenses would definitely be included in the stock valuation, i.e. indirect fixed manufacturing overheads, although non-manufacturing expenses (such as research and development, marketing) could still be treated as period expenses. Indeed, for a specific contract, such as in this example, the company would be able to spread the development and marketing costs (£120,000) over the period of contract under the rules of SSAP 9. If we break down the indirect

	Year 1		Year 2		Year 3		Total
	£000	£000	£000	£000	£000	£000	£000
Sales		400		720		880	2000
Opening stock	—		160		160		
Direct production costs	360		360		280		
	360		520		440		
Less: Closing stock	160	200	160	360	—	440	1,000
Contribution		200		360		440	1,000
Less: Indirect expenses		300		150		110	560
		(100)		210		330	440

Figure 5.1   *Marginal costing approach to stock valuation*

expenses for this contract, this will enable us to calculate profit using the absorption costing approach:

	Year 1 £000	Year 2 £000	Year 3 £000	Year 4 £000
Fixed production overhead @ £7 per unit	126	126	98	350
Non-production expenses	174	24	12	210
	300	150	110	560

Direct production costs	£20 per unit
Fixed production overhead	£7 per unit
Total absorption cost	£27 per unit

The impact of using an absorption costing based stock valuation is illustrated in Figure 5.2. Although total profit has not been affected, the timing of the reporting of this profit has, such that there is a more favourable loss forecast in year 1 because of the increased stock value. If development and marketing costs had been spread over the sales revenue in the three years as well, a profit would have been shown in year 1. This has the effect of decreasing the year 2 and 3 results when this higher valued stock is sold.

	Year 1		Year 2		Year 3		Total
	£000	£000	£000	£000	£000	£000	£000
Sales		400		720		880	2000
Opening stock	—		216		216		
Total absorption cost	486		486		378		
	486		702		594		
Less: Closing stock	216	270	216	486	—	594	1,350
Cost of sales		130		234		286	650
Less: Non-production costs		174		24		12	210
		(44)		210		274	440

Figure 5.2 *Absorption costing approach to stock valuation*

Analysing the impact on profit

If, in any period, production and sales are equal (i.e. no increase or decrease in stocks during the period) and there is no inflation, the profits should be the same for both the absorption costing and marginal costing systems. This is because (provided opening stocks exist) the same proportionate amount of overheads will have been carried forward as an expense to be included in the current period in the opening stock valuation as will be deducted in the closing stock valuations from the production cost figure. The overall effect is that even with an absorption costing system the only overheads which will appear to be included as a cost for the period will be those which are incurred in the period.

When production exceeds sales, stated profits for the period are higher under the absorption costing approach, because physical stocks are increasing. This means that there is a greater amount of overhead in the closing stock, which is being deducted from the expenses of the period, than the brought forward overheads in the opening stock, which is sold during the period.

When sales exceed production a higher profit is shown by the marginal costing system. This is because physical stocks decline and a greater amount of brought forward overhead will therefore need to be expensed as the opening stock is sold, than is being carried forward in the closing stock held at the period end.

Impact of sales fluctuations

Even if sales volumes increase and both selling prices and cost structures remain the same, under an absorption costing system, profits may still decline from one period to the next. This is because under absorption costing profit is a function of both sales volumes and production volumes.

Profit and stock valuation is affected not only by changes in the level of sales, but also by changes in the level of production because increases or decreases in overheads which arise as a result of the change in the level of production are reflected in the stock valuation. Also, adjustment for the under- or over-recovery of overheads can distort profit figures. Therefore, a situation might arise where, even though sales volumes are rising, profits may still decrease because production volumes and overhead costs are also increasing. However, because manufacturing overheads are regarded as period costs under marginal costing, an increase in manufacturing overheads is not reflected in the stock valuation.

Another complication of absorption costing is caused by the need to estimate cost levels for budgeting purposes. Because the calculation of overhead absorption rates is based on estimated overhead expenditure during the budgeted period, it is highly unlikely that the forecast overhead charged to a responsibility centre will be the same as the actual overhead incurred. Thus, there will be either an overcharge or undercharge of overhead which must be recovered. For example, if annual overheads are estimated at £250,000 and the annual activity is forecast to be 100,000 direct labour hours, the estimated overhead rate will be £2.50 per hour. Actual overheads incurred turn out to be £250,000 as estimated, but actual activity is only 85,000 direct labour hours. Therefore only £212,500 will be charged, giving an under-recovery of overheads of £37,500. The adjustment, for the purposes of external profit reporting, is normally treated as a period cost and written off against the profit and loss account in the current accounting period. None of the adjustment would therefore be included in the stock valuation.

Arguments in support of marginal costing

One argument in favour of marginal costing is that it removes from profit the effect of stock changes. Where stock changes are likely to fluctuate significantly, profits may be distorted if they are calculated on an absorption costing basis as the stock changes will affect the amount of manufacturing overheads charged to a particular accounting period. This will be particularly true if the company is measuring profit on a frequent basis (i.e. monthly or quarterly). Hence, for regular presentation to management, marginal costing should ideally be used; but, for annual reporting, absorption costing has to be used. So far as managerial performance measurement is concerned, managers could try to alter their stock levels so as to affect reported profits when an absorption costing system is used. Consequently, financial performance may be principally affected by movements in stock levels rather than by changes in sales activity.

The inclusion of overhead costs in stock, as is the case with absorption costing, can encourage stock building because the actual costs incurred can be 'hidden' and not reflected in profit. The use of marginal costing also avoids any possibility of overheads being capitalized in slow-moving or unsaleable stocks. If surplus stocks exist, where an absorption costing system is in use, a proportion of overheads may be tied up in these stocks, which may never be recovered if the stocks cannot be sold at their original selling price. A stock write-off will be necessary in a later accounting period, although under absorption costing stocks should be valued at the lower of cost and net realizable value. Consequently the stock value of these items should have been reduced below their full cost to reflect their lower selling prices if appropriate. This would also be done, if necessary, under marginal costing, but it is less likely to be needed due to the lower cost base under marginal costing. Consequently there is a risk that, under absorption costing, the current period's profits may be overstated.

The biggest argument in favour of marginal costing is that separating fixed and variable costs provides more useful and relevant information for management decision-making. The projection of future costs and revenues for different activity levels and the use of the relevant decision-making techniques are much easier if a marginal costing system is adopted. However, it is quite possible for an absorption costing system to be used for external financial reporting and for these costs also to be analysed into their fixed and variable elements in order to support internal decision-making, as is done by many companies.

Arguments in support of absorption costing

The importance of overheads is not underestimated with absorption costing. All costs must be met in the long run; e.g. if a pricing decision is based on variable costs only, there is a risk that the sales revenue achieved may be insufficient to recover all the costs and the business will make a loss. However, merely apportioning fixed costs to a product does not by itself ensure that these fixed costs will be covered. This could happen if the actual sales volume achieved is less than the estimated level which was used to calculate the fixed overhead rate, on which these indirect costs were apportioned.

Absorption costing is argued, by its proponents, to be the superior system because it recognizes the importance of product costs, and links them, through the accounting principle of matching, to the relevant products in the actual period of their sale. The definition of an asset is critical to this debate. One interpretation put forward by absorption costing proponents distinguishes between assets and expenses according to whether or not the costs incurred will contribute to the realization of sales revenue in the future. This concept assumes that any cost which needs to be incurred to make a product which is expected to be sold in the future constitutes a cost of obtaining that future sales revenue. Hence these costs should be carried forward in stock valuation and matched against the future sales revenue, i.e. they are included in the calculation of the profit for the period of the sale.

However, with fixed costs it can be argued that no such future benefit exists, since these costs will be incurred regardless of the level of operation. Thus, marginal costs are more relevant to future periods and management decision-making because they are the true level of product costs. Fixed costs are irrelevant because they are period costs. If we refer back to the earlier example, a particular decision has to be made about a three-year contract. We need information (about product costs) that allows us to analyse performance over the three years as a whole and not just in the first year. Therefore we advocate marginal costing as the superior decision-making technique, although if properly applied over the total period of the project, both systems will give the correct result.

Another important consideration is whether the overhead allocation system motivates employees to work in harmony with the company's objectives. A lot can be learned from the Japanese approach to management accounting which helps to create an environment in which the organization can compete in the future; it does not merely judge the performance of the organization to the present date.

Stock valuation: a problem area for analysis?

As has already been discussed reported profits can be significantly affected by the values placed on stocks. Stocks may be valued at:

1 Prime cost, which is made up of direct material, direct labour and direct expense.
2 Factory marginal cost, which is prime cost plus direct variable factory overhead.
3 Total factory cost, which is prime cost plus fixed and variable factory overhead.

Prime cost is the most prudent valuation. When stock levels are increasing, profits will be understated because other costs which are normally carried forward to a future period will be written off in the current period.

Factory marginal cost is favoured under the marginal costing system where fixed expenses are considered period costs. With the total factory cost approach, however, (as used in absorption costing), the partial costs of the marginal or differential methods are not considered to reflect fully the expenditure that has been incurred in bringing the product to its present location and condition. This expenditure should include purchasing costs and the costs of conversion appropriate to that location and condition. Costs of conversion include direct production costs (direct labour, direct expenses) and production overheads based on the normal level of activity.

Stocks and work-in-progress are valued for financial reporting purposes at the lower of cost and net realizable value. Long-term contract work-in-progress is valued at cost plus attributable profit less any foreseeable losses.

There are also a number of ways of assessing what cost means when used for stock valuation purposes:

1   First-in, first-out (FIFO), where the cost of the most recently purchased items will be reflected in the valuation. Thus, during times of inflation the earliest items with the lowest prices will be issued first, leading to a lower cost of sales calculation and a higher profit.
2   Last-in, first-out (LIFO), where the latest and highest prices are charged to production resulting in a higher cost of sales figure and lower profits compared with using FIFO, as well as a lower stock valuation.
3   Average cost, where the value of stock at any one time is the average of all the items of cost, although the average method will always be most affected by the latest stock purchases and issues.
4   Replacement cost, which is the present cost to replace the asset with the same productive capacity and a similar cost base.

The four bases for valuation can best be compared by looking at a simplified example over a short period. In Figure 5.3 details of stock receipts and issues in a department over a one month period are shown. If it is assumed that the first item of input raw material to be received was also the first item to be issued then stock will be valued on a 'first in, first out' (FIFO) basis.

A particular type of clay is required to manufacture earthenware pots. During September purchases and issues of this raw material were as follows:

1 September	Received	280 kg @ £18 per kg (cost price)
8 September	Received	70 kg @ £19.50 per kg
12 September	Issued	260 kg
15 September	Received	100 kg @ £19 per kg
16 September	Issued	120 kg
17 September	Issued	30 kg
22 September	Received	200 kg @ £18.50 per kg
28 September	Issued	210 kg

Figure 5.3

From Figure 5.4 it can be seen that the clay issued on 16 September is at three different purchase prices. This is because after the first issue on 12 September there still remains 20 kg purchased at £18 per kg plus the 70 kg purchased on 8 September at £19.50 per kg. However, on 16 September, 120 kg are to be issued and this still leaves an issue requirement of 30 kg which must be taken out of the 100 kg purchased on 15 September at £19 per kg. The 30 kg of stock which is left at the end of the period will be valued at £18.50 per kg, i.e. at the price of the last clay received.

However, if it is assumed that the last item to be received in stock is the first item to be issued, then the stock is being valued on a 'last in, first out' (LIFO) basis. Thus from Figure 5.5 it can be seen that the 16 September issue is now only at two purchase prices. This is because all of the 8 September purchase of 70 kg at £19.50 was consumed in the 12 September issue because it was the last stock received. We can also see that the closing stock consists of 30 kg left over from the 1 September receipt.

	Receipts			Issues			Stock		
Date	Qty kg	Price per kg £	Amount £	Qty kg	Price per kg £	Amount £	Qty kg	Price per kg £	Amount £
1 Sept	280	18	5,040				280		5,040
8 Sept	70	19.50	1,365				350		6,405
12 Sept				260	18	4,680	90		1,725
15 Sept	100	19	1,900				190		3,625
16 Sept				20	18	360			
				70	19.50	1,365			
				30	19	570			
				120		2,295	70		1,330
17 Sept				30	19	570	40		760
22 Sept	200	18.50	3,700				240		4,460
28 Sept				40	19	760			
				170	18.50	3,145			
				210		3,905	30		555

The closing stock represents: 30 kg @ £18.50 per kg = £555

Figure 5.4 *FIFO method of valuing stocks*

Date	Receipts Qty kg	Receipts Price per kg £	Receipts Amount £	Issues Qty kg	Issues Price per kg £	Issues Amount £	Stock Qty kg	Stock Price per kg £	Stock Amount £
1 Sept	280	18	5,040				280		5,040
8 Sept	70	19.50	1,365				350		6,405
12 Sept				70	19.50	1,365			
				190	18	3,420			
				260		4,785	90		1,620
15 Sept	100	19	1,900				190		3,520
16 Sept				100	19	1,900			
				20	18	360			
				120		2,260	70		1,260
17 Sept				30	18	540	40		720
22 Sept	200	18.50	3,700				240		4,420
28 Sept				200	18.50	3,700			
				10	18	180			
				210		3,880	30		540

The closing stock represents: 30 kg @ £18.00 per kg = £540

Figure 5.5 *LIFO method of valuing stocks*

With the average cost method items are issued at the average cost per unit. This is calculated by dividing the total cost of the stock by the total quantity in stock after each new purchase. In practice this average cost calculation may only be updated monthly. It can be seen from Figure 5.6 that the closing stock value is similar to that obtained under the FIFO method. This is because the average method is always most affected by the latest stock receipts and issues, as is FIFO.

Under certain circumstances a fixed asset such as a steel rolling mill may be valued at the lower of replacement cost or market value. Thus, we are dealing with a present cost, i.e. the cost of replacing the asset with another with the same productive capacity and a similar cost base. However, the technology of the existing asset is likely to be outdated and so it will not be possible to replace the asset directly. Hence the market value of the existing asset will have fallen, although the replacement cost will not.

Date	Receipts			Issues			Stock		
	Qty kg	Price per kg £	Amount £	Qty kg	Price per kg £	Amount £	Qty kg	Price per kg £	Amount £
1 Sept	280	18	5,040				280	18	5,040
8 Sept	70	19.50	1,365				350	18.30	6,405
12 Sept				260	18.30	4,758	90	18.30	1,647
15 Sept	100	19	1,900				190	18.67	3,547
16 Sept				120	18.67	2,240	70	18.67	1,307
17 Sept				30	18.67	560	40	18.67	747
22 Sept	200	18.50	3,700				240	18.53	4,447
28 Sept				210	18.53	3.891	30	18.53	556

The closing stock represents: 30 kg @ £18.53 per kg = £556

Figure 5.6   *Average cost method of valuing stocks*

In our stock valuation example the 30 kg of clay left at the end of the period might have a replacement cost of £18 per kg (i.e. £540), although its market value may only be £16 per kg (£480) for financial reporting purposes.

During times of rising prices the method of stock valuation chosen could have a major bearing on the profit reported by the organization. Using FIFO a higher closing stock figure will arise thereby inflating the reported profit figure. Hence SSAP 16 (1980): *Current cost accounting* recommended that for financial reporting stocks be valued at their FIFP cost or their net realizable value, whichever was the lower. This would give the nearest approximation to current value of stock.

Stock management

Stocks represent a major investment of funds for most businesses which needs to be managed both efficiently and effectively. This involves the firm in determining its optimum level of investment in stocks. To do this two conflicting requirements must be met: first, the firm must ensure that there are sufficient stocks of raw material and work-in-progress to meet the requirements of the production department and sufficient stocks of finished goods to satisfy sales demands; second, it must avoid holding surplus stocks which are an unnecessary cost burden on the organization and which increase the risk of obsolescence and pilferage.

The relevant costs for determining the optimum level of investment in stocks using quantitative modelling consist of holding costs and ordering costs. Holding costs are usually made up of the following items:

- opportunity cost of investment in stocks
- incremental warehouse and storage costs
- incremental insurance costs
- incremental material handling costs
- costs of obsolescence and pilferage of stock

The relevant holding costs should include only those items which will vary with the levels of stocks. Hence the analysis should only be concerned with the incremental costs of storage, handling and insurance arising from a change in the level of stocks. As capital is invested in stocks, there is an opportunity cost of holding stocks which should be included in the analysis. This cost is the incremental return which is foregone from investing in stocks rather than some alternative investment.

Ordering costs are the costs of preparing purchase orders for stocks, receiving deliveries and paying invoices. Again the analysis focuses only on the incremental costs of ordering. Those costs which are common to all stock decisions are not relevant. Stock acquisition costs are also irrelevant if they remain unchanged irrespective of the order size or stock levels (e.g. there may be discounts for large orders). However, the ordering and holding costs may change in relation to the order size and these will be relevant for decision-making models.

Determining the economic order quantity

A business may decide it wants to differentiate its level of service by holding high inventory levels near to its customers to allow quick delivery. It is essential therefore that the full stockholding costs, which could be particularly high if the products require special handling or storage conditions (e.g. frozen storage), are included in the financial justification of this strategy. It is not impossible to have stockholding costs as high as 30 per cent of the total value of the stock. Thus, the effective control of these costs is vital and hence stock management systems are now very sophisticated. Required stockholding levels are often calculated using computerized models which take account of the entire range of factors which affect the optimum stockholding level. Most of these models are based on the economic order quantity (EOQ) or optimum order size which shows the volume of any stock item it is most economical to purchase using the factors included.

The EOQ is a function of the holding and ordering costs discussed above. If a large amount of stock is ordered at one time, fewer orders will be required per year. This will reduce ordering costs, but larger average stocks will have to be maintained thereby increasing holding costs. There is therefore a trade-off between the costs of carrying large stocks and the costs of placing more orders. The optimum order size will result when the total amount of the ordering and holding costs is minimized.

The formula for the EOQ (Q) is:

$$Q = \sqrt{\frac{2 \times \text{total demand for period} \times \text{cost per order}}{\text{Holding cost per unit}}}$$

$$Q = \sqrt{\frac{2DO}{H}}$$

(see Appendix for mathematical derivation)

There are a few key assumptions inherent in the EOQ formula:

1   It is assumed that the holding cost per unit will be constant. In practice some costs might increase on a step basis as stock levels increase.
2   In calculating the total holding cost it is assumed that the average balance in stock is equal to one half of the order quantity. However, if a constant amount of stock is not used per day (seasonal and cyclical factors may produce an uneven usage over time) this assumption will not hold.
3   Safety stocks have been ignored in the analysis because it has been assumed that the level would stay the same irrespective of the order size. However, the size of safety stocks is unlikely to be independent of order quantity as relatively larger safety stocks are likely to be associated with smaller order quantities.

Bearing in mind these assumptions EOQ is a useful tool for analysis. Figure 5.7 illustrates the relationship between holding and ordering costs as order quantity increases. A graphical representation is given in Figure 5.8.

Figure 5.8 shows that the lowest level of total cost will be at the point where holding costs are equal to ordering costs.

The EOQ formula can be adapted to determine the optimum length of the production runs. This is done by balancing set-up costs (rather than ordering costs) with stockholding costs. There is an assumption that a set-up cost is incurred only once for each batch produced. Set-up costs include incremental labour and material costs, machine down-time and other costs of making facilities ready for production.

In the example in Figure 5.7 total set-up cost (S) is £160. Therefore:

$$\text{Optimal production run (P)} = \sqrt{\frac{2DS}{H}}$$

$$P = \sqrt{\frac{2 \times 9,000 \times 160}{2}}$$

$$P = 1,200 \text{ units}$$

Example

A pot maker buys a raw material from an outside supplier at a cost of £12 per unit. The total demand during the period of this product is 9,000 units. Relevant cost information is as follows:

Opportunity cost of capital = 15%

Therefore, required return on investment in stocks (15% × £12)	£1.80	
Other holding costs per unit	£0.20	
Holding costs per unit		£2.00
Ordering costs per order		£4.90

Calculate the EOQ

$$Q = \sqrt{\frac{200}{H}}$$

$$= \sqrt{\frac{2 \times 9000 \times 4.9}{2}}$$

$$= 210 \text{ units}$$

Figure 5.7

Thus with a demand of 9,000 units and an optimum production run of 1,200 units 7.5 production runs will be needed during the period.

Up to now we have assumed a degree of certainty with the ordering, delivery and usage of stocks. In practice this is not the case, and to protect itself from conditions of uncertainty a firm will maintain a level of safety stocks for its raw materials, work-in-progress and finished goods.

Safety stocks are the level of stocks which are carried in excess of what is expected to be used during the lead time (the time between ordering and receiving new stocks). They therefore provide a buffer against running out of stocks. For example, a company could have an average lead time of three weeks. With average weekly usage of stocks of 100 units it would re-order when stocks fall below 300 units. However, demand and lead time are not certain so the firm needs to have a level of safety stocks. If the maximum weekly usage is 150 units and lead time might

Relevant cost data for pot maker

Order quantity	50	100	150	200	210	250	300
[1] Average stock (units)	25	50	75	100	105	125	150
[2] Number of purchase orders	180	90	60	45	43	36	30
[3] Holding cost £	50	100	150	200	210	250	300
Ordering cost £	882	441	294	221	210	176	147
Total relevant cost £	932	541	444	421	420	426	447

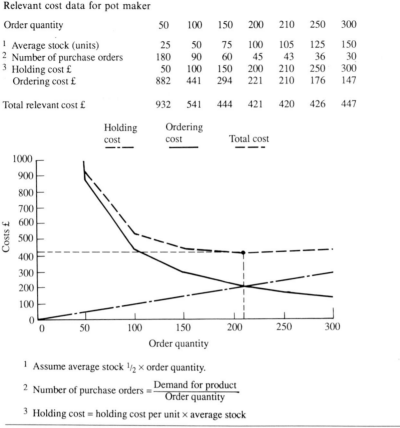

[1] Assume average stock $\frac{1}{2}$ × order quantity.

[2] Number of purchase orders $= \dfrac{\text{Demand for product}}{\text{Order quantity}}$

[3] Holding cost = holding cost per unit × average stock

Figure 5.8   *Determining the economic order quantity*

extend to four weeks, then the safety stock level would be an additional 300 units [(150 units × 4 weeks) − (100 units × 3 weeks)]. The level of safety stock will depend on the firm's perception of risk. Maintaining high safety stocks may not be a sensible policy if the cost of holding the excessive stocks exceeds the costs that should be incurred if the company ran out of stocks. Thus if the probability of demand reaching 150 units a week or of lead time extending to four weeks is low, the management may decide to keep a lower level of safety stocks.

Japanese management accounting

Although cost measurement and control plays an important role in management accounting, it is not the only role. Japanese manufacturing strategy, for example, places a high premium on quality and timely delivery in addition to low-cost production. Thus managers need non-financial measures to evaluate performance;

a management accounting system that measures only costs tends to focus management's attention exclusively on cost control. There needs to be a direct link between management accounting practices and the objectives of the company (e.g. improved quality, timely delivery).

The traditional approach to stock management has been to try to optimize the level of investment in stocks by analysing the EOQ which provided an optimum balance among set-up or ordering costs, storage and holding costs and stock-out costs. The mathematics of optimum inventory policy have become quite complex. The Japanese, however, have always approached the problem from a broader and more fundamental perspective. They view inventory as a form of waste. Therefore they do not wish to optimize the level of stocks; rather to get rid of them altogether. In analysing the problem, the Japanese tried to understand why they held stock in the first place. One reason was to protect against poor quality and consequent interruptions to production. For example, if a machine in the production line broke down, those workers further down the line needed a stock item so that they could continue working. Another reason was long set-up times which of necessity drove up the required level of stocks to cope with the disruption. Japanese managers have set about reducing set-up times so that the EOQ is nearly equal to one.

The Japanese just-in-time (JIT) theory on controlling stocks is now well disseminated. The goal of zero work-in-progress requires that no item is produced until the next stage of production is ready to work on it. As a result, holding costs are greatly reduced as well as there being more spare factory floor space after the factory layout is improved. However, not only were savings made, but other previously hidden problems emerged – quality problems, bottle-necks, supplier unreliability – which had to be solved.

The use of JIT systems changes the accounting requirements of managers. In order to support the objectives of JIT non-financial measures (such as average set-up times and throughput times, which are the times taken to manufacture and distribute the product from order to delivery to customer and supplier lead times) are required, and these are totally integrated into the management accounting process. This is discussed further in Chapter 13.

Stock valuation and pricing

Stock valuation also plays an important role in pricing policy. As a starting point for price fixing, managers often estimate the full cost for each product at normal capacity. This is an attractive approach (in the eyes of accountants at least) when conditions of uncertainty prevail. To the full cost figure is added a margin which will allow for a profit to be made and cover any abnormal capacity. This is the 'cost plus' approach.

This full cost estimate will include costs of holding and ordering stocks. However, in order to know what stocks are needed, demand has to be forecasted. Therefore management must have an understanding of the market, its customers and the competition.

Different price levels should be set for different stages of the product life-cycle; e.g. a lower relative price in the growth stage to achieve an increasing market share and a higher one in the mature stage to maximize sales revenues and profits. Pricing and planning is discussed in greater depth in Chapters 8 and 9.

Questions

1 The Nitelife portable telescope is the only product of Tranzfar Ltd. It sells the product direct to the customer via mail-order at a price of £95. The company normally sells 7,200 telescopes over a 12-month period.

Below is a budgeted profit and loss statement for 12 months based on sales and production at this normal level of activity.

	£000	£000
Sales		684
Costs:		
Direct material	232	
Direct labour	86	
Variable production overheads	10	
Fixed production overheads	98	
Selling and advertising	86	
Administrative overheads	70	582
Net profit		102

Budgets have been prepared for years 3 and 4. In the budget for year 3 production has been included at the normal level of activity but sales are only expected to reach 90 per cent of the normal level, although they are expected to reach 100 per cent in year 4. Production will be reduced in this year so as to utilize all the available stock carried forward from the previous year.

You are required to prepare a budgeted profit and loss account for each of the two years using:

a) absorption costing
b) marginal costing.

(You can assume that there is no stock carried forward to the beginning of year 3.)

Discuss the effect on profit of these two costing approaches.

2 Discuss whether marginal costing or absorption costing is the more appropriate approach to cost allocation for the following businesses:

    a) computer software
    b) oil exploration
    c) vehicle leasing/car hire
    d) construction of a nuclear reactor
    e) ball-bearing manufacturer.

3 A discount motoring shop sells sets of car mats at £25 a set. The shop has a choice of three main suppliers, but it only ever buys from one supplier each month depending on which offers the best deal. Stocks are replenished on a monthly basis. From January to June the deliveries and sales of the mats were as shown below. Fifteen sets, which had been purchased in December the previous year at £17 a set, were in stock at the beginning of the year.

Month	Sets of mats purchased		No. of sets
	No.	Cost £	sold
January	50	15	56
February	30	17	29
March	30	17	37
April	45	19	36
May	35	16	28
June	20	16	21

You are required to
(a) prepare stock records for the above transactions using the following methods:

    i) LIFO
    ii) FIFO
    iii) average cost.

    b) Recommend which method you would advise the shop management to use and why.

Appendix: mathemical derivation of EOQ formula

The total relevant cost (TC) for any order quantity can be expressed as follows:

$$TC = \frac{DO}{Q} + \frac{QH}{2}$$

where $\dfrac{DO}{Q} = \dfrac{\text{Total demand for period} \times \text{Ordering cost per order}}{\text{Quantity ordered}}$

and $\dfrac{QH}{2} = \dfrac{\text{Quantity ordered} \times \text{holding cost per unit}}{2}$

A minimum for this total cost function can be determined by differentiating the above formula with respect to Q and setting the derivative equal to zero.

$$TC = \frac{DO}{Q} + \frac{QH}{2}$$

$$\frac{dTC}{dQ} = \frac{-DO}{Q^2} + \frac{H}{2}$$

If $\dfrac{dTC}{dQ} = 0$, then $\dfrac{H}{2} = \dfrac{DO}{Q^2}$

$$Q^2 = \frac{2DO}{H}$$

$$Q = \sqrt{\frac{2DO}{H}}$$

Part Three

Planning

Relevant costs for decision-making

Overview

There are many kinds of management decisions involving the analysis of alternative courses of action. These decisions can broadly be categorized into investment, disinvestment, and cost reduction or profit enhancement decisions. Although profits are important in understanding the financial performance of a business, cash flows give a more accurate picture of the impact of any potential decision. Therefore only cash flow items are included as relevant costs. Decisions relate to the future, and therefore only future costs are relevant for decision-making purposes. Costs which have been incurred in the past (sunk costs) or costs which have already been committed (committed costs) are, therefore, not relevant to financial decisions. Costs that are common or which will be incurred whether or not a particular option is chosen are excluded from the decision-making process. Only the additional costs (the incremental costs) are necessary for decision-making. The costs that are relevant take into account the impact on the whole enterprise. Therefore opportunity costs have to be considered for decision-making purposes.

Introduction

Most management decisions involve analysis of the alternative courses of action which are available to the organization. These alternatives are then ranked in accordance with pre-determined criteria and the final decision is made to select the alternative which sets the business on the best course of action to attain the organization's specific objectives. In order to make the best decisions, managers obviously require supporting information which is accurate and relevant to the particular decision they are currently facing. Obviously the costs and benefits of the various alternatives being considered are an essential part of the financial information required. The Chartered Institute of Management Accountants (CIMA) defines these costs (and benefits) as those appropriate to aiding the making of specific management decisions, i.e. relevant costs.

This chapter addresses the process which needs to be gone through to identify those costs which are not relevant and those which are relevant to any planning or decision-making process. In doing so, it illustrates why financial accounting and absorption cost accounting, as discussed in Part Two, do not really help in relevant cost analysis for decision-making.

Decisions

It is perhaps best to start by trying to identify the major categories of decisions made by managers in organizations. Obviously not all types of decisions made by managers in all organizations can be classified here, but we will try to categorize them into three broad areas:

- Investment decisions
- Disinvestment decisions
- Cost saving/profit enhancement decisions

Investment decisions

Decisions in this category perhaps have one of the highest impacts on the achievement of the organization's objectives and financial goals. At all stages in the life-cycle of any organization decisions have to be made about entering into new markets, launching new products or extending existing products and markets. These decisions can involve expenditure on research and development and marketing activities, as well as investment in the purchase or replacement of fixed assets. Fixed assets may be either tangible (e.g. plant and machinery) or intangible, such as brands, technical know-how, product licences, etc.

It is normal that most decisions in this category involve substantial expenditure in the short term as well as possibly the long term. Companies have to invest immediately in plant and machinery and research and development, as well as possibly having to incur increased expenditure on the operating activities over the life of the project they are evaluating.

The impact of these additional capital and revenue costs on the organization's financial objectives can obviously be substantial. These costs are not always limited to only the direct costs that are incurred. Quite often there are other knock-on costs incurred as a result of a decision to invest, which also need to be considered in arriving at a decision whether to go ahead with the investment or not, and these are illustrated in the example given below. The decision-making process is further complicated by the fact that in many cases the benefit to the organization of such an investment decision accrues over several accounting periods, and possibly over many years. The uncertainty involved in forecasting the value of these prospective future annual benefits requires a high level of judgement from the decision-maker. This is further complicated by the fact that the same amount of money received at different points in time will have different present values to the organization, as will be discussed further in Chapter 7. Perhaps for this reason managers involved are at times accused of 'creative' accounting to justify investments they favour.

A simple example may be useful to illustrate the concepts involved in this type of investment decision. Fast Dig plc, which manufactures, sells and distributes industrial excavators, has a 30 per cent share of its local national market. Three other major competitors (two of whom are based overseas) control the vast majority of the remaining market. Although Fast Dig is market leader in supplying excavators, the potentially lucrative market for after-sale maintenance and service is very fragmented with a large number of small companies providing these services. Fast Dig has a small service business itself, but it is based at its main factory and hence it only services customers located nearby. There is also a limited number of large customers who have their own in-company maintenance facility. The current net profit margin on supplying excavators is 10 per cent, while the potential margin on components and service is over 25 per cent.

The company is evaluating whether to set up a new wholly owned subsidiary which would actively sell branded replacement components for Fast Dig excavators, as well as for competitors' excavators. The foreign competitors currently ship replacement components direct to the small service companies but in small batches, which result in relatively high unit costs. At present a high proportion of replacements are made using alternative cheaper components, purchased direct by these small maintenance contractors.

The decision-making process involves identifying the obvious direct, and possibly easily identifiable, costs involved in investing in any required additional plant capacity, particularly to produce the components for competitive products, as well as acquiring suitable sales outlets, staffing these outlets and holding adequate levels of stocks of Fast Dig components and competitors' components. However, there are other knock-on financial effects which need to be taken into account in arriving at the final decision.

Although there may be financial benefits from the extra contribution which can be generated from the sale of competitors' components, there may be more important implications caused by the potential improvements in the effectiveness of the supply chain for competitors. Customers may find the improved availability of competitors' components a substantial incentive to purchase the competitors' excavators. It is possible therefore that there will be a change in the sale of Fast Dig's own excavators and components as a result of the decision to invest in the subsidiary due to a loss in market share. The possible changes to the sales and profits of the existing service department of Fast Dig should also be considered. The increased convenience and ease of access to parts and components of all equipment manufacturers may attract new entrants into the maintenance business or encourage more of the larger customers to provide their own service facility. Fast Dig's managers also have to decide the time period over which to evaluate the financial benefits of the potentially increased sales revenues. There is a risk that if this period is long, the market may undergo significant changes during this period. However, by reducing the company's dependence on initial product sales, the volatility of profits during the inevitable economic downturns may be reduced and this may reduce the perceived risk profile of the business.

The company also has to consider several other options which include aggressively selling branded replacements for their own machines only.

Disinvestment decisions

The disinvestment decision, the opposite of the investment decision, is also important in the impact it has on the organization's objectives and financial goals.

The financial and non-financial effects of a decision to disinvest, whether it involves closing down a plant or selling a brand, can be quite substantial and, because of the possible adverse consequences, should be considered very carefully. The fear of possible adverse consequences should not deter management from making this decision because, unfortunately for organizations, most products and technologies do eventually come to the end of their economic life-cycle. It is even possible that, although a particular technology or product is quite profitable, it may not fit into the organization's current strategies and objectives. Grand Metropolitan's decision to sell off a number of businesses was influenced more by 'strategic' factors than lack of profitability, as evident from the fact that none of the disposals made by Grand Metropolitan from 1987 to 1990 was unprofitable. The decision to withdraw from a market or activity is referred to as the disinvestment decision. These decisions, because of the long-term impact on the core business, require a clear understanding by the manager of the benefits that would accrue to the organization by maintaining support for a particular product or technology, versus the benefits that could accrue to the organization by disinvesting from the obsolete product or technology.

Although it is relatively easy to identify the 'direct' benefits of disinvesting and to compare them with the 'direct' costs of continuing with the activity, as discussed in the investment decision, the 'indirect' or knock-on costs and benefits are difficult to identify and quantify. What would be the costs and benefits of, for example, Guinness deciding to sell off Kaliber, its non-alcoholic beer? The 'direct' costs associated with Kaliber's production (such as marketing expenses) would be saved and this benefit can be compared with the contribution which would no longer be earned from continuing production of Kaliber. However, as a consequence of the decision, the costs of producing the normal alcoholic lager from which the alcohol is removed to produce Kaliber would also be affected. In the long term the increased costs of producing lower volumes of 'normal' lager could possibly outweigh any benefits of disposing of the Kaliber brand, even if this brand were not making a positive net contribution on its own. Unlike investment decisions, with disinvestment decisions the benefits could be immediate but the costs, quite often, are not direct and could be incurred over a long period.

Therefore, a clear understanding is needed by the manager of the future benefits or costs that will accrue to the organization if it continues producing and selling existing products or using the current technology, versus the alternative benefits of exiting from the product or technology including all the knock-on costs and benefits. An example may make this clearer.

There is an increasing trend in many industries for companies to concentrate on what are defined by them to be core activities and disinvest those activities which are felt to be peripheral, thus not only saving costs but freeing management time to focus on enhancing performance of the core activities. A number of companies, including BET, have taken advantage of the trend in other organizations to focus on core activities and BET therefore provides 'peripheral' services such as security, cleaning, recruitment, etc. to these organizations. What would be the costs and benefits, for example, of the National Health Service (NHS) deciding to concentrate on its core activity of providing health care to patients and consequently deciding to use a company like BET to provide cleaning services at their hospitals?

The obvious potential benefits to the NHS are the saving in operating costs of labour and material, and the proceeds of disposing of cleaning equipment and materials. The clearly evident costs are the annual charges made by BET for providing the cleaning service. However, in arriving at a decision the NHS management would also need to consider the impact of this decision on the quality of service provided, and the possible loss of control. Even more importantly the NHS will have to consider what best alternative benefit could be achieved from the space and other resources freed. This 'opportunity cost, as defined in Chapter 2, or the value/cost of the next best alternative course of action, is an essential element in the decision process and should therefore be evaluated in order to arrive at the 'best' decision.

Cost saving/profit enhancement decisions

Managers in any organization, with profit or cost efficiency and effectiveness as an objective, will be looking either to maximize profits or at least to achieve a satisfactory level of return, or to reduce costs and so optimize the effective use of the resources of the organization. To this end perhaps, most financial decisions made by managers fall into this category and quite often result in the comparison of short-term costs and short-term benefits to the organization. This short-term focus is influenced by the nature of the decision itself which is often aimed at enhancing performance in the short term. However, it must be emphasized that in making decisions in this category managers need to be aware that actions which may yield short-term profit growth or cost reduction may not necessarily lead to the best long-term benefit for the organization. The full implications of decisions, whatever the category, need to be considered in arriving at the final decision.

Returning to the previous example of the NHS, although it may be clear that the immediate benefits of subcontracting cleaning services to an outside contractor are lower costs than the immediate costs of continuing the cleaning service within the NHS, it is equally possible that in the long term the quality of cleaning from any subcontractor may deteriorate and adversely affect the quality of service to National Health Service patients, who are the ultimate customers. These possible adverse consequences or, for that matter, the possible favourable consequences in the long term must be taken into account in evaluating any cost saving/profit enhancement decision.

There are numerous examples of companies which, when faced with a need to enhance profits or reduce costs in the short term, decide to reduce, or perhaps cancel altogether, expenditure on those activities which do not have a direct immediate impact on sales, i.e. discretionary activities. A good example of a discretionary cost/activity is that of the NHS cleaning as discussed above. In the short term it is clear that reduction in 'quality' of cleaning will not have an immediate impact on 'sales' of the business. The avoidance of discretionary costs, which are incurred at the discretion of management, will perhaps increase profits in the short term if those costs do not have an immediate impact on sales, but the medium to long-term impact may be quite adverse. Similarly in other organizations and industries the avoidance of discretionary costs such as advertising, research and development, training, etc. will obviously increase profits in the short term but the impact of this in the long term must also be considered.

Incurring additional discretionary expenditure may also have the opposite effect in that a profit enhancement decision to spend on a discretionary activity, with a view to achieving the benefit of increased earnings, may also not necessarily lead to these benefits in the short term. A recent example was the headline of a news item in the financial press 'Bulmers hit by increased advertising costs', where the company had in the current financial year spent substantial amounts on national advertising, the benefits of which should accrue in the form of increased sales in future years. This kind of adverse external publicity can, in many other cases, deter a manager from making a decision which, although not favourable in the short term, will lead to benefits in the long term.

The reason for this short-term focus and the consequent unwillingness to take management decisions which are best for the company in the long term can in part be attributed to the traditional financial accounts orientation of many companies and managers. This issue is discussed further in the next section of this chapter.

Financial accounts and cost accounts

Managers making decisions falling into any of the above categories would in many cases look initially at the profit and loss account and the impact on this account in the short term. The profit and loss account which is consulted could be for the organization as a whole or for any product group or other segment within the organization, depending on the scope of the role of the manager and the particular decision being considered. Managers attribute this overall need to their desire to satisfy their investors and the fact that these investors look at the profit and loss account in judging the company's performance. Thus they have created the current profit and loss/financial accounts orientation. But in doing so managers also need to appreciate that, as discussed in Chapter 2, externally published financial accounts for the whole company are prepared on a historical basis covering a specific period of time and produced in accordance with well accepted accounting concepts and rules. Unfortunately accounting policies, such as depreciation policies, and the use of historical costs, which may be totally out of date, do not assist the decision-making process. Nor do periods, over which management decisions need to be considered, fit with the traditional financial accounting period of 12 months.

There are many examples of companies where the short-term profit and loss orientation of managers has led to the wrong decisions. Necessary expenditures which could lead to profit enhancement over a period of time have been put off to a future accounting period purely because incurring the expense in the tail end of the current period would not lead to profit enhancement in the same period.

Together with budgetary 'gameplaying, as discussed in Chapter 9, this short-term financial accounts orientation, focusing on 'arbitrary' accounting periods, has in many cases led to the wrong decisions being made.

Financial accounting, as well as traditional cost accounting, relies on historical costs as the basis for preparing a profit and loss account and for reporting on performance such as in variance reports or in profit and loss statements for comparison against pre-set budgets. These budgetary 'constraints which may have been set a number of periods ago can and do in many cases deter managers from making the 'right' decision. These accounting systems also rely on the accruals or matching concept of matching sales and expenses to the period in which the sales transactions occur. The custom of having 12 month accounting periods, the ends of which are chosen at random or for tax and other unconnected reasons, together with the application of the matching principle, leads again to an accurate set of financial accounts being prepared, which comply with financial accounting regulations and principles, but does not lead to the best decision necessarily being made.

Cost accounts using historical standard costs applied to absorption costing or marginal cost statements are also often used to arrive at management decisions. Absorption costing leads to the allocation of overheads and fixed costs to individual products or product groups as discussed in chapters 4 and 5. This can quite often not be helpful in the decision-making process. Let us consider the example of a three product company manufacturing products A, B and C and selling to various customers, as set out in Figure 6.1, which may help to illustrate this.

	A	B	C	Total
Sales	100	80	70	250
Labour	30	20	10	60
Materials	20	20	30	70
Prod dept overheads	20	27	20	67
Central overhead (apportioned)	10	8	7	25
Marketing expenses	5	3	4	12
Total absorption cost	85	78	71	234
Profit/loss	15	2	(1)	16

Central overheads of £25,000 are the general administration expenses of the head office which would not be saved unless the whole company was closed down.

Marketing expenses, although product specific and therefore normally avoidable if a product were to be discontinued, have already been paid and are not recoverable.

Figure 6.1 *Apportioned cost example: discontinued production*

The company wanted to identify any unprofitable products so that they could be considered for discontinuation. Based on the basic information shown in Figure 6.1 the company would want to discontinue product C as it appears to show a net loss. Further examination using the relevant financial information however reveals that this would have been quite the wrong decision to take.

First, the fixed expenses apportioned to individual products would not be avoided if product C were to be discontinued. Consequently as a result of the discontinuation, the costs which had been previously charged to product C would now have to be absorbed by products A and B. This would then indicate that product B has now apparently become unprofitable as can be seen in Figure 6.2. If we carry on this process of bottom-slicing the unprofitable products, a company could find itself eventually losing its head!

Second, as can be seen from the example, marketing expenses, although avoidable in theory if product C were to be discontinued, have already, in this case, been incurred and are therefore 'sunk costs' and not recoverable. Sunk costs are discussed further later on in this chapter.

Third, production department overheads would normally include a charge for depreciation of machinery dedicated to each product. Although, again in theory, the depreciation is avoidable; in fact the machinery has already been purchased in a previous period and no portion of this historic cash outflow on machinery will be saved as a result of closing product C down. On the other hand, it is quite possible that there may be a further cost involved in dismantling and disposing

	A	B	Total
Sales	100	80	180
Labour	30	20	50
Materials	20	20	40
Prod dept overheads	20	27	47
Central overhead (reapportioned)	14	11	25
Marketing expenses	5	3	8
Marketing expenses (reapportioned)	2	2	4
Total absorption costs	91	83	174
	9	(3)	6

As a result of absorbing the central overhead by products A and B and writing off the marketing expenditure on product C to products A and B, product B now appears unprofitable.

Figure 6.2 *Apportioned cost example: post discontinuation of product C*

of the machinery! Clearly, the 'relevant costs', i.e. the costs which will be saved or incurred as a result of the decision, are the proceeds of sale of the machinery netted off against the disposal expenses. Relevant costs are discussed in detail later in this chapter.

Quite clearly, therefore, absorption cost accounting information is of no value in management decision-making regarding disinvestment decisions, unless the information can be adjusted for a number of irrelevant factors.

If we now consider an investment decision, so as to examine the impact of the launch of a new product D on our previous company, the situation changes again, as shown in Figure 6.3.

As central overheads are allocated to products based on sales revenue values in this company, the new product D would attract £7,000 of overheads. The charging of these central overhead costs to product D could possibly lead to product D appearing to be an unprofitable option and therefore the investment decision may be quite wrongly taken not to launch product D. However, launching product D would reduce the share of overhead borne by existing products and hence improve their profitability; apparently making product C now appear to be profitable!

	A	B	C	D	Total
Sales	100	80	70	100	350
Labour	30	20	10	20	80
Materials	20	20	30	30	100
Prod dept overheads	20	27	20	30	97
Central overhead (apportioned)	7	6	5	7	25
Marketing expense	5	3	4	14	26
Total absorption costs	82	76	69	101	328
Profit/loss	18	4	1	(1)	22

Figure 6.3 *Apportioned cost example: additional product*

Committed costs and sunk costs

These examples clearly indicate that even cost accounting principles are of limited value and can be misleading in making financial decisions. The alternative of using marginal costing as discussed in Chapters 4 and 5 is more useful that absorption cost accounting but still does not enable managers to make the most effective management decisions. This can be seen by looking at the marginal costing statement for products X, Y and Z as illustrated in Figure 6.4.

	X	Y	Z	Total
Sales	250	120	150	520
Variable costs:				
labour	100	30	70	200
Materials (committed)	80	40	90	210
Contribution	70	50	(10)	110
Advertising	20	20	10	50
Promotion	1	1	1	3
Depreciation	5	3	5	13
Fixed overhead (apportioned)	25	12	10	47
Profit/loss	19	14	(36)	(3)

Figure 6.4 *Apportioned cost example: decision whether to discontinue product Z*

Traditional marginal costing principles suggest that product Z does not make a positive contribution even at the level of only charging direct costs and should therefore be discontinued. The decision taken would in fact be wrong because in this case there are other expenses, such as the materials expenditure, which have already been committed and therefore will not be saved if production of product Z were to be discontinued. Committed expenses are, as the name suggests, those costs which will have to be paid for irrespective of whether the organization enters into, or does not enter into, a particular course of action. As a result it can be seen that although by discontinuing product Z a loss of £10,000 at the contribution level is saved, the committed payment of £90,000 for materials changes the economics of the decision. When taken together with the fact that apportioned overheads and depreciation are book costs which also are not saved, a true economic loss of a further £69,000 would result from the discontinuance decision. This will be true unless an alternative use can be found for the materials and real savings made in the expenditure on fixed overheads.

Basing the decision on marginal costs and thus discontinuing Z will not financially benefit the company due to the committed costs which will have to be paid anyway. This does not mean that the marginal costing analysis is wrong, just that it is not appropriate for decision-making unless a proper understanding of the various cost components leads to the identification of the true decision costs, i.e. the relevant costs and relevant benefits of the decision.

On further inspection of product Z it can be seen that there is an amount of £5,000 for depreciation in Figure 6.4 itemized as a cost for this particular product. Depreciation, as discussed in Chapter 2, is the writing off, over the economic life of the asset, of the cost of the asset which was incurred at some point in the past, so as to match the expense of using the asset against the benefits received by using it in the business. It is evident therefore that depreciation is not a cost to the organization in cash flow terms in each period, but is part of the accounting concept of matching expenses to the sales in the period in which they are generated. The only cash flow benefit to the company as the result of discontinuing product Z would be if the equipment on which the depreciation amount is being charged could be sold and the proceeds of the sale would therefore become a benefit to the company.

It can also be seen that, at the point when the decision is being taken, the original cost of the asset does not enter the decision-making process. This can be illustrated with a personal example. In financially evaluating a decision to travel to London from Milton Keynes either by car or by train, the costs which would need to be included in the process are the train fare compared to the fuel cost for the car and an estimate of the wear and tear on the tyres and engine of the car. The fact that the car was purchased for £12,000 two years ago will not affect the decision in any way.

A further decision could also be considered, with the alternatives being to sell the car now for £8,000 or to spend £500 on a major service and sell it after a further year's use for £7,500. Again it can be seen that, although further information is necessary to make the final decision, the original cost of the car is not in any way relevant to the decision. Whether the car is sold now for £8,000 or in a year for £7,500, the original cost of £12,000 has already been incurred and will not affect the decision in any way.

Therefore it is evident that the original cost of the asset which was incurred many periods ago is a sunk cost and not relevant to the decision-making process. A sunk cost is a cost which has already been incurred and will not be recovered as a result of the decision now being made. This cost of the asset and any associated depreciation charge is sunk and has no relevance to the decision made or in the decision-making process. The only 'cost' arising from the disposal that is relevant is in fact the benefit that would accrue to the company as a result of selling the asset.

From the above examples and discussion on the various kinds of decisions, it can be seen that in making management decisions it is necessary to consider only the 'true cost' or benefit of the decision. It can also be seen that this 'true cost' is the *cash* cost or benefit of the decision.

A question that often arises is: surely the cost or benefits that are relevant to a decision are arrived at by looking at the profit or loss that arises purely as a result of the particular decision?

The following section, once again, discusses the critically important distinction between profits and cash so as to reinforce the fact that, although both are important, profits are not the same as cash. It is further argued that cash costs and benefits are the fundamental factors in any decision-making process, and therefore in using relevant costs for decision-making, the relevant cash flows should be the primary consideration.

The importance of cash flows to decision-making

Although both profits and cash are important it is quite clear that, by comparing the sources and application of funds statement and the profit and loss account for any company, as was done in chapter 2, profits are not the same as cash for any organization. As previously stated financial accounting and cost accounting are both based on the matching concept, and match sales and costs to the period in which the sales transactions occur.

In preparing financial accounts and internal profit and loss statements managers apply these fundamental accounting concepts, and similarly investors who receive this information accept that these accounts have been prepared historically by applying these concepts. Despite a clear understanding and acceptance of these concepts by both the managers and investors, the results are reports indicating only how the company has performed in the past periods. Although the underlying accounting concepts are the basis for both the profit and loss accounts and the balance sheets in published financial statements, the various depreciation policies and differing accounting conventions which are adopted by companies can lead to difficulty in comparing various projects for management decision-making purposes.

It is also necessary to appreciate that accounting profits are purely the increase in net assets resulting from the trading activities of the company and unless they have been translated into cash they may have no tangible value at present, depending on what form these assets take. For example, a finance company may, by applying various perfectly acceptable accounting conventions, show a substantial profit from leasing or selling on hire purchase a variety of long-term assets to its customers. These 'credit' sales will not generate funds for the company, until subsequently translated into cash when these customers pay. It is therefore important in managerial decision-making to use cash flows as the relevant costs for decisions, thus overcoming the vagaries of accounting conventions and clearly focusing on the true costs and benefits of each decision.

It should be realized that, although profits and cash may not be the same during individual periods, they must come to the same amount in total over the life of the project. However, cash received at different times has different values to the business and, as a consequence, decision accounting concentrates on cash flows and the changes in those cash flows which result from any particular decision. A detailed example should make these differences clearer.

Decision-making example

A company has very recently bought a motor car for the sales and marketing director, who does around 40,000 miles per year, with annual operating costs of £6,000. The car cost £21,000 and because of the high mileage it was expected that the car would be sold after three years for £6,000. Very soon after buying the car, an innovative company brought out a new fuel economy device which dramatically improves fuel consumption and halves petrol usage. This is forecast to produce a saving of £2,000 per year for the new car and this new device is priced at £4,500.

As a result of this new device and other breakthroughs in engine maintenance, a rival car manufacturer very quickly announces a new model with a similar specification to the director's car. It deliberately prices its car below the existing model at £18,000 and the annual operating savings (including the benefit of the fuel economy device which is fitted as standard to the new model) are forecast to be £4,000 per year. This new model is also expected to have a 3-year life and a final trade-in value of £6,000. The company is naturally interested in this new model and these potential savings, and so the sales and marketing director calls in to the dealer and inquires about the trade-in value on his nearly-new, spotless executive car which cost £21,000. The dealer is very polite but apologetic, and points out that the car is now outdated technology; therefore he is being very generous by offering a trade-in against the fabulous new car of £10,000.

Thus a loss of £11,000 has been made on the existing model in a very short time and some companies would argue that they could not afford to make such a loss by trading in the car. They would be completely wrong in their logic. The loss has been made whether the car is traded in or not – trading the car in merely *realizes* the loss, it does not make it. (This is like arguing that shareholders are *not* worse off if their shares go down in price *unless* they sell their shares. The value of the shareholdings have reduced and hence the shareholders are worse off, whether they choose to realize the loss or not.)

In decision-making terms the original cost of the car is irrelevant to this decision as it is an historic (or sunk) cost and should not affect the future choice as to keeping the car, buying the new device to add to the car or trading in the car to buy the new model. Following the discussion earlier in this chapter on various management decisions, it should now be possible to identify the relevant costs of this car example and the criteria for identifying them. The decision can be based on the total cash flows over the life of the two cars, and these are shown below.

Impact on cash flows

Option 1: Keep car and do nothing

	Cash flows				
	Year 1 £	Year 2 £	Year 3 £	Year 4 £	Total £
Fixed assets purchased	(21,000)	–	–	–	(21,000)
Fixed asset sale proceeds	–	–	–	6,000	6,000
Operating costs	(6,000)	(6,000)	(6,000)	–	(18,000)
Total	(27,000)	(6,000)	(6,000)	6,000	(33,000)

Option 2: Keep car and add fuel device

Cash flows

	Year 1 £	Year 2 £	Year 3 £	Year 4 £	Total £
Fixed assets acquired	(25,500)	–	–	–	(25,500)
Fixed assets sale proceeds	–	–	–	6,000	6,000
Operating costs	(4,000)	(4,000)	(4,000)	–	(12,000)
Total	(29,500)	(4,000)	(4,000)	6,000	(31,500)

Comparing Options 1 and 2 shows that the impact over three years is £33,000 of expense if nothing is done and £31,500 of expense if the new fuel device is bought. Thus there is less of an impact on cash flows by choosing Option 2.

Option 3: Sell the car and buy new model

Cash flows

	Year 1 £	Year 2 £	Year 3 £	Year 4 £	Total £
Fixed assets acquired (£21,000 + £18,000)	(39,000)	–	–	–	(39,000)
Fixed assets sale proceeds	10,000	–	–	6,000	16,000
Operating costs	(2,000)	(2,000)	(2,000)	–	(6,000)
	(31,000)	(2,000)	(2,000)	6,000	(29,000)

Net expenses at £29,000 show an improvement of £4,000 against the 'do nothing' alternative.

Impact on profit and loss account

An alternative approach to evaluating the decision is to look at the impact on the profit and loss accounts.

Option 1: Keep car and do nothing

Profit and loss account

	Year 1 £	Year 2 £	Year 3 £	Total £
Operating expenses	(6,000)	(6,000)	(6,000)	(18,000)
Depreciation expenses	(5,000)	(5,000)	(5,000)	(15,000)
	(11,000)	(11,000)	(11,000)	(33,000)

Note: depreciation expense is calculated as follows:

$$\frac{£(21,000 - 6,000)}{3} \text{ p.a.} = \begin{array}{l} £5,000 \text{ p.a., i.e. reduction in value} \\ \text{from £21,000 to £6,000 spread over the 3 years} \end{array}$$

Option 2: Keep car and add fuel device

Profit and loss account

	Year 1 £	Year 2 £	Year 3 £	Total £
Depreciation expense				
car	(5,000)	(5,000)	(5,000)	(15,000)
fuel device	(1,500)	(1,500)	(1,500)	(4,500)
New operating expenses	(4,000)	(4,000)	(4,000)	(12,000)
	(10,500)	(10,500)	(10,500)	(31,500)

Option 3: Sell the car and buy new model

Profit and loss account

	Year 1 £	Year 2 £	Year 3 £	Total £
Loss on sale of car:				
(Cost £21,000 – proceeds £10,000)	(11,000)	–	–	(11,000)
Depreciation expense on new car $\dfrac{(18,000 - 6,000)}{3}$	(4,000)	(4,000)	(4,000)	(12,000)
Reduced operating expenses	(2,000)	(2,000)	(2,000)	(6,000)
	(17,000)	(6,000)	(6,000)	(29,000)

The differential cash flow approach

The above example clearly illustrates that, although profits and cash flows may vary substantially in individual years, over the life of the project the profits and cash flows will be necessarily equal. The same decision can be arrived at much more quickly and easily however by looking at just the relevant cash flows, i.e. the future differential cash flows.

Keep car or buy new model

Differential cash flows: buy the new model and trade-in the existing car

Cash outflows – purchase of new model	(£18,000)
Less: Trade-in of existing model	£10,000
Cash outflow	(£8,000)
Cash inflows – annual savings in operating costs of new model (£4,000) p.a. for 3 years	£12,000
Net cash inflow	£4,000

Keep existing car and fit fuel device

Cash outflow – purchase of fuel device	(£4,500)
Cash inflow – annual savings in operating costs at £2,000 p.a. for 3 years	£6,000
Net cash inflow	£1,500

The benefit of trading-in is £4,000 which is greater than the opportunity cost (fitting fuel device) benefit of £1,500, and hence the best option is to trade-in the existing car and buy the new model, as is explained in more detail below.

One alternative is to keep the car and do nothing while another is to keep the car and fit the fuel economy device (for this example the time value of money is ignored). Looking at the differences in cash flows here is quite simple; £4,500 is spent now to buy the device and £2,000 is saved each year for the three years that the company intends to keep the car. The total cash inflow is £6,000 against an expenditure of £4,500 and so the company is better off buying the new device than keeping the car and doing nothing (net gain £1,500).

The other alternative is to buy the new model and trade-in the existing car. The opportunity cost of this decision is the cost of buying the fuel economy device which made the company £1,500 better off (in this case, less badly off) than doing nothing. If a comparison is made between buying the new car and doing nothing, a net benefit of more than £1,500 is needed to justify the decision.

Again, looking at the future cash flow differences is quite easy. If the new model is bought, £18,000 must be paid out; but with the trade-in value of the existing car of £10,000, the net payment is only £8,000. We are only interested in future cash flows and so the sale proceeds of the current car are a cash inflow, despite the sale making an accounting loss of £11,000. The annual operating savings of £4,000 achieved by owning the new more efficient car can be offset against this cost of £8,000. With an expected life of three years, savings will total £12,000 for a net financial benefit of £4,000. Thus buying the new car is more attractive than keeping the existing car even if the fuel efficiency device is added.

Several important points should be noted from this differential cash flow approach. In concentrating on future cash flows we do not include depreciation expenses as these are not a movement of cash but simply an accounting expense. Instead we include the actual cash outflows to buy the fixed assets where they are *future* costs. We do not include past expenditures, so the original cost of the car is irrelevant and the decision would have been the same if the historic cost had been £121,000. We are able to make the evaluation without knowing all the other costs to do with the business and even without needing to know the absolute cost of running the cars. As long as the changes in cash flows can be forecast sensible financial decisions can be made.

Relevant costs

As a working definition, relevant costs can be regarded as those future cash flows of the company which change (compared to the present situation) directly as a result of the decision.

Management decisions will have an impact on the future profits of the company, and it is important to remember that only costs that are going to be incurred in the future and revenues that will be earned in the future matter to the decision. Costs which have been incurred already, i.e. sunk costs, are not relevant because they do not affect the final decision.

The fact that a property developer bought a piece of land during the boom days of 1989 for £10 million is not relevant if the decision now is whether to sell the land for £7 million or wait for two years when prices are expected to go up and the land could be sold for £8 million. The only costs which are relevant are the £7 million now compared to the £8 million in two years time.

Similarly, if the property developer had contracted to pay £500,000 to prepare the land for development, and had committed his company to this payment irrespective of whether the land is sold or not, then this £500,000 is considered a committed cost and will not affect the final decision in any way. A committed cost has already been defined as a cost which has not yet been incurred, but which will be incurred whether the decision is taken to go ahead with the particular project or not. Committed costs can include fixed costs such as lease and hire purchase costs, advertising contractual expenses and maintenance contract payments for plant and machinery. It is important to realize that apparently variable costs such as wages and materials, if contracted for in bulk in advance, may be committed costs too. Although wages are traditionally seen as variable costs along with materials, for decision-making purposes it can be seen that categorizing costs into variable and fixed is not necessarily of much use. It is on the other hand more useful to identify those costs which are committed and not relevant to the decision, from those which are not committed and which are, therefore, relevant to management decisions.

In making decisions the key questions are:

- Has any particular cost being considered in the decision process already been incurred? If so, the cost is a sunk cost and should not be included in the decision.
- Do the remaining costs to be incurred in the future result directly from the particular decision?
- How many of these future costs would have been incurred anyway? If any, they should not be included as they are committed costs.
- Are all the costs being considered cash costs? If not, they are not relevant and should not be included in the decision-making process.

We can see from the previous examples that all decisions start from the base point of the current situation, then the particular alternative under consideration is looked at and the relative benefits or costs of entering into that alternative are evaluated, in terms of the impact on future cash flows rather than accounting costs. For this reason, a number of alternative terms are used to describe relevant costs.

Differential costs

Additional cash costs incurred directly as a result of going into a particular course of action are called differential costs. The amount of this cost will be the additional expense incurred on top of the current position. For example, in considering a new product launch the options might be to launch in East Anglia, the whole of the South East, or the whole country with total promotional costs of, respectively, £1 million, £2 million and £5 million, compared to the present situation of a promotional spend of £750,000 per annum. Therefore the *incremental* cost of launching in East Anglia alone would be £250,000, in the South East it would be £1,250,000, and nationally £4,250,000. Differential cost is very similar to incremental cost, but considers the difference between any two options. For example, the *differential* cost of promotion nationally compared to the alternative of the South East would be £3,000,000.

Although considering total costs instead of incremental or differential costs may lead to the same decision being made, the application of the principles of differential costs discussed above will help focus management attention on those costs that matter, i.e. those costs which will change as a result of the decision – the relevant costs.

Avoidable costs

Avoidable cost is a term usually associated with disinvestment decisions, but it can be applied to cost saving decisions too. Avoidable costs are defined as those costs which can be directly identified with a particular activity and which will be avoided if that activity did not exist, i.e. the cost will not be incurred. Avoidable costs are, like committed costs, not necessarily only variable costs. Going back to a previous example it can be seen from Figures 6.1 and 6.2 that if product C were to be discontinued, in addition to the variable labour and material costs of manufacture that would be avoided, the production overhead cost of £20,000 would also be avoided, although it would normally be classified as a fixed overhead. This is because the plant which had been dedicated to the manufacture of product C would now be closed down and associated costs such as repairs and maintenance would be avoided.

Opportunity costs

In management decision-making the key objective must be to improve the position of the organization as a whole. It is therefore essential that in analysing relevant costs the alternative uses to which the resources could be applied must be considered.

If the space freed up by subcontracting cleaning had no alternative use for the NHS and could not be disposed of, there is no cost saving on space for the NHS. On the other hand, if the NHS currently occupies a building rented on a short-term basis at £200,000 p.a. and the space would not be needed as a result of subcontracting the cleaning operations, the relevant cost saved would be £200,000 p.a.

The opportunity cost of allocating a resource to a particular activity is the benefit foregone by not entering into the best alternative activity. Intuitively it is clear that the cost of acquiring something is what must be given up to get it; but in practice however it is sometimes difficult to consider opportunity costs as one of the relevant costs in decision-making. The logic of opportunity costs is that in all financial decisions as in life there is no such thing as a free lunch. All organizations need to understand and financially evaluate what is being given up as a consequence of any potential course of action; at the very least any funds released could be placed on deposit in the bank as discussed in Chapter 1.

Summary

Although financial information is of great importance in planning and decision-making, we should also appreciate that many business decisions are primarily based on qualitative factors. This chapter has looked at the financial information necessary for decision-making and the presentation of that information, but the relevant qualitative factors obviously need to be taken into account in arriving at the final business decision.

The main advantages in using cash flows rather than profits for decision-making are illustrated in the next chapter, which discusses the time value of money and discounted cash flows.

A comprehensive example designed to draw together the various aspects of relevant costs is now given, with an answer included as an appendix to the chapter.

Consumer Products Ltd: out-sourcing

The senior managers of Consumer Products Ltd were even more agitated and aggressive than usual. At the monthly executive meeting the buying manager, John Jackson, had tabled a proposal to out-source several company functions. Unknown to most members of the executive committee the managing director, Charles Grady, had instructed Jackson to look at reducing the cost base of the business by obtaining price quotations from external suppliers for a range of services and non-core manufacturing operations, all currently performed internally. Grady's objective had been partially to try to save costs but primarily he had wanted to shake up his departmental heads, whom he believed had become relatively fat, happy and complacent. Consequently he had deliberately selected one area from each director's field of responsibility and he was confident that Jackson would obtain some keen quotations; not least because he had indicated that a good performance could lead to a position on the board, not necessarily as buying director!

However, not even Grady's provocative management style could have foreseen the mayhem that would ensue at the actual meeting when Jackson tabled his recommendations. From the areas examined he argued that sizeable savings, totalling 25 per cent of the current year's budgeted profit, could be achieved by ceasing internal operations and using outside suppliers. Some of the proposals were for only partial cessation and out-sourcing; but in the area of distribution, Jackson recommended the exclusive use of outside hauliers and outside storage for finished goods warehousing. This suggestion had caused the commercial director, Bernard Garrett, to explode as finished goods storage and distribution represented most of his area of responsibility, having lost buying in an earlier reshuffle. He was even more apoplectic when it became apparent that Pat Orsay, the financial director to whom Jackson now reported, had assisted with some of the financial analysis.

He did manage a cynical grin at Pat Orsay, as she turned crimson when Jackson suggested closing down her beloved systems development department and using outside software houses instead.

Charles Grady broke up the meeting, not that it really needed breaking up, and said 'I appreciate that this may have come as quite a shock to some of you but I think John has done a good job. I'd like your responses to his proposals within forty-eight hours and then we'll consider the time-scales for implementation.' He was a great believer in considering people guilty until they were proven innocent!

Bernard Garnett picked up Jackson's proposal regarding storage and distribution, and stormed out of the meeting. The proposal was very simple, consisting of a price quotation from Bell's Transport and Storage Ltd together with an analysis of the current costs of carrying out the functions internally. These are given below:

Internal costs		£000
Direct labour – drivers and warehouse staff		550
Consumables		
Fuel and other materials	450	
Pallets	100	550
		1,100
Overheads		
Depreciation of lorries	200	
Maintenance	100	
Rent of warehouse	150	
Occupancy costs (rates, lighting, heating, etc)	100	
Indirect wages	40	
Manager's salary	35	
75% share of director's costs	75	700
Share of general administration overheads		250
Total costs of distribution department		£2,050

Quotation from Bell's for a 3-year contract: £1,500,000 p.a. (not fixed price).

Bernard had to concede that the gap looked amazingly large but he was sure that there must be some differences in the way the figures were calculated. He was particularly concerned that three-quarters of his costs (himself, secretary and personal assistant) were included in the analysis, and he quickly raised this point with Charles Grady. Charles was overwhelmingly reassuring about having no plans at all for getting rid of Bernard whatever decision they finally came to, but Garrett still felt that uneasy, gnawing feeling in his stomach and a certain dryness in the back of this throat as he went back to his own office.

There were other areas that he thought needed adjustment and these included pallets, lorries and fork lift truck hire. They had purchased in bulk a large quantity of wooden pallets last year and still had a stock of 10,000 with a cost of £20 each. Current annual usage was 5000 pallets and the price had already increased to £30 for purchases of normal quantities. However, it was a specialized market and selling their existing stock would probably only realise £15 per unit.

The lorry fleet was also quite new, having been replaced last year and had a total cost of £1 million. They had forecast a residual value after four years of £200,000 and were depreciating the balance on a straight line basis. However, if the lorries were sold now, they would realise only £400,000. Also, as part of last year's complete review of the distribution function, Garrett had entered into a four-year hire contract for fork lift trucks at an annual rental of £20,000 (this was included in 'other materials'). If the company wanted to terminate the contract it had to pay an immediate cancellation fee of £30,000 in order to save these annual costs.

He felt that this information actually made the position worse because, having spent a lot of money last year, it still appeared that an outsider could provide the same service at a much lower cost, while presumably making a profit! In desperation he went to see Pat Orsay to seek some advice regarding these items as well as the warehouse and general administrative overheads. Pat felt that the existing warehouse, which was rented on a 25-year lease and was located next door to the factory, was not a problem as it could be re-used by the company as extra production space with a minimal cost of conversion. The company was severely constrained in terms of available production space and was, in fact, using outside contractors for certain operations, which led to double handling of products and other production inefficiencies. She did not feel that the general administrative costs would be reduced whatever happened, because most of these costs were incurred in her departments and they were already cut to the bone and ran themselves very efficiently. 'She would say that, wouldn't she', muttered Bernard as he walked back to his office again. Even his parting shot had rebounded badly. 'How much of these costs represent the *existing* systems development area?' he asked on his way out; but Pat was still too quick for him as she replied, 'A lot less than 75 per cent!' Perhaps he should check his biorhythms, he thought!

Before looking at the answer supplied in the appendix, readers are recommended to prepare an analysis using both cash flows and profit and loss accounts in order to decide whether to go outside for distribution services. You should also consider what other issues should be taken into account.

Questions

1 In the case of Fast Dig plc, discussed in this chapter, the company found that it would need to invest £500,000 in plant, and set up five distribution outlets at various locations in the UK if it were to opt for a new, wholly owned subsidiary which would sell its own and competitors' spare parts and provide a service facility. Present turnover from this activity is £1 million p.a., but this is expected to double if the new subsidiary is set up.

The products of a Japanese competitor have up to now been very successful in the market. With the changing economic and political environment, Fast Dig plc feels that it will have to make adequate returns from the new subsidiary over the next five years.

Market research indicates that sales of Fast Dig excavators are likely to fall by 10–15 per cent as a consequence of better availability of competitors' spare parts encouraging customers to switch to competitor products. Fast Dig's turnover at present is £10 million p.a. The market growth is expected to be around 5 per cent p.a. Fast Dig's turnover has been fairly static for a number of years.

a) What action would you recommend to Fast Dig plc?
b) What other factors need to be considered?

2 The managing director of your company, as a consequence of the 'recession' and its impact on profits, is considering whether to cut marketing and other discretionary spending across the board by 20 per cent. Draft a report outlining your views on cutting discretionary expenditure and possible consequences.

3 'This company has to generate an income in excess of all its costs, both variable and fixed. Marginal costing and contribution analysis is both misleading and dangerous. I believe the only appropriate costing system is a "full cost" system.' How would you respond to this statement by a managing director?

4 In the decision-making example discussed in this chapter, on page 136, the company is not totally convinced that the latest model will in fact generate a saving of £4,000 p.a. over the current vehicle's operating costs. By how much will the savings have to fall annually before it is not advisable to buy the new car?

Appendix: Solution to Consumer Products Ltd

A   Using total cash flows

	Year 0 £000	*Year 1* £000	*Year 2* £000	*Year 3* £000	*Total* £000
Savings from outside contract:					
Labour	–	550	550	550	1,650
Fuel and other consumables[1]	(30)	450	450	450	1,320
Pallet costs[2]	150	–	–	150	300
Depreciation[3]	400	–	–	(200)	200
Maintenance	–	100	100	100	300
Rent of warehouse	–	150	150	150	450
Occupancy costs	–	100	100	100	300
Indirect wages	–	40	40	40	120
Manager's salary	–	35	35	35	105
Director's costs[4]	–	–	–	–	–
	520	1,425	1,425	1,375	4,745
Outside contract costs	–	1,500	1,500	1,500	4,500
	520	(75)	(75)	(125)	245

Workings to above calculations

[1] The forklift truck contract can be cancelled by paying £30 k now and this will generate a saving of the £20 k p.a., which is a sound decision. Thus all the savings have also been included, but this would be invalid without the £30 k initial payment.

[2] The stock of pallets can be sold, which generates £15 per unit. No cash is payable in years 1 and 2 due to the existing stock, but a saving of the replacement cost per unit would be achieved in year 3.

[3] The existing lorries can be sold now for £400 k but it was expected that they would be sold at the end of Year 3 for £200 k, and this cash inflow cannot be received.

[4] No cash flow savings are forecast from the apportioned costs as it is assumed that these costs have not been saved.

B Using profit and loss accounts

	Year 0 £000	Year 1 £000	Year 2 £000	Year 3 £000	Total £000
Savings from outside contract:					
Labour	–	550	550	550	1,650
Fuel and other consumables[1]	(30)	450	450	450	1,320
Pallet costs[2]	(50)	100	100	150	300
Depreciation[3]	(400)	200	200	200	200
Maintenance	–	100	100	100	300
Rent of warehouse	–	150	150	150	450
Occupancy costs	–	100	100	100	300
Indirect wages	–	40	40	40	120
Manager's salary	–	35	35	35	105
Director's costs[4]	–	–	–	–	–
	(480)	1,725	1,725	1,775	4,745
Outside contract costs	–	1,500	1,500	1,500	4,500
	(480)	225	225	275	245

Workings to above calculations

[1] Cancellation payment on fork lift truck hire contract is financially a good idea and so this £30 k is shown as an initial cost, and full saving on contract payment is also shown. If this payment is not made, no saving is achieved because contract is fixed for three years and thus total cost of £20 k pa is committed.

[2] Existing 10,000 stock of pallets can be sold for £15 each which represents a loss of £5 per unit. In year 3, new pallets would have to be bought at the replacement cost of £30 each.

[3] The lorries can be sold for £400 k against a book value of £800 k (cost one year ago of £1 million), thus a book loss is generated of £400 k.

[4] The apportioned costs have been excluded (including the proportion of the commercial director's costs) on the assumption that these costs would not be saved, but all other direct costs would.

Techniques for capital investment appraisal

Overview

Long-term investment decisions must be financially justified using the relevant costs and associated incomes. This means concentrating on cash flows rather than profits. However, because these cash flows will take place over a considerable period of time, the investment appraisal technique should take into account the timing of the cash flows as well as being able to cope with several other factors. These other factors include the size of the initial investment, the economic life of the project, the certainty of the returns (or the relative risk of the project) and the strategic importance to the company.

There are several methods of capital investment appraisal, namely:

- Payback
- Discounted cash flow
  - Net present value
  - Internal rate of return
- Discounted pay back.

The most sophisticated methods adjust future cash flows back to their 'present value' by applying an appropriate 'negative interest', or discount, rate. This makes all the cash flows directly comparable, i.e. they become additive, and is the same type of process as converting different foreign currency values to a single currency so that the items can be added directly. Money received at different points in time clearly has different values, and the discounted cash flow technique adjusts for these relative differences.

Introduction

The previous chapter looked at the various decisions that are taken by organizations, without particularly differentiating between short-term and long-term decisions but identifying the costs and benefits that are relevant to the decisions that need to be taken. Various categories of decisions were discussed and the need to identify carefully all of the relevant costs of these options in order to arrive at the best decision was also emphasized. As a result of this evaluation process it will be possible to identify the stream of cash flows, i.e. focusing on cash and not profit, that are expected to arise as a consequence of management decisions. These cash flows can clearly arise over a number of periods or a single accounting period.

This chapter addresses capital investment appraisal, considering the specific issues that arise in long-term decisions as a result of identifying the relevant cash flows which take place over a relatively long period of time. These issues necessitate not only having to identify the relevant costs and associated incomes as previously discussed but also require development of techniques specific to long-term decisions, which take into account a number of factors including the consideration of the time value of money; i.e. that money, whether paid out or received, at different points in time has different economic values.

Timing of returns

Intuitively we know that an organization which invests relatively large sums of money in a project would prefer to receive the returns from the project sooner rather than later. Thus, in analysing the relevant costs and associated sales revenues, a project which has net cash inflows coming in during its earlier stages would be preferred to a similar project where the net inflow comes in at the later stages. This intuitive knowledge arises from the fact that, given the risky environment in which most businesses operate, the risk level is reduced if the returns come in at an earlier stage.

Consider, for example, the authors' experience with a company in the softdrinks industry. The company is considering two alternative projects both involving an initial investment of £500,000, as shown in Figure 7.1. Project 1 is a product line extension, and consequently sales revenues should commence immediately after the initial investment is made and the returns should cumulatively exceed the original investment by the end of year 2. Project 2 involves a new product development where the initial sales revenues should commence only from year 2 onwards and the cumulative cash flow returns are not expected to lead to a total repayment of the original investment until year 4.

As stated, project 1 involves an extension to the company's current range of soft drinks, and due to the rapidly changing nature of this market, sales revenues and consequent cash inflows are expected to peak quickly, but decline rapidly thereafter as the market changes.

Project 2 is a new product which, following a period of sustained development and marketing, should generate healthy cash flows for a number of years before eventually declining by the end of year 10 to zero cash flows, as in project 1.

Due to the highly competitive nature of the industry and its associated risks, the company should prefer to invest in project 1 if it wished to minimize the overall risk involved for the organization. Furthermore, if the inflows from a project were to come in at an earlier stage in the life of the project, these inflows could be

	Project 1	Project 2
Initial investment	− 500	− 500
Cash inflows		
Year 1	+ 200	0
Year 2	+ 350	+ 100
Year 3	+ 400	+ 200
Year 4	+ 200	+ 250
Year 5	+ 100	+ 350
Year 6	+ 100	+ 500
Year 7	+ 100	+ 400
Year 8	+ 100	+ 300
Year 9	+ 100	+ 200
Year 10	0	0

Figure 7.1 *Soft drinks company (projected cash flows in £000s)*

invested in other projects or repaid to the bank, if funds have been raised on a loan, yielding either an incremental saving or additional source of income for the organization. It is therefore necessary for any capital investment appraisal technique to take into account the timing of returns from the project in addition to considering the actual relevant cash flows.

Initial investment

The previous chapter discussed how to identify relevant costs and associated incomes from any project in order to enable management to decide on the viability of the project; but this does not necessarily mean that all the apparently viable projects, i.e. where the relevant costs are less than the associated incomes, will be taken on by the company. Although the financial analysis of the relevant costs and benefits may indicate that a certain project is acceptable, few businesses will have available the large volume of funds needed in order to be able to invest in all these acceptable projects which it may have in the pipeline. It is an unfortunate fact that in business, as in personal life, there is a limit to the amount of money available for investment. Current funds available within a company will therefore necessarily influence the size and number of projects which can be invested in.

It is true that most organizations should have access to additional external funds, and therefore if there are a number of very financially attractive projects the company should be able to raise the required funds externally from either shareholders or lending institutions. If the organization has a current shortage of available funds the initial investments will need to be funded externally, which may mean the company having to incur additional interest costs on any borrowed funds. If the required funds are raised from shareholders, they will also expect a return on their increased investment which will take the form of a mixture of dividend income and capital appreciation in the value of their shares.

However, a substantial initial investment in a new project will probably also have a significant internal impact on the existing material, labour, financial and other resources of the organization, which may need to be reallocated. This can have an impact not only on managers, but also on the shareholders and other financiers. They may perceive the company to be changing direction strategically and therefore possibly moving into a higher risk profile with a consequent demand for a higher return/interest payment. The company's (potentially changing) risk profile is shown in Figure 7.2. This shows that as risk increases expected return will also increase (this is discussed further in Chapter 8).

It is of course possible that the new project may be perceived as reducing the overall risk of the business and the expected, or demanded, return will become lower than at present. It is therefore necessary to understand the risk/return relationship of the specific investment opportunity and the consequent impact, favourable or otherwise, on the expected level of return for the business as a whole.

As mentioned above, a major decision criterion is the amount of money that is required to be invested in the project in its initial stages. However, it is not only the limited amount of funds available to most organizations that will lead to the size of the investment being a major criterion. The impact a significant investment will have on the business profile is also a key issue.

Even when there are sufficient funds available, the opportunity cost of funds needs to be taken into account. As discussed in Chapter 6 the initial investment involves an opportunity cost; i.e. if the organization has surplus funds, these

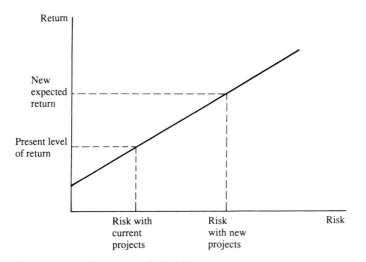

Figure 7.2 *Risk-return relationship*

amounts could be invested elsewhere to yield an alternative return. The following example illustrates this.

Roxanne Clay plc (which has existing net assets of £2,000 million) is considering two possible new investment projects. Project A involves investing £50 million in another quarry (the company owns and excavates a large number of existing quarries). Project B arose from the increasing desire by the management of the company to diversify away from the traditional single core activity of quarrying. The particular diversification project identified was an investment of £250 million, which was needed to bid for and acquire Cave Homes plc, a regional property development company. Roxanne Clay company has only £40 million of internal funds available for investment at present and even if potential sources of external funds were utilized the company would be unable to implement both projects at once. Thus a decision to select either project involves giving up the potential benefit of the other. This example, based similarly on the authors' practical experiences, also illustrates various other issues that need to be taken into consideration in deciding whether to go for project A or B. The cash flow forecasts for the two projects are shown in Figure 7.3.

Managers within the company may feel that diversifying into property development is a good strategic move, as it reduces the overall risk of the company. However, the external investors may feel that diversifying into an area which is not familiar to the existing management of Roxanne Clay may, in fact, increase the risk profile of the company, and thus the investors may not be very favourably disposed towards project B. However, the project involving investment in another quarry,

Cash flows in £ millions

	Project A	Project B
Initial investment	− 50	− 250
Year 1	0	+ 20
Year 2	0	+ 25
Year 3	0	+ 25
Year 4	+ 5	+ 25
Year 5	+ 10	+ 25
Year 6	+ 15	+ 25
Year 7	+ 20	+ 25
Year 8	+ 25	+ 25
Year 9	+ 25	+ 25
Per year 10–13	+ 25	+ 25
Per year 14–50	0	+ 25

Figure 7.3 *Roxanne Clay plc: projected cash flows*

which is seen as acceptable to the existing investors, may not be found to be suitable by the managers of Roxanne Clay.

Life of the project

Continuing with the example of Roxanne Clay, it is forecast that in project A the new quarry would have an economic operating life of ten years. Due to the need to develop the site before quarrying operations could start, the quarry would not be operational until year 4 with returns rising slowly but steadily over the next ten years' life of the quarry, as shown in Figure 7.3. Project B on the other hand, as explained previously, involves buying an existing very profitable company and consequently the existing cash inflows are expected to stay at their present high level. As a result, project B is forecast to be in a position to commence repaying the original investment from the very first year and has a very long economic life-cycle. It is also expected that project B would take longer to repay the much higher original investment but would have a much higher repayment over its total life, as illustrated in Figure 7.4.

Clearly it is not correct to look just at the time taken to recover the original investment. The process of long-term financial decision-making should therefore look at the financial returns over the entire life of the project.

Certainty of returns – risk

In developing suitable techniques for evaluating projects, managers need to take account of risk for two main reasons. First, as risk increases, rational investors, be they shareholders or lenders, will expect a correspondingly increased return

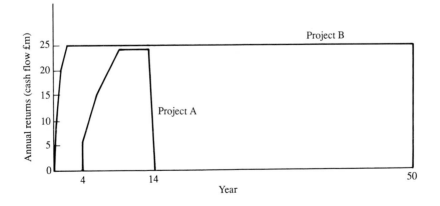

Figure 7.4 *Roxanne Clay plc: comparison of returns over life of project*

from their investment (as shown in Figure 7.2). Even at the personal level, it is clear that the expected return from a low risk investment, e.g. index linked government bonds (Gilts), is far lower than an 'investment' in a speculative share or, for that matter, from a flutter on an outsider at the races! Managers therefore have to take into account the increased return demanded by investors when evaluating a risky project.

Second, managers need to take account of the various factors which affect the certainty of returns from a project. Certainty of return is normally reduced as the life of a project increases due to the wide range of various external factors which can influence the future returns from a project, as illustrated in Figure 7.5.

Each capital investment project has its own associated unique combination of risk factors which influences returns. It is obviously not possible to identify all such factors here, but broadly they can be categorized in relation to most projects as:

- Technology risk – the risk that the technology which is applied to a project may, if new, not work, become obsolete or become relatively inefficient.
- Cash flow risk – partly because of the impact of inflation, there is often a lack of ability to forecast accurately the actual cash flows a long way ahead. For this and a number of other reasons, this cash flow forecasting risk is perhaps the most important of all the risk factors. The cash flow risks of long-term projects, will be discussed in Chapter 8.
- Risk of competitor reaction – In many competitive marketing orientated companies it is often found that even the best planned projects with supposedly 'certain' cash flows can be thrown awry by an unexpected reaction from competitors. Although it can be argued that good managers should be able to anticipate these reactions, the project risk is still increased if it can be significantly affected by possible competitor reactions.
- Learning curve – The experience curve or learning curve is based on the well proven, practical link between increased output levels and average costs of the

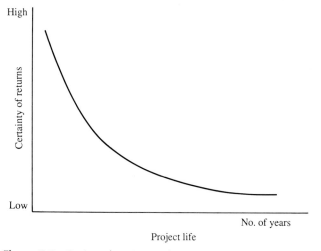

Figure 7.5 *Project duration and certainty of returns*

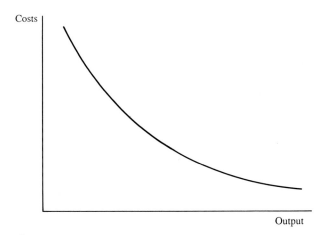

Figure 7.6 *Learning curve*

producer. As cumulative output increases and experience is gained of the production process involved the average real costs of this total output should correspondingly decrease, as shown in Figure 7.6. Although this relationship has been proved for many industries, there are also many examples of companies who have not built on these potential efficiency improvements, and thus they have not succeeded in reducing their costs. Therefore they have not gained a competitive advantage. Not being able to move down the learning curve as expected will have significant adverse reactions on a project, and hence the risk of the project is increased if the financial justification is based on such a cost decrease.

- Market risk – the market, i.e. the customers, may not react as expected to a new product, or other changed output resulting from a project. This type of risk could perhaps be reduced by using appropriate market research information, but is still a significant risk.

Strategic importance to company

In capital project evaluation, the long-term allocation of funds within the business is not merely a question of selecting the most obviously profitable projects and investing in these exclusively. Quality improvement projects, recently carried out in a number of companies, are an example of projects where even though the specific financial benefits may be unclear, the long-term strategic benefits have helped management to decide in favour of the projects. The financial analysis of even these projects can still have a vital role to play in the system of allocating funds. However, it is also important to recognize that the easily identifiable financial criteria are not the only issues to be considered. Management should be concerned with the long-term viability of the business, and as such, should be seeking to maximize long-term financial returns so as to ensure the long-term success of the organization itself. The initial financial analysis and ranking of the investment proposals often involve the specific relevant costs and income for the projects, but a second further level of analysis would involve the strategic analysis of the company's activities by the board or senior management, and lead to the prioritizing of investment proposals based on their contribution to the long-term strategy of the company. It must be stressed that, as seen in the above section on risk, the financial calculations of relevant costs and returns, however precisely they may be made, and however definite the answer they may seem to give, are not guaranteed to lead to successful investment decisions. They are just another facet in the decision-making process and are based on future forecasts, which are inevitably subject to error. They do not replace the judgmental process that is essential to successful management and, indeed, most of the forecasts involved are themselves based on such managerial judgements. Managerial judgement is influenced by a number of factors, the most significant of which are now discussed.

Non-quantifiable factors

In financially analysing the relevant costs and associated inflows, only those factors which can be measured in terms of money can be built into the calculations. Although these are important, they may not be the only issues which should be considered. It may, for example, be financially worthwhile to invest in sophisticated computing equipment for an office. However, it could be strategically disastrous if the resulting redundancies in the office lead to bad industrial relations, which may cause severe business problems for years to come, particularly if people are the key asset of the business.

ICL, for example, have invested millions of pounds in a company wide quality improvement programme. The benefits in the form of more reliable products, greater customer satisfaction, higher employee and management pride and commitment should lead to increased sales and profits. With such a long-term quality improvement programme, the financial benefits are very difficult to quantify and in fact in this case the management do not believe that their commitment to quality should be geared toward only short-term sales growth. Consequently no specific financial evaluation was carried out. Even if companies do attempt to quantify such benefits, the uncertainty surrounding them will often invalidate the financial analysis produced.

Uncertainty

Calculations on relevant costs and inflows are based on predictions of the future. If we consider our earlier example of the soft drinks manufacturer, the cost of the initial investment is evident, but we cannot be certain as to when and how much will be the future yield from the investment. An apparently sound decision, based on the best presently available information, will therefore sometimes turn out to be disastrously incorrect because of unexpected factors.

Managerial preferences regarding profits or cash flows

In evaluating projects based on the criteria discussed above, we could use either profits or cash in the evaluation process. However, as discussed in Chapter 6, profits are influenced by accounting conventions, such as depreciation policy, and the decision on what is considered a capital investment and what is considered revenue expenditure. Depending on the accounting practices prevalent in various organizations, various conventions can be applied to 'creatively account' and provide the profit level that is required. This has been discussed in detail earlier, but is re-emphasized here because it can lead to poor economic evaluations of potential investments if managers are wrongly motivated by being set targets expressed exclusively in terms of profits, rather than cash flow.

In discussing the criteria for capital investment appraisal it was found that cash flows have a real opportunity cost because only cash can be invested in alternative new projects. Profits on the other hand cannot be invested in any project unless they are first translated into cash. For this reason, cash flow is used in arriving at relevant decision costs and in evaluating capital investment projects. This obviously leads to a conflict with the traditional accounting return on investment method of evaluating both economic and management performance used by the majority of organizations. This conflict will be considered further in Chapter 8.

As discussed in the preceding sections, in developing and applying any technique for capital investment appraisal managers need to consider the following:

- Timing of returns
- Initial investment
- Life of the project
- Certainty of returns - i.e. Risk
- Strategic importance to company.

Various techniques have been developed which consider the above factors to different degrees. In choosing among these techniques, managers have often taken into account their relative convenience in application as well as the practical relevance of the information produced using each technique. The various techniques are discussed below.

Basic methods of capital projection evaluation

Payback

The long established simplest method for the evaluation of capital investment projects is known as the payback period. This method is based on the calculation of the time it takes to recoup the initial expenditure made on a project. Individual companies use their own slight variations of this technique to calculate the payback periods. The technique is based on calculating the cash flows arising from the

£000s

	Project A	Project B
Initial investment	− 5000	− 5000
Cash inflows Year 1	+ 2000	+ 3000
Cash inflows Year 2	+ 3000	+ 2000

Figure 7.7   *Payback example 1*

project in each of the years of its life, which measures the amount of cash that will be released each year from the project and thus becomes available for use in other areas of the business. These cash inflows will be related to the year in which they will occur and a project is judged according to the amount of time it takes for the initial investment to be paid back. The payback method requires the summation of the net cash inflows year by year until they equal the amount of the original investment. The length of time this process takes gives us the payback period for the project. For example, for project 1 in Figure 7.1 it takes just under two years to payback the original investment, while project 2 has a payback period of just under four years.

The decision-making criterion used under the payback method is that the shorter the payback period the better. Therefore, using only the payback method of evaluation, project 1 would be chosen because of its shorter payback period.

The payback method has a number of obvious advantages. First, it is very simple to calculate for most projects, as it is quite easy visually to examine the project cash flows and work out the payback period with very simple calculations. Second, it does take into account the timing of returns to an extent by considering how long it takes to return the original investment. Also, very importantly, it measures the amount of time the company is exposed as a result of going into an investment project.

However, the payback method does also have a number of significant disadvantages in relation to the ideal decision criteria we discussed for capital investment appraisal. Although it does to an extent take into account the timing of cash flows, it does not adequately reflect the importance of timing within the cash flows. For example, in projects A and B, which are illustrated in Figure 7.7 it can be seen that project B pays back a larger sum of money earlier than project A. Therefore with this simple example it is easy to decide that project B is preferable to project A, but the payback method in itself does not indicate this even in this simple example as both projects have a payback of two years. Clearly the situation is even less clear with complicated projects.

Also a project may pay back the investment earlier than another project, and therefore appear preferable using the payback method of evaluation, but the rejected

£s

	Project C	Project D
Initial investment	− 10,000	− 10,000
Cash inflow Year 1	+ 4,000	+ 2,000
Cash inflow Year 2	+ 6,000	+ 5,000
Cash inflow Year 3	+ 4,000	+ 6,000
Cash inflow Year 4	+ 2,000	+ 6,000
Cash inflow Year 5	+ 2,000	+ 4,000

Figure 7.8   *Payback example 2*

project could in fact give a substantially higher cash flow after the payback period. The example in Figure 7.8 illustrates this possibility.

In Figure 7.8 project C pays back the initial investment of £10,000 earlier than D and would be chosen purely on payback criteria. On further inspection it can be seen that the total financial return over the five years is greater on project D (£23,000) than on project C (£18,000). Therefore all other things being equal (risk, etc.) D should perhaps be preferred to C.

It can further be argued that project C, with higher cash flows coming in earlier, will generate funds which can be re-invested profitably. Therefore, because money has a higher value earlier than later, it is once again possible that project C will be preferred. These obvious and serious disadvantages of the simple payback method have led to the development of the more sophisticated Discounted Cash Flow model which is discussed in the next section.

Time value of money and compound interest

The proper evaluation of the impact of the timing of the relevant cash flows is the key to satisfactory evaluation of any long-term project. The earlier the funds are made available, the sooner they can be used to make a further contribution to profits by being redeployed. Accounting for the time value of money and the application of the theory of compound interest is now discussed.

Cash can be used in many ways. It can be deposited in a savings account and earn interest for the organization, or it can be lent to other companies and/or invested in projects which can in turn generate funds for the organization. If, for example, £100 is invested in a building society where it can earn interest at 10 per cent p.a., at the end of one year the original £100 will have grown to £110. If this amount of money is not withdrawn, but left to accumulate still at 10 per cent p.a., then at the end of the second year the original capital will have grown from £100 to £121. This process of 'compounding' will continue until such time as the money is withdrawn from the building society. It is easy to see how the original £100 compounds to £121 over a two-year period, and it can be shown that any initial sum of money (P) will grow over any period of time (*n*) at any interest rate (i) using the following formula:

$$S = P(1 + i)^n$$

where S is the sum of money in the future.

Therefore with our investment of £100 placed at 10 per cent p.a., in a building society, the sum at the end of two years is $S = 100(1.1)^2 = £121$.

Compound interest can be used to solve a number of business problems. A property company, for example, investing £1 million in some development land, could be expecting to make a profit when it disposes of the land at the end of five years. If the £1 million has been borrowed at an interest rate of 15 per cent p.a., the company can quite easily work out at what price the land has to be sold at the end of five years in order for the company to make a profit.

Minimum selling price to make a profit

$$S = 1(1 + 0.15)^5$$

$$= \underline{£2.01} \text{ million}$$

This price would be the minimum the company needs to receive in five years to cover its costs. Additionally the company would want to make a profit as compensation for the risk taken. Building in an expected annual rate of return to allow this would be relatively easy.

£s

	Project P	Project Q
Initial investment	− 2000	− 8000
Cash inflows Year 1	+ 600	+ 2000
Cash inflows Year 2	+ 600	+ 2000
Cash inflows Year 3	+ 600	+ 2000
Cash inflows Year 4	+ 600	+ 2000
Cash inflows Year 5	+ 600	+ 2000
Cash inflows Year 6	—	+ 2000

Figure 7.9   *Projected cash flows*

For many companies, the long-term capital investment decision-making process involves projects where fresh outflows and inflows take place at various points in time and requires comparisons of different types of projects with various economic lives. Therefore it would be preferable for the company to work out how much these various cash flows would be equal to in 'present value terms'. The example shown in Figure 7.9 shows how this can be handled.

Project P has a life of five years while project Q has a life of six years. Appropriate annual costs of capital for both projects are 12 per cent, The net value of in five years can be calculated by working out how much each year's cash flow of £600 would be worth at the end of the project and deducting the original investment, which is also expressed at the end of the project. Therefore for project P, assuming as normally done in practice that cash flows all arise at the end of each year for convenience, the net terminal value is:

$$
\begin{array}{lcr}
-2000 \times 1.12^5 & = & -3524.60 \\
+600 \times 1.12^4 & = & 944.11 \\
+600 \times 1.12^3 & = & 842.96 \\
+600 \times 1.12^2 & = & 752.64 \\
+600 \times 1.12^1 & = & 672.00 \\
+600 \times 1.12^0 & = & 600.00 \\
\hline
\text{At end of year 5, net terminal value} & = & +287.11
\end{array}
$$

Similarly for Project Q the net terminal value:

$$
\begin{array}{lcr}
-8000 \times 1.12^6 & = & -15790.58 \\
+2000 \times 1.12^5 & = & +3524.68 \\
+2000 \times 1.12^4 & = & +3147.04 \\
+2000 \times 1.12^3 & = & +2809.86 \\
+2000 \times 1.12^2 & = & +2508.80 \\
+2000 \times 1.12^1 & = & +2240.00 \\
+2000 \times 1.12^0 & = & +2000.00 \\
\hline
\text{At end of Year 6, net terminal value} & = & +439.80
\end{array}
$$

Unfortunately these terminal values cannot be directly compared as project P has a terminal value at the end of year 5, while Q's terminal value is at the end of year 6. Both values have to be calculated at the end of the same year for a direct comparison to be made. Although it is possible to compound forward the net terminal value of project P for one more year to the end of year 6, it is normally found to be more helpful to find out what today's value of both streams of cash flows are and then compare the net present values of the two alternative projects. This is helpful because it places the comparable net cash flows into a time frame where managers have a sense of relative values. Is a net terminal value of £440 in 6 years time really a good return for an investment now of £8,000?

Discounted cash flow (DCF)

Calculating the present value of a future cash flow involves the inverse process from compounding and is not surprisingly referred to as 'discounting', because it involves applying a negative rate of interest. Thus the present value of £121 to be received in two years time at 10 per cent p.a. interest as discussed above must be equal to £100. We can rearrange the compound interest formula derived above to arrive at the appropriate discounting formula:

$$P = S \times \frac{1}{(1 + i)^n}$$

The discounting formula can be used to work out the present value of any future cash flows at any interest rate (i) over a period of n years. The factor $1/1(1 + i)^n$ can be identified by looking at the discount tables at the end of this Chapter. (For those readers who possess sophisticated calculators, the factors can be generated by pressing the relevant buttons on the calculator.)

Using discounted cash flows, therefore, we can identify for any project the present value of all future cash flows over the life of the project. The present value of all the required investments when taken away from the present value of all the cash inflows will produce the net present value of the overall project. This net present value indicates the value of the financial benefits of going into a project in today's cash terms. A key advantage of the present value method of using discounted cash flows, is that a number of projects with various economic lives can be satisfactorily compared. By properly reflecting the impact of the timing of cash flows, as well as including the initial investment and the life of the project, a decision can be reached which takes into account all the criteria discussed earlier as desirable in a method of capital project evaluation.

The higher the positive net present value achieved, the more financially attractive the project. Using the cash flows given in Figure 7.9 as an example, they can be discounted at a rate of 12 per cent to arrive at Net Present Values (NPV) as follows:

Project P	Cash flows £	Discount factors	Present value £
Initial investment* Year 0	− 2000	1.0	− 2000.0
Cash flows Year 1	+ 600	0.893	535.8
Cash flows Year 2	+ 600	0.797	478.2
Cash flows Year 3	+ 600	0.712	427.2
Cash flows Year 4	+ 600	0.636	381.6
Cash flows Year 5	+ 600	0.567	340.2
Net present value			163.0

* The initial investment is assumed to take place now, at a single point in time for arithmetic convenience, and in practice this point in time is called Year 0.

Project Q	Cash flows £	Discount factors		Present value £
Year 0	−8000	1.0		−8000
Year 1	+2000	0.893		
Year 2	+2000	0.797		
Year 3	+2000	0.712	× 4.111**	8222
Year 4	+2000	0.636		
Year 5	+2000	0.567		
Year 6	+2000	0.507		
Net present value				222

The two projects can now be directly compared using the net present value (NPV) today. The decision would be to opt for project Q as it has a higher NPV, and thus appears the more financially attractive, although both projects have a positive net present value.

The discount rate applied in the net present value calculation is obviously of critical importance. It should be intuitively obvious, and can be seen by trying different discount rates on the above example, that the higher the discount rate the lower the net present value of the project. As it is essential to achieve a financial return which is higher than the cost of the funds of the company which is considering going into a project, the discount rate should be based on the rate of return that the company would have to pay to any source of such funds. Also the more risky a project is, the higher the return that the investors in the company would expect and therefore the riskiness of a project would also influence the discount rate to be applied.

The decision on the appropriate discount rate to be applied if a net present value is required is not only of great importance, but is also a process which should be gone through very carefully. This is discussed in further detail in Chapter 8.

Internal rate of return (IRR)

It was found in the previous section that the net present value is inversely proportional to the discount rate, i.e. as the discount rate increases, the net present value will decrease. This can be tested by the reader applying various discount rates to the above projects P and Q. These rates can be tabulated on a graph.

In the above example, at any discount rate below approximately 13 per cent project Q has a positive net present value, as is shown in Figure 7.10. If the required discount rate is below 13 per cent, the project offers a wealth creating opportunity to the company. The project therefore generates more value than it costs as it

---

** Whereas Table 1 in the Appendix gives the annual discount factor, Table 2 gives the annuity factor which can be applied to all equal annual cash flows received for a number of years and is in effect the addition of the individual factors given for each year in Table 1.

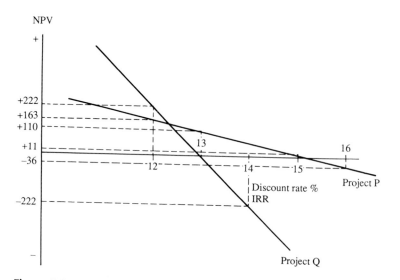

Figure 7.10 *Projects P and Q: internal rate of return*

offers a positive net cash flow. Similarly, if the required discount rate is above 13 per cent we find that the net present values are negative and therefore in today's cash terms the project costs more than the present value of the income it generates. At discount rates above 13 per cent therefore, the project is unacceptable because clearly, it would not be wise to accept a project where any outflow today generates future cash inflows which have a lower present value.

From the above, it can be seen that if the required discount rate is applied to the relevant cash flows for any project, managers clearly can decide whether a project is viable or not. At the appropriate discount rate, projects which have a positive net present value would be acceptable and those projects with a negative net present value would be rejected. It must be emphasized again that these are only quantitative analyses of the project and there may be other reasons for going into a project, even if the net present value is negative, or for rejecting a project with a positive net present value.

It was also seen in the above example that at a discount rate of 13 per cent the net present value is equal to zero. This is to say that at a discount rate of 13 per cent the present value of cash inflows equals the present value of cash outflows. If all the cash flows related to the project were to take place today in today's cash terms, then the project will yield neither a surplus nor a deficit – the project breaks even in real terms. The discount rate at which the net present value is equal to zero or where the present value of cash inflows is equal to the present value of cash outflows is called the internal rate of return (IRR), or the internal yield of the project.

To identify the IRR, alternative rates of discounts are applied until the project makes neither a profit nor a loss. In the absence of electronic assistance to compute the IRR, the process of working out the IRR involves applying these various discount rates so as to identify a small positive net present value and the associated discount rate, and a small negative net present value with its discount rate. As can be seen in the preceding example, a process of linear interpolation will then help to identify the internal rate of return with reasonable accuracy.

The IRR method of evaluating projects has become very popular because of the ease of calculation now possible due to the use of computer software, but it has a number of conceptual shortcomings which need to be noted:

1 Multiple solutions to IRR. In a number of situations it is possible to arrive at more than one internal rate of return, i.e. discount rate at which the net present value is zero, for any project. Multiple solutions occur where the cash flows go from negative to positive and back again to negative or vice versa. Under these circumstances, the real internal rate of return may not easily be identified and IRR should not be used to assess these projects. Therefore NPV is the preferred method for such projects.
2 Conflict between NPV and IRR. Considering projects P and Q, the graph in Figure 7.10 reveals that while project P has a higher internal rate of return (about 15 per cent) than project Q (13 per cent), it may not necessarily lead to the higher net present value at any specific discount rate required by the company. This obviously leads to a potential conflict between the net present value and the internal rate of return. The net present value method indicates more clearly the ranking for projects that are mutually exclusive.

If these mutually exclusive projects require the same initial investments, the simple ranking according to the net present values of the projects is satisfactory. However, if the initial investments needs of the project differ considerably, this must be taken into account in the relative ranking. For example, project 1 may generate a NPV of £1m using a discount rate of 20 per cent while project 2, using the same discount rate, gives a NPV of £2m. An initial ranking for these mutually exclusive investment opportunities would put project 2 above project 1, but if the initial investments required are, for project 1, £10m and, for project 2, £40m the position changes.

The simplest way of incorporating this into the evaluation process is to calculate the profitability indices for the projects and to compare these. The profitability index divides the net present value by the initial investment and is normally expressed as a percentage.

Thus for our two projects the position is:

Discount rate used = 20 per cent

	Project 1	*Project 2*
NPV	£1m	£2m
Initial investment	£10m	£40m
Profitability index	10%	5%

The internal rate of return is not as straightforward as the net present value method in evaluating projects, and therefore needs to be adapted if it is to be used in evaluating mutually exclusive projects, where the initial investments are not equal, or the lives of the projects differ significantly.

In spite of this, the internal rate of return method is now more popular with managers in UK companies than the net present value method, as has been found in a number of research studies. A number of reasons can be given for this, but the most commonly stated reason is that managers feel that IRR is a very appropriate and convenient method for ranking mutually exclusive projects, simply according to their relative internal rates of return. However, this is exactly the area where IRR has major shortcomings.

The IRR method has these shortcomings for a number of reasons. It does not fully take into account the scale of the project, either in terms of the initial investment or in the period for which the project will continue. As discussed, the use of the Profitability Index overcomes this shortcoming for NPV based calculations. More importantly, the IRR makes an assumption that the cash flows produced by the project are reinvested at the calculated IRR; whereas in the NPV method the assumption is that these funds are reinvested at the appropriate cut-off rate for NPV calculations. Clearly it is wrong to assume that cash flows produced from any project can be reinvested at whatever IRR is produced by the project. Cash flows will be reinvested at the opportunity cost of capital for the company, which has no direct connection to the IRR of any project, but will normally be lower.

If IRR is to be used in evaluating projects and ranking mutually exclusive projects with differing initial investments, the method should involve:

1   Compare the IRR's, if the larger investment has the greater IRR and this is above the cut-off rate, accept this project; if not,
2   Calculate the differential cash flows between two mutually exclusive projects, and
3   Identify the internal rate of return on these differential cashflows, and
4   If the IRR on these differential cash flows is higher than the cost of capital, accept the project with the *smaller* IRR, i.e. the larger initial investment, and vice versa.

Another stated reason for IRR being more popular with managers is the problem discussed above of identifying the appropriate discount rates to use in calculating the net present value. Managers appear to favour the calculation of IRR for a project whereby the investment decision can be made subsequently depending on the cut-off rate which is established, above which projects will be accepted and below which projects will be rejected. It is very important to remember that IRR cannot be used to accept or reject projects unless this hurdle rate of return is established. Thus IRR does not avoid selecting an overall cost of capital for the business, but it enables businesses to delay the decision and to carry out individual project evaluations before this has been fixed. A third more emotive reason for the preference appears to be simply that managers like to see the financial measure of their project investment performance in percentage terms which are easy to understand, discuss and relate to the existing return on investments achieved in the business.

Discounted payback

In surveying the usage of capital investment evaluation methods in industry, it was found that payback was the most popular method. Obviously this is because it is easy and convenient to use. As discussed earlier it has a number of disadvantages. One version of the payback method which is increasingly popular and overcomes a number of these shortcomings is the discounted payback period. The cash flows involved in a project are discounted back to present value terms as discussed above. The cash inflows are then directly compared to the original investment in order to identify the period taken to pay back the original investment in present value terms. This method overcomes one of the main objections to the original payback method in that it now fully allows for the timing of the cash flows, but it still does not take into account those cash flows which occur subsequent to the payback period and which may be substantial.

Taxation and capital investment appraisal

Tax laws vary from country to country, and varying types of allowances can distort the impact of taxation on particular types of projects. However, tax payments represent a cash outflow from the business and therefore these tax cash flows are a critical part of the project evaluation process. Because of the time allowed to companies to pay their taxes (in the UK approximately 1 year) tax cash flows normally occur in the year following the project cash flows to which they relate.

Practical considerations

In project appraisal, managers work with uncertain future events and estimated cash flows expected to occur in future years. This involves a substantial amount of estimation which, in practical terms, means that spurious accuracy is something which needs to be avoided. The discount figures used can be calculated with great accuracy but, when they are applied to these future estimated cash flows, the resultant calculation is only as accurate as the cash flow estimates. In many companies there is a tendency to produce discounted cash flow computations with several decimal places on each of the present values. This creates a totally fallacious appearance of accuracy in the evaluation process.

Also, to enable convenient calculations to be performed, it is normal practice in capital project evaluations to assume that all cash flows take place at the end of the year. The initial cash outflow or investment in a project is assumed to take place now. The cash flows which go out now are taken to be at year 0. The concept of year 0 does not mean a year in general terms, but a point in time, i.e. today. Year 1 cash flows are assumed to take place at the end of the first year with the second year cash flows occurring at the end of year 2, and similarly for subsequent years.

It may now be useful to look at a comprehensive example of capital project evaluation.

Peter Piper is puzzled

Peter Piper picked three proposed projects to illustrate how projects can be appraised using net present values and internal rates of return in financial decision making.

The group used both net present values and internal rates of return as the main method of approving capital expenditure proposals. The divisional financial targets were based on the previous year's achievement and the external environment, whereas the group IRR criteria for new investments were closely attuned to the expected Return on Equity demanded by shareholders and the level of risk associated with the project.

Peter Piper's division was achieving a better than average return (last year 25 per cent against a group average of 20 per cent) but it was well aware that a number of its products were very mature and that new investments were needed (another objective was growth in absolute profits in real terms) and these potential projects had recently been put up to the divisional board for consideration. The impact on the profitability of the division differed dramatically and the decision regarding which, if any, should be put up to the group did not seem obvious.

(All IRR calculations are done at today's cash flow levels and NPV calculations are done using a discount rate of 25 per cent. The tax allowances on plant, etc., have been ignored for these calculations.)

Project A. An existing retail operation within the division (one of their relatively new and growing operations) had identified new branches which would enhance profitability significantly but required investment in freehold property plus additional stock levels. The net cash flow after tax from these new branches was forecast at £3m p.a., and the life of the project was taken (under group guidelines) to be ten years. The property investment of £10 million would obviously have a high residual value and in the absence of better information it was assumed to be the same as cost, i.e. £10 million. The stock investment of £4 million was also assumed to be recovered at the end of the ten year period.

Project B. One manufacturing part of the operation had proposed a spin-off from one of their main product lines. The new product was acknowledged as having a short product life-cycle (estimated at five years) but because of the existing presence in the market it was forecast that profitability would be achieved in year 1 and maintained thereafter at £3 million after tax. The investment required was £10 million for plant and equipment, £2 million for stock and £2 million for debtors. The residual value of the plant was negligible and the fashion nature of the product indicated a risk of not recovering all the stock value at the end of the project. The group uses straight line depreciation, and thus the profit of £3m is calculated after charging £2m p.a. for depreciation.

Project C. Another area of the business had developed a new exciting product which would take the company into new markets. As such it would take time to build into profitability but would then become very profitable for the rest of its estimated ten year life. An investment of £10 million in plant was required (nil residual value) and £4 million was estimated as needed for working capital (all reclaimed in year 10). The profit/(loss) after tax was forecast as:

Year	*1*	*2*	*3*	*4–10*
£	(3m)	(2m)	Nil	10m

Project A – NPV calculations at 25 per cent

Timing	*Cash flow item*	*Amount*	*Discount factor @ 25%*	*Present value*
Year 0	Investment	(£14m)	1	(14m)
Years 1–10	Profit stream	£3m	3.571	10.7m
Year 10	Return of investment	£14m	0.107	1.5m
			NPV	£(1.8m)

Project A – IRR calculations

IRR = 22 per cent

Timing	*Cash flow item*	*Amount*	*Discount factor @ 22%*	*Present value*
Year 0	Investment	(£14m)	1	(14m)
Years 1–10	Profit stream	£3m	3.923	11.8m
Year 10	Return of investment	£14m	0.137	1.92m
			NPV	£(0.3m)

Project B – NPV calculations at 25 per cent

Timing	Cash flow item	Amount	Discount factor @ 25%	Present value
Year 0	Investment	(£14m)	1	(14m)
Years 1–5	Profit (add back depreciation)	£3m + £2m	2.689	13.45m
Year 5	Debtors recovered	£2m	0.328	0.66m
			NPV	£0.11m

Project B – IRR calculations

IRR = 25 per cent

Timing	Cash flow item	Amount	Discount factor @ 25%	Present value
Year 0	Investment	(£14m)	1	(14m)
Years 1–5	Profit (add back depreciation)	£3m + £2m	2.689	13.45m
Year 5	Debtors recovered	£2m	0.328	0.66m
			NPV	£0.11m

Project C – NPV calculations at 25 per cent

Timing	Cash flow item	Amount	Discount factor @ 25%	Present value
Year 0	Investment	(14m)	1	(14m)
Year 1	Loss (add back depreciation)	(2m)	0.800	(1.6m)
Year 2	Loss (add back depreciation)	(1m)	0.640	(0.6m)
Year 3	Break-even (add back depreciation)	1m	0.512	0.5m
Years 4–10	Profit (add back depreciation)	11m	(3.571–1.952)	17.81m
Year 10	Recovery of working capital	4m	0.107	0.43m
				£2.54m

Project C – IRR calculations

IRR = 28 per cent

Timing	Cash flow item	Amount	Discount factor @ 28%	Present value
Year 0	Investment	(14m)	1	(14m)
Year 1	Loss (add back depreciation)	(2m)	0.781	(1.56m)
Year 2	Loss (add back depreciation)	(1m)	0.610	(0.61m)
Year 3	Break-even (add back depreciation)	1m	0.477	0.48m
Years 4–10	Profit (add back depreciation)	11m	(3.269–1.868)	15.41m
Year 10	Recovery of working capital	4m	0.085	0.34m
				NPV £0.06m

Since Peter Piper has established a cut-off rate of 25 per cent based on last year, it appears that at this rate NPV is just positive for Project B and acceptable for Project C. Using the NPV as the criterion, Project A would be rejected and the choice for the company would be Project C. The IRR calculations also support this conclusion.

But the company must take into account the risk involved in these three projects and question whether the return is adequate for the risk. Although Project C gives the highest IRR and a positive NPV it would appear that it is also the project which faces the highest levels of risk. It involves the development of a new product which is going into a new market and cash flow do not become positive until year 3. The consequent uncertainty may result in the return being not adequate for the risk.

It is in fact quite feasible that Project A, although giving a low return, is still giving a return commensurate with the risk and may be preferred!

Project evaluation therefore does not stop after calculating NPV and IRR. Further strategic analysis is also necessary. It will be useful for the company to adjust the discount rate for risk and thus evaluate the NPV. This adjusting for risk is considered in Chapter 8.

Summary

In evaluating a capital project, the following stages have to be gone through.

1 Identify the annual relevant cash flows
   - only cash costs will be included
   - only relevant incremental costs will be included
   - exclude sunk costs
   - opportunity costs to be included, where appropriate.
2 Identify clearly the timing of these cash flows and assume that cash flows in any one year take place at the end of year.
3 Identify the appropriate discount rate using the net present value method to evaluate the capital project.
4 Discount all annual cash flows to their present values, using the appropriate discount rate.
5 Compute the net present value by netting off the annual cash flows against the original investment, which will have the same present value. If net present value is positive, the project is acceptable to the company at the given discount rate.
6 If the IRR method is used, calculate the appropriate IRR for a project either by interpolation or with a computer.
7 Identify the cut-off rate for the company using the company's cost of capital as the base and adjusting for the risk profile of the project.
8 If the project has an IRR higher than the cut-off rate, then the project is acceptable on the given criteria.
9 If ranking mutually exclusive projects, using the NPV method, the higher the net present value, the greater the acceptability of the project if the original investments are equal. If using the IRR method, take great care and use differential cash flows discussed above in using IRR to rank capital projects. If the original investments are not equal, the profitability indices of the mutually exclusive projects should be compared in order to rank the projects.

Questions

1 How would your decisions on Peter Piper be influenced if the company was allowed to depreciate the capital investment (capital allowance) on a straight line basis for tax purposes over the life of the project and tax was payable lagged by one year on profits at 30 per cent?
2 A company wishes to replace a mature product with a 'mark 2' new product. The existing plant, with a tax written down value of £15 million and which can be sold for £5 million, will have to be replaced at a cost of £10 million with zero residual value and will qualify for 20 per cent capital allowances on a reducing balance basis. Initial incremental investment on working capital is £1.6 million, and a further £0.5 million is needed in year 2. No increase in profit

is expected immediately but in year 2 profits will increase by £2 million, and £3 million p.a. subsequently.

If the company expects a return of 20 per cent, how many years will the project have to run to make it viable?

3 Discuss the issues to be considered in using expected NPVs as a criterion for evaluating investment projects under conditions of uncertainty?

Appendix 1: discount factors – present value tables

Present value of £1 received n years hence, at a discount rate of $r\%$ per year $= \dfrac{1}{(1+r)^n}$

Discount rate (r) per year

Years (n)	1%	2%	3%	4%	5%	6%	7%	8%	10%	12%	14%	15%	16%	18%	20%	22%	25%	28%	30%	35%	40%	50%
1	0.990	0.980	0.971	0.962	0.952	0.943	0.935	0.926	0.909	0.893	0.877	0.870	0.862	0.847	0.833	0.820	0.800	0.781	0.769	0.741	0.714	0.667
2	0.980	0.961	0.943	0.925	0.907	0.890	0.873	0.857	0.826	0.797	0.769	0.756	0.743	0.718	0.694	0.672	0.640	0.610	0.592	0.549	0.510	0.444
3	0.971	0.942	0.915	0.889	0.864	0.840	0.816	0.794	0.751	0.712	0.675	0.658	0.641	0.609	0.579	0.551	0.512	0.477	0.455	0.406	0.364	0.296
4	0.961	0.924	0.888	0.855	0.823	0.792	0.763	0.735	0.683	0.636	0.592	0.572	0.552	0.516	0.482	0.451	0.410	0.373	0.350	0.301	0.260	0.198
5	0.951	0.906	0.863	0.822	0.784	0.747	0.713	0.681	0.621	0.567	0.519	0.497	0.476	0.437	0.402	0.370	0.328	0.291	0.269	0.223	0.186	0.132
6	0.942	0.888	0.837	0.790	0.746	0.705	0.666	0.630	0.564	0.507	0.456	0.432	0.410	0.370	0.335	0.303	0.262	0.227	0.207	0.165	0.133	0.088
7	0.933	0.871	0.813	0.760	0.711	0.665	0.623	0.583	0.513	0.452	0.400	0.376	0.354	0.314	0.279	0.249	0.210	0.178	0.159	0.122	0.095	0.059
8	0.923	0.853	0.789	0.731	0.677	0.627	0.582	0.540	0.467	0.404	0.351	0.327	0.305	0.266	0.233	0.204	0.168	0.139	0.123	0.091	0.068	0.039
9	0.914	0.837	0.766	0.703	0.645	0.592	0.544	0.500	0.424	0.361	0.308	0.284	0.263	0.225	0.194	0.167	0.134	0.108	0.094	0.067	0.048	0.026
10	0.905	0.820	0.744	0.676	0.614	0.558	0.508	0.463	0.386	0.322	0.270	0.247	0.227	0.191	0.162	0.137	0.107	0.085	0.073	0.050	0.035	0.017
11	0.896	0.804	0.722	0.650	0.585	0.527	0.475	0.429	0.350	0.287	0.237	0.215	0.195	0.162	0.135	0.112	0.086	0.066	0.056	0.037	0.025	0.012
12	0.887	0.788	0.701	0.625	0.557	0.497	0.444	0.397	0.319	0.257	0.208	0.187	0.168	0.137	0.112	0.092	0.069	0.052	0.043	0.027	0.018	0.008
13	0.879	0.773	0.681	0.601	0.530	0.469	0.415	0.368	0.290	0.229	0.182	0.163	0.145	0.116	0.093	0.075	0.055	0.040	0.033	0.020	0.013	0.005
14	0.870	0.758	0.661	0.577	0.505	0.442	0.388	0.340	0.263	0.205	0.160	0.141	0.125	0.099	0.078	0.062	0.044	0.032	0.025	0.015	0.009	0.003
15	0.861	0.743	0.642	0.555	0.481	0.417	0.362	0.315	0.239	0.183	0.140	0.123	0.108	0.084	0.065	0.051	0.035	0.025	0.020	0.011	0.006	0.002

n																						
16	0.853	0.728	0.623	0.534	0.458	0.394	0.339	0.292	0.218	0.163	0.123	0.107	0.093	0.071	0.054	0.042	0.028	0.019	0.015	0.008	0.005	0.002
17	0.844	0.714	0.605	0.513	0.436	0.371	0.317	0.270	0.198	0.146	0.108	0.093	0.080	0.060	0.045	0.034	0.023	0.015	0.012	0.006	0.003	0.001
18	0.836	0.700	0.587	0.494	0.416	0.350	0.296	0.250	0.180	0.130	0.095	0.081	0.069	0.051	0.038	0.028	0.018	0.012	0.009	0.005	0.002	0.001
19	0.828	0.686	0.570	0.475	0.396	0.331	0.277	0.232	0.164	0.116	0.083	0.070	0.060	0.043	0.031	0.023	0.014	0.009	0.007	0.003	0.002	
20	0.820	0.673	0.554	0.456	0.377	0.312	0.258	0.215	0.149	0.104	0.073	0.061	0.051	0.037	0.026	0.019	0.012	0.007	0.005	0.002	0.001	
21	0.811	0.660	0.538	0.439	0.359	0.294	0.242	0.199	0.135	0.093	0.064	0.053	0.044	0.031	0.022	0.015	0.009	0.006	0.004	0.002	0.001	
22	0.803	0.647	0.522	0.422	0.342	0.278	0.226	0.184	0.123	0.083	0.056	0.046	0.038	0.026	0.018	0.013	0.007	0.004	0.003	0.001	0.001	
23	0.795	0.634	0.507	0.406	0.326	0.262	0.211	0.170	0.112	0.074	0.049	0.040	0.033	0.022	0.015	0.010	0.006	0.004	0.003	0.001	0.001	
24	0.788	0.622	0.492	0.390	0.310	0.247	0.197	0.158	0.102	0.066	0.043	0.035	0.028	0.019	0.013	0.008	0.005	0.003	0.002	0.001	0.001	
25	0.780	0.610	0.478	0.375	0.295	0.233	0.184	0.146	0.092	0.059	0.038	0.030	0.024	0.016	0.010	0.007	0.004	0.002	0.002	0.001		
26	0.772	0.598	0.464	0.361	0.281	0.220	0.172	0.135	0.084	0.053	0.033	0.026	0.021	0.014	0.009	0.006	0.003	0.002	0.001			
27	0.764	0.586	0.450	0.347	0.268	0.207	0.161	0.125	0.076	0.047	0.029	0.023	0.018	0.011	0.007	0.005	0.002	0.001	0.001			
28	0.757	0.574	0.437	0.333	0.255	0.196	0.150	0.116	0.069	0.042	0.026	0.020	0.016	0.010	0.006	0.004	0.002	0.001	0.001			
29	0.749	0.563	0.424	0.321	0.243	0.185	0.141	0.107	0.063	0.037	0.022	0.017	0.014	0.008	0.005	0.003	0.002	0.001	0.001			
30	0.742	0.552	0.412	0.308	0.231	0.174	0.131	0.099	0.057	0.033	0.020	0.015	0.012	0.007	0.004	0.003	0.001	0.001				
40	0.672	0.453	0.307	0.208	0.142	0.097	0.067	0.046	0.022	0.011	0.005	0.004	0.003	0.001	0.001							
50	0.608	0.372	0.228	0.141	0.087	0.054	0.034	0.021	0.009	0.003	0.001	0.001										

Appendix 2: cumulative discount factors – annuity tables

Present value of £1 received each year for n years $= \dfrac{1}{r} - \dfrac{1}{r(1+r)^n}$

Years (n)	1%	2%	3%	4%	5%	6%	7%	8%	10%	12%	14%	15%	16%	18%	20%	22%	25%	28%	30%	35%	40%	50%
1	0.990	0.980	0.971	0.962	0.952	0.943	0.935	0.926	0.909	0.893	0.877	0.870	0.862	0.847	0.833	0.820	0.800	0.781	0.769	0.741	0.714	0.667
2	1.970	1.942	1.914	1.886	1.859	1.833	1.808	1.783	1.736	1.690	1.647	1.626	1.605	1.566	1.528	1.492	1.440	1.392	1.361	1.289	1.224	1.111
3	2.941	2.884	2.829	2.775	2.723	2.673	2.624	2.577	2.487	2.402	2.322	2.283	2.246	2.174	2.106	2.043	1.952	1.868	1.816	1.696	1.589	1.407
4	3.902	3.808	3.717	3.630	3.546	3.465	3.387	3.312	3.170	3.037	2.914	2.855	2.798	2.690	2.589	2.494	2.362	2.241	2.166	1.997	1.849	1.605
5	4.853	4.713	4.580	4.452	4.329	4.212	4.100	3.993	3.791	3.605	3.433	3.352	3.274	3.127	2.991	2.864	2.689	2.532	2.436	2.220	2.035	1.737
6	5.795	5.601	5.417	5.242	5.076	4.917	4.767	4.623	4.355	4.111	3.889	3.784	3.685	3.498	3.326	3.167	2.951	2.759	2.643	2.385	2.168	1.824
7	6.728	6.472	6.230	6.002	5.786	5.582	5.389	5.206	4.868	4.564	4.288	4.160	4.039	3.812	3.605	3.416	3.161	2.937	2.802	2.508	2.263	1.883
8	7.652	7.325	7.020	6.733	6.463	6.210	5.971	5.747	5.335	4.968	4.639	4.487	4.344	4.078	3.837	3.619	3.329	3.076	2.925	2.598	2.331	1.922
9	8.566	8.162	7.786	7.435	7.108	6.802	6.515	6.247	5.759	5.328	4.946	4.772	4.607	4.303	4.031	3.786	3.463	3.184	3.019	2.665	2.379	1.948
10	9.471	8.983	8.530	8.111	7.722	7.360	7.023	6.710	6.145	5.650	5.216	5.019	4.833	4.494	4.192	3.923	3.571	3.269	3.092	2.715	2.414	1.965
11	10.368	9.787	9.253	8.760	8.306	7.887	7.499	7.139	6.495	5.938	5.453	5.234	5.029	4.656	4.327	4.035	3.656	3.335	3.147	2.757	2.438	1.977
12	11.255	10.575	9.954	9.385	8.863	8.384	7.943	7.536	6.814	6.194	5.660	5.421	5.197	4.793	4.439	4.127	3.725	3.387	3.190	2.779	2.456	1.985
13	12.134	11.348	10.635	9.986	9.393	8.853	8.358	7.904	7.103	6.424	5.842	5.583	5.342	4.910	4.533	4.203	3.780	3.427	3.223	2.799	2.469	1.990
14	13.004	12.106	11.296	10.563	9.899	9.295	8.745	8.244	7.367	6.628	6.002	5.724	5.468	5.008	4.611	4.265	3.824	3.459	3.249	2.814	2.478	1.993
15	13.865	12.849	11.938	11.118	10.380	9.712	9.108	8.559	7.606	6.811	6.142	5.847	5.575	5.092	4.675	4.315	3.859	3.483	3.268	2.825	2.484	1.995

Interest rate (r) per year

16	14.718	13.578	12.561	11.652	10.838	10.106	9.446	8.851	7.824	6.974	6.265	5.954	5.669	5.162	4.730	4.357	3.887	3.503	3.283	2.834	2.489	1.997
17	15.562	14.292	13.166	12.166	11.274	10.477	9.763	9.122	8.022	7.120	6.373	6.047	5.749	5.222	4.775	4.391	3.910	3.518	3.295	2.840	2.492	1.998
18	16.398	14.992	13.754	12.659	11.689	10.828	10.059	9.372	8.201	7.250	6.467	6.128	5.818	5.273	4.812	4.419	3.928	3.529	3.304	2.844	2.494	1.999
19	17.226	15.678	14.324	13.134	12.085	11.158	10.335	9.604	8.365	7.366	6.550	6.198	5.877	5.316	4.843	4.442	3.942	3.539	3.311	2.848	2.496	1.999
20	18.046	16.351	14.878	13.590	12.462	11.470	10.594	9.818	8.514	7.469	6.623	6.259	5.929	5.353	4.870	4.460	3.954	3.546	3.316	2.850	2.497	1.999
21	18.857	17.011	15.415	14.029	12.821	11.764	10.835	10.017	8.649	7.562	6.687	6.312	5.973	5.384	4.891	4.476	3.963	3.551	3.320	2.852	2.498	2.000
22	19.660	17.658	15.937	14.451	13.163	12.042	11.061	10.201	8.772	7.645	6.743	6.359	6.011	5.410	4.909	4.488	3.970	3.556	3.323	2.853	2.498	2.000
23	20.456	18.292	16.444	14.857	13.488	12.303	11.272	10.371	8.883	7.718	6.792	6.399	6.044	5.432	4.925	4.499	3.976	3.559	3.325	2.854	2.499	2.000
24	21.243	18.914	16.936	15.247	13.798	12.550	11.469	10.529	8.985	7.784	6.835	6.434	6.073	5.451	4.937	4.507	3.981	3.562	3.327	2.855	2.499	2.000
25	22.023	19.523	17.413	15.622	14.094	12.783	11.653	10.675	9.077	7.843	6.873	6.464	6.097	5.467	4.948	4.514	3.985	3.564	3.329	2.856	2.499	2.000
26	22.795	20.121	17.877	15.983	14.375	13.003	11.825	10.810	9.161	7.896	6.906	6.491	6.118	5.480	4.956	4.520	3.988	3.566	3.330	2.856	2.500	2.000
27	23.560	20.707	18.327	16.330	14.643	13.211	11.986	10.935	9.237	7.943	6.935	6.514	6.136	5.492	4.964	4.524	3.990	3.567	3.331	2.856	2.500	2.000
28	24.316	21.281	18.764	16.663	14.898	13.406	12.137	11.051	9.307	7.984	6.961	6.534	6.152	5.502	4.970	4.528	3.992	3.568	3.331	2.857	2.500	2.000
29	25.066	21.844	19.188	16.984	15.141	13.591	12.277	11.158	9.370	8.022	6.983	6.551	6.166	5.510	4.975	4.531	3.994	3.569	3.332	2.857	2.500	2.000
30	25.808	22.396	19.600	17.292	15.372	13.765	12.409	11.258	9.427	8.055	7.003	6.566	6.177	5.517	4.979	4.534	3.995	3.569	3.332	2.857	2.500	2.000
40	32.835	27.355	23.115	19.793	17.159	15.046	13.331	11.925	9.779	8.244	7.105	6.642	6.233	5.548	4.997	4.544	3.999	3.571	3.333	2.857	2.500	2.000
50	39.196	31.424	25.730	21.482	18.256	15.762	13.800	12.233	9.915	8.304	7.133	6.661	6.246	5.554	4.999	4.545	4.000	3.571	3.333	2.857	2.500	2.000

Long-term decision-making

Overview

Long-term decisions enable the business to plan without being significantly constrained by its existing resources and commitments. However, their very long-term nature makes it much more difficult to predict their outcomes and consequently increases the risks associated with these decisions.

Business planning is based on the financial analysis and evaluation of alternatives which utilize all the appropriate techniques discussed in Chapters 3–6. However, the most relevant analytical approaches for long-term decisions are the discounted cash flow techniques considered in the previous chapter, due to their ability to cope with the impact of the time value of money. Long-term planning should be a hierarchical process which starts with the overall mission statement of the business and develops through to very specific objectives and strategies for the sub-divisions of the business which will actually implement the plan.

This planning process should highlight the major risks associated with particular strategic options and, as far as possible, outline contingency plans which can be implemented if necessary. Where the risk cannot be removed or allowed for, in this way, the business must ensure that the expected financial return adequately compensates for the risk associated with the selected plan. This can be done by using a risk adjusted discount rate or cut-off rate when carrying out the financial evaluations of long-term planning decisions. The level of this rate must be related to the effective cost of capital for the company and this cost of capital should reflect the available sources of capital which need to be utilized in order to finance the plan.

The most common method of establishing the cut-off rate is to compute the weighted average cost of capital for the business and to adjust this rate for the relative risk profile of the specific projects involved in the long-term business plan.

Introduction

We have considered many financial decision-making techniques in the previous chapters and it is now time to place them fully into the planning cycle of the business. Business planning is, not surprisingly, a combination of long-term and short-term issues with a great deal of interaction between these different time-scales. Thus a short-term action may decrease the prospects of the organization achieving one of its long-term aims, and it is consequently dangerous to separate the planning cycle into completely discrete units. However, there are significant differences between planning for the long-term and short-term time-frames; perhaps the most obvious being that in the short term the option open to the business are severely constrained because of the high level of fixed, committed costs which cannot be altered in this short-term period. Another critical difference is that in short-term decisions, the impact of the time value of money is much less significant than it is for long-term decisions. Consequently these different time-scales are considered separately, with short-term budgeting issues being dealt with the following chapter, while here we concentrate on long-term decisions.

Long-term decisions are the result of probably the most complex yet most important decision-making process for the management of any organization. It is complex because of the unpredictable nature of future events, particularly long distant events, and the uncertainty of future returns for present investments. It is also complex because of the perceived conflict between the short-term and the long-term goals and objectives of the business and the impact which long-term decisions have on both of these sets of objectives. Long-term decisions are also particularly important because of the significant effect they have on the overall performance of the business.

This chapter is primarily concerned with the two main separable aspects of long-term decisions; investment and financing decisions within organizations. The investment decision, which is also referred to as the capital budgeting decision, is the process by which business decisions are made to invest in both tangible and intangible assets. The fundamental questions facing the manager concerning these decisions are:

1 How much should the firm invest, and
2 What projects should the firm invest in?

The financing decision on the other hand, looks at how the company should raise any externally needed funds for the selected projects. It also considers both the cost of and the period over which the funds should be raised for these projects. The cost of these funds, including the opportunity cost of any internally available, will constrain the types of projects which can be financially justified. However, this chapter does not deal with the intricacies of modern financial products as this is outside the scope of management accounting, as discussed in Chapter 1.

A fundamental objective of a business is to carry out activities and generate future cash flows in a way that optimizes the position of the stakeholders in the business. It is normally supposed that the shareholders are the primary group of such stakeholders as they are the residual claimants to the profits that remain after all other expenses have been paid. Interest on debt funding represents one of the expenses which need to be paid before arriving at the residual income available to shareholders. Lenders can therefore be seen as stakeholders in the business too. A conflict that also sometimes arises is that these stakeholders and lenders are not restricted to shareholders of the business, but extend to include management, employees and other interested parties, as was discussed in Chapter 1, and is illustrated in Figure 10.1 in Chapter 10.

Priorities, nevertheless, need to be established and, for the purposes of the discussion in this chapter, we assume that the fundamental objective of the business is maximizing the wealth of shareholders. Settling on this objective of maximizing shareholder wealth is relatively easy, but deciding exactly what these shareholders' objectives are and how the company can maximize shareholder wealth, is more difficult. Is the shareholder's wealth maximized by earnings, dividends, or capital gains and over what time-scale should this wealth be maximized?

Capital budgeting process

Applying the discounted cash flow techniques discussed in the previous chapter as the method of financially evaluating long-term investment decisions should lead to the maximization of the long-term value of the business. This is the objective of many capital investment budgeting (CIB) systems used within companies, but, in practice, their operation tends to become more complex and less clear-cut.

All companies have limited funds to invest in their business and most companies have an excess of potential investment projects. Consequently the CIB acts as a capital rationing process in directing funds to those projects which generate the highest financial returns. This could be achieved by ranking all the potential projects according to their financial returns and accepting them in descending order until the available investment funds have been used up. The most simple way of ranking for this purpose would be to use net present values but, as discussed in Chapter 7, the absolute size of the NPV does not reflect the relative return being achieved on the initial investment required for each project.

Thus the overall return may not be maximized unless the ranking uses the profitability index (PI) measure which places the NPV properly into the context of its usage of the available investment funds. This can be illustrated by considering a very simplified CIB consisting of four projects as shown below:

Project	*NPVs @ 20%*	*Ranking on NPV*
A	£10m	1
B	£5m	2
C	£4m	3
D	£3m	4

Using only the absolute NPVs, the company would rank the projects as shown. If a total investment budget of £50m were available, the company would then allocate these funds to the projects in descending order of priority, but this could create a conflict if the initial investments required were not equal. For our four project the position is:

Project	NPV	Initial investment	PI
A	£10m	£50m	20%
B	£5m	£20m	25%
C	£4m	£18m	22.2%
D	£3m	£12m	25%

If the company selects project A, this project will use up all the available funds and none of the other projects can be implemented; therefore the total NPV of the CIB will be £10m. However, if the company selected projects B, C and D, which can all be implemented as they have a total investment requirement of £50m, the total potential NPV is increased to £12m. Hence the long-term value of the investment decisions has been increased, and this decision could be made easier by using profitability indices rather than absolute NPVs. As shown the PI for each of B, C and D is higher than for A. Alternatively, the projects could have been graded by using their IRR percentage but there are potential problems involved with this technique, some of which are dealt with in Chapter 7.

Unfortunately, even making this modification to the capital project evaluation process does not resolve all of the problems of ranking and grading projects. Long-term decisions should be taken in order to achieve the long-term objectives of the business and, consequently, the business may want to place a higher priority on a particular project which has greater strategic importance than others being considered at the same time. Also, as discussed earlier, not all the benefits arising from long-term decisions can be financially quantified and therefore the qualitative factors involved should form part of the overall evaluation process.

A further complication is caused by the long-term nature of these decisions and the high degree of flexiblilty which is consequently available to the business. In this section so far, we have been discussing investment decisions and the constraints placed on the business because of limited available funds. If a large number of acceptable projects are identified the company could attempt to increase the funds available for investment, and this could be done by raising new external funds as mentioned in the previous chapter. Alternatively, this could be achieved by disinvesting from some existing areas of activity or by instigating short–term payback cost-saving projects at the same time, which will rapidly increase the funds available for longer-term strategic investments. A major potential benefit of a large well-diversified conglomerate style group should be that it can change the way it manages some of its business units, if necessary, in order to produce a greater cash flow from some of them, which can be productively redeployed in other areas of the group.

Thus the management of the overall capital investment budget is by no means a question of simply ranking the potential investment projects according to their discounted cash flows. Another complicating criterion, which has been mentioned before and is considered in detail later in the chapter, is that this wide range of available investment alternatives is unlikely to have exactly the same uniform risk profile. Risk can be dealt with by adjusting the discount rate applied to the cash flows or increasing the required hurdle rate, but this deals only with individual project risk. The CIB should try to evaluate the overall risk involved in the selected portfolio of projects and assess the overall return which is expected in the context of this overall risk profile.

This overall risk profile may not be just a weighted average of the individual project risks as some of the projects may have interlinked risk profiles. Thus if two high risk projects are implemented at the same time, the overall risk may be compounded, if the risks are complementary and positively correlated, whereas, if the business risks are counter-cyclical the overall risk profile may be reduced. This risk evaluation should ideally be done taking into account the impact of the proposed new investment budget on the whole existing investment portfolio of the business as this should show the total change in risk which will result.

It is this overall risk assessment which should be done by the investors, because they obtain a proportionate interest in all the projects, both existing and new, undertaken by the company. If investors are to assess the present value of the future returns which will be produced by these investments, they need to adjust their discount factors for changes in the overall risk profile of the company. However, this is assuming that investors do value companies based on their long-term returns.

Critics of the stock markets argue that shareholders do not know what is in their own best interests and therefore are guilty of short-termism whereas clearly, they argue, the value of their investment could be enhanced by a longer-term view. Short-termism is usually defined as meaning that shareholders look for returns over a short-term horizon, say one or two years. Even if a capital investment project is financially acceptable in the long term, the short term effect could be that the company's profits fall and as a consequence the share price falls due to the concentration of investors on short-term results, although profits will rise in the longer term as the benefits of the project start to show in the published accounts. It is argued that the share price fall in the short term may make the company liable to a hostile take-over bid. Consequently, many companies place great emphasis on increasing their annual returns on shareholders' investment as well as the internally based returns on capital employed (or return on net assets). These companies seem to believe that the return to shareholders and lenders should be optimized annually as a percentage of their investment. Therefore managers sometimes argue that any long-term project entered into by the company should also be compatible with these short-term objectives and show the best possible return on investment in both the short and long term.

Conflict of short term and long term

This has led to the use by many companies of an accounting based, project evaluation technique, despite all the previously mentioned problems of using profits for evaluating financial decisions. The accounting rate of return method of evaluating projects employs the normal accounting and budgeting techniques to calculate the increase in profit that would result from any new investment. This increase in profit is then compared with the incremental amount of capital required for the project. Annual profits from individual projects are divided by the required investment (which is normally either defined as the initial investment or the average investment over the life of the project) to arrive at a return on investment measure. It must be remembered that the discussion is about profit at this stage, not cash. Therefore the accounting return on investment is calculated on accounting profits, and is illustrated in Figure 8.1. The obvious disadvantages with this method in

Capital Investment Appraisal
Accounting Return on Investment

	Project A		Project B	
	£	£	£	£
Capital cost		10,000		10,000
Profit after depreciation				
Year 1	6,000		2,000	
Year 2	4,000		2,000	
Year 3	2,000		4,000	
Year 4	1,000		6,000	
	13,000		14,000	
Average per annum	3,250		3,500	

$$\text{Rate of return} \quad \frac{3,250}{0.5 \times 10,000} = 65\% \qquad \frac{3,500}{0.5 \times 10,000} = 70\%$$

If an additional £5,000 for working capital is required, how will this affect the calculation?

$$\text{Rate of return} = \quad \frac{3,250}{10,000} = 32.5\% \qquad \frac{3,500}{10,000} = 35.0\%$$

Note: The working capital investment is included at its full value since it does not depreciate over the life of the project as is the case for the initial investment.

Figure 8.1

comparison to the discounted cash flow methods discussed in the previous chapter are that:

1 This method takes no account of the timing of cash flows, and the different values money has at different points in time.
2 The accounting measure of return is not normally equal to the cash inflows.
3 The results are open to misinterpretation depending on the accounting policies employed by the company.

The return on investment method has its advantages in that it is simple to calculate and the rate of return of various projects can be totalled and compared to the existing or required corporate rate of return. However, as can be seen from the example of Project B from Peter Piper in Figure 8.2 the accounting return on a project can increase from 25 per cent in the first year to 50 per cent in the later years because of depreciation and other accounting policies.

This obviously creates problems in evaluating project performance from year to year and consequently many companies calculate only the average accounting

---

Project B – Accounting rate of return over time

Part of our earlier example company, Peter Piper plc, had, as mentioned at the end of Chapter 7, proposed a spin-off from one of their main product lines. The new product was acknowledged as having a short product life-cycle (estimated at five years) but because of the existing presence in the market it was forecast that profitability would be achieved in year 1 and maintained thereafter at £3m after tax. The investment required was £10m for plant and equipment, £2m for stock and £2m for debtors. The residual value of the plant was negligible and the fashion nature of the product indicated a risk of not recovering all the stock value at the end of the project.

Accounting return:

Year	1	2	3	4	5	
Net book value of investment	£8m	£6m	£4m	£2m	£0m	
Working capital	£4m	£4m	£4m	£4m	£2m	(stock write-off)
	£12m	£10m	£8m	£6m	£2m	
Profit after tax	£3m	£3m	£3m	£3m	£3m	
Return on investment	25%	30%	37.5%	50%	150%	

Figure 8.2

rate of return over the life of the projects, rather than using the fluctuating annual levels. If this average rate exceeds the expected return of the shareholders, the managers can argue that over the project a viable return has been achieved from the new investment. More vehement advocates believe that the very short-term impact of the project on the reported accounting results is what is important, and therefore they compute the annual accounting rate of return, with greater prominence being given to the results of the early periods. These supporters of the accounting return on investment method of evaluating projects argue that, due to the short-termism of the stock market, ROI is a very effective method of focusing attention on the organization's objectives of maximizing shareholder wealth, *in the short-term*. Fortunately, the short-termism argument can be quite easily refuted.

Shareholders will not knowingly sell their investments at depressed prices simply because short-term profits are low if, in the long-term, profits are expected to grow substantially due to current investments in some good projects. If they did so, it would lead to the next buyer of these shares realizing substantial gains from the investments of the company, as the anticipated profits were achieved. If, as does happen in some cases, a company's share price falls when a long-term strategic investment is announced, this is because shareholders do not believe that the company will make the substantial profits which are forecast from this investment. Therefore the share price is correspondingly and appropriately lowered. The investors knock down the share price because they do not agree with the management's estimate of what the long-term benefits will be, not because of the short-term impact on profitability. If this was not true, the shares of loss-making companies would have a negative value!

Share values are actually a very good example of the application of the discounted cash flow process explained in Chapter 7. A prospective shareholder in a company is buying a share in the future returns of that company and is trying to value those future returns today. This is simply a present value calculation of the potential income stream which will be received by the investor (i.e. the dividend per share paid out by the company during this investor's period of ownership) added to the capital value of the share, which is only received when the share is eventually sold. Clearly this present value calculation represents a long-term valuation of the share in the company; however, the value may change rapidly if the expectations regarding this future cash flow stream change or the perceived risk of the company alters (this would alter the discount rate applied to the forecast future cash flows).

Management therefore have to ensure shareholders see eye to eye with them on their investment strategies by improving their communication process with the stock market, and explaining to shareholders their management policies for long-term investment, highlighting the benefits to the organization. The argument that shareholders in general are short-termists, and that therefore short-term ROI is the best method of evaluating financial performance of various long-term projects, does not hold water.

An argument that does hold water is based on the conflicting objectives of the organization, the investors and the managers of the organization itself. It is increasingly argued that the organization's objectives do not always coincide with individual manager's performance objectives and targets. As a result of this lack of goal congruence, investment decisions are sometimes taken which do not match with the organization's overall objective. It can be argued that if ROI meets the investors' objectives and also is an acceptable way of defining the organization's objectives, it can be translated into managerial targets. The process of linking company objectives to managerial objectives is discussed in the next section.

The planning cycle

Prior to engaging in any long-term capital investment decision, the managers of the organization have to agree with shareholders on the organization's goals or mission. The question, 'why are we in business?' needs to be understood and the purpose of the business accepted by the organization's managers and shareholders together. Corporate missions, such as 'Our purpose shall be not solely to gain wealth nor to show industrial strength, but to contribute to the progress and welfare of the community and the nation', (Matsushita Corporation) and, 'The basis of our business is the goodwill of our customers' (Cadbury Schweppes), indicate the unquantified and everlasting nature of many large company vision statements. These rather general and grandiose statements of why these companies exist need to be translated into much more finite objectives, which can be used to measure the performance of the organization, and against which to evaluate potential investments.

The overall objectives or goals should be communicated to the stakeholders in the business and agreed by them. In order to achieve these corporate missions or goals, the organization will need to establish clear objectives for the business in total and for the various sub-divisions, which will help achieve this goal. The objectives may range from maximizing sales revenues to increasing profitability over a given period of time. It is impossible to determine whether management is behaving rationally without clear and explicit statements of the organization's objectives. The lack of clear overall objectives can lead to an excessive emphasis on sub-activities which, in turn, can lead to the neglect of certain activities which are vital to the long-term success of the firm.

These objectives need to be translated into the long-term strategy of the organization, and an action plan should be developed of activities which need to be entered into in order to achieve the objectives. The long-term strategy and planning process will be clearly influenced by a number of internal and external factors. Gaining competitive advantage may, for example, be one long-term strategy which needs to be addressed in order to achieve the organization's objectives. Gaining such a competitive advantage may need a substantial investment in new technology. Many organizations find that the process of gaining competitive advantage leads inevitably to a decline in short-term profits of the organization. For example, to reach its present state as a leading player in the retailing industry, Tesco had to go through a period of relatively low profits while it invested heavily in new developments, new technologies and rationalizing its existing activities.

These factors need to be taken into consideration in the strategic planning process of the organization.

Any level of business planning can be broken down into two principal stages:

1 Deciding what to do, and
2 Deciding how to do it.

Thus the business needs goals and objectives to aim at, but these must be followed up by developing strategies which will enable the business to achieve these objectives. This can be represented diagrammatically as in Figure 8.3 which shows, once again, how planning and decision-making are a continuous process.

Financial analysis is a key element in the process of setting corporate objectives, but managerial judgment is clearly required in, for example, predicting how the future external environment will differ from that existing at present. The objectives must be realistic if they are to have a positive motivational impact on the managers who have to try to achieve the business plan. However, equally the role of managers is to make decisions and therefore the plan should not merely be an extrapolation of the existing state of affairs until the end of the planning cycle.

One of the key elements in long-term planning is that the business has the opportunity to remove existing constraints and to change elements which are currently adversely affecting the performance of the business. It is this critically important process of reallocating existing resources and acquiring any new resources which are needed which justifies the effort and cost involved in financially evaluating long-term plans and decisions.

Strategic planning and long-term investment decisions therefore involve managers in trying to identify ways of bridging the 'gap' between the results which the company is likely to achieve without any action, and the company's long-term objectives. In carrying out this 'gap' analysis, managers not only need to understand the 'costs' of gaining competitive advantage, as discussed above, but also have a clear view of the resources required and costs involved in bridging the 'gap' as is illustrated in Figure 8.4.

As stated these planning objectives have to be realistically established if they are to have any practical value, but this means that they will be regularly modified in line with changes in the external business and competitive environment. Having

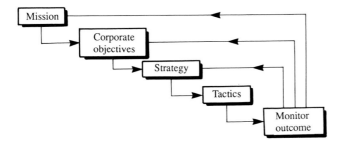

Figure 8.3 *Integrated view of planning (as a continuous process)*

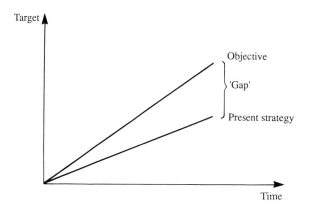

Figure 8.4 *Gap analysis*

a constantly shifting long-term target could be confusing for managers and, consequently, many companies now split their long-term aims into a mission statement and corporate objectives. The mission statement, as previously illustrated, may be general and unquantified so that it does not need constant updating, whereas the corporate objectives can be modified, as necessary, without risking that the company will lose the sense of strategic direction.

The long-term plans should establish strategies and action plans which indicate how these corporate objectives are to be achieved. Included within these strategies and action plans will be specific investment opportunities which are needed to reallocate resources, improve the performance of existing resources or, very commonly, to increase the resources which are employed in particular areas. It is these long-term decisions which require the application of the sophisticated evaluation techniques previously discussed.

However, these action plans cannot all be long term, as there must be short-term actions taken in order to achieve the long-term objectives. 'The longest journey cannot be completed until the first step has been taken' is (or should be!) an old Chinese proverb.

Short-term plans therefore need to be prepared and budgets produced which take into account the long-term strategy of the organization. These should take into account any possible decline in profits or need for increase in investments in the short term. Short term planning and budgeting will be considered in detail in the next chapter.

An obvious area that is often overlooked is the need to provide feedback which monitors performance against budgets and short-term plans, in order both to provide information to senior management on the overall viability of the long-term strategy and the achievement, in the short-term, of critical objectives which will lead to the achievement of long-term objectives. This area is considered in more detail in Chapter 10.

Assumptions need to be made, both in preparing short-term plans and in the long-term strategy planning process, about the market and competitive reactions to the activities proposed by the company. The effects of these potential competitor and market reactions need to be evaluated and used in the feedback process. This ensures that the process of strategy development and long-term planning is carried out in a dynamic iterative manner, using the best information available on the external environment. This enables the plan to be changed if the environment changes significantly.

If the planning cycle of the organization and the resulting strategies and plans are clearly understood by managers, and communicated broadly but effectively to the shareholders who accept the implications of these strategies, there is no reason why shareholders should have a short-term attitude. However, both shareholders and managers are concerned with the relationship between risk and return, and how this is forecast to change during the period of the plan.

Risk and return

Risk occurs where future outcomes of current actions are unknown, but the probabilities of these future outcomes can be reasonably estimated from a knowledge of past and current events. Risk is therefore normally measured by volatility of returns, because a certain outcome has no variance and, hence, no volatility.

Uncertainty on the other hand occurs where the probabilities of future outcomes cannot be predicted from past or current events, because no probability estimates are available.

As a working definition, risk can be regarded as the gap between what an organization realistically wishes, or expects and plans, to achieve and the probability of what it might achieve in the existing business environment. Increased volatility in future events and the consequent difficulty in forecasting future outcomes increases risk. For example, the risk of companies not achieving their target levels of profitability may be increased by uncertainty surrounding the government's economic policy prior to the next general election.

Because of the wide fluctuations surrounding the many different variables which contribute to risk, investors, lenders, and managers all look to increase their returns to compensate for the increased level of risk. This relationship between risk and return and the various other components of expected return have been discussed earlier in the book but are considered in more detail in this chapter.

The expected return from an investment is influenced by a number of factors in addition to risk. Even a totally risk-free investment, or a very low risk investment such as an index-linked government bond, is expected to yield a return to compensate for the pure time preference value of money. The fact that the investor is giving up the opportunity to spend the money now in return for a future sum of money requires compensation. This pure time preference expected return is obviously influenced by prevailing rates of inflation, as this reduces the deferred purchasing power of money, and the desired balance between consumption and saving on the part of the investor. Thus, if investors have a strong preference for saving rather than immediate consumption, the rate of return demanded on low or nil risk investments will be lower. However, if, as in the USA and the UK during the 1980s, there is a change towards a preference for immediate consumption (i.e. a reduction in the savings ratio when expressed as a percentage of net disposable income), it is probable that this rate of return will increase. This means that higher returns need to be offered in order to attract investors or savers; this creates higher interest rates in those economies which have lower savings ratios.

There is therefore a risk free rate of return (R_f) which is demanded by investors to compensate for giving up immediate consumption.

A model which relates to the return demanded by investors, known as the capital asset pricing model, was developed initially as an approach to analysing the stock market value of shares and the returns that are expected on investments. This model can also be applied to capital investment appraisals within companies.

Whenever a company invests in a project, there are risks involved. Some risks are unique to the business of the specific company, e.g. an ice cream manufacturer. However, the company can diversify its activities by investing in projects with different unique risks, and thus it is possible to diversify a proportion of these risks; e.g. the ice cream manufacturer can diversify into sausages so as to reduce the seasonality risk of its original business. By investing in a number of projects, a company will normally find that some projects do well and some do badly but as a portfolio of investments, the average return on all the projects together should turn out more or less as expected.

This portfolio theory is most clearly illustrated by reference to the investment in shares and other marketable types of investment by an intelligent rational investor. The risk of shares in individual companies is obviously related to the type of company and the strategy that it is implementing. Therefore investors who want low risk could invest only in shares of an appropriately low risk business,

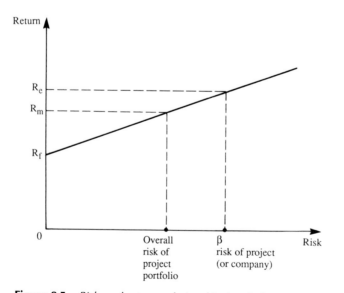

Figure 8.5 *Risk and return relationship (capital asset pricing model)*

such as monopoly utility type companies. However, due to the low risk, there will be a compensatingly low return, but if anything did go wrong with the single specific investment, the investors will have lost all their money. For example, an investor could have owned shares in USA based electricity utility companies which were seen as low risk until the problems of the nuclear power plant on Three Mile Island occurred, when the perceived risks increased dramatically.

Consequently a better investment strategy is for all investors to diversify their risk by holding a range of shares, rather than concentrating on one. Because this is easy and cheap to do, the level of returns achieved in the stock market assume that all shareholders do this and thus they get rid of the specific (or non-systematic, as it is called) risk of individual shares. However, there is still a risk that all the shares on the stock market will decline in value, as happened on 19 October 1987, and it is impossible to diversify away this market risk. The investors logically therefore demand a premium for investing in the stock market to compensate them for bearing this systematic, nondiversifiable risk. This logic can be applied to internal capital project opportunities for a business

Unique specific project risks that can, on the whole, be spread out or diversified away are called diversifiable, or non-systematic, risks. There are some project risks that cannot be diversified away because of the intimate nature of all projects within this company. These risks are referred to as unavoidable, or systematic, risks. The capital asset pricing model is mainly concerned with measuring these risks and how this risk affects the returns on projects and hence the value of projects.

A particular project can be more or less risky than the average project, and should therefore attract a risk premium. The capital asset pricing model is based on this relationship.

The risk-free rate of return is expressed as R_f but to compensate for increased risk, the company demands a premium return. R_m is used to express the return expected on the overall project portfolio, and can be regarded as the market return demanded by the shareholder when the model is applied to stock markets. $(R_m - R_f)$ is therefore the premium return for the overall project portfolio. The return demanded for any particular project is related to the risk for the particular project and the premium for all projects. Mathematically this gives the relationship:

$$R_e = R_f + \beta (R_m - R_f)$$

where R_e = Return on any project

and β = Particular risk of that project

This is most commonly shown graphically, as is illustrated in Figure 8.5.

There is an obvious but very significant use for this risk adjusted expected return on the project and that is as the discount rate to be applied to the forecast cash flows arising from the project. It is therefore important that the methods of analysing project risks are clearly understood and the first stage is to start to break down the overall risk associated with any investment.

Business risk and financial risk

The total risk of a company can be broken down into business risk and financial risk. A company's business risk is determined by how it invests its funds, i.e. the type of projects which it undertakes, while financial risk is determined by how it finances these investments.

A company's competitive position, the industries in which it operates, the company's market share, the rate of growth of the market and the stage of maturity all influence business risk. Financial risk on the other hand is primarily influenced by the level of financial gearing, interest cover, operating leverage, and cash flow adequacy.

The logical inter-relationships between business risk and financial risk can be highlighted, as in Figure 8.6.

Companies in the top right hand box of Figure 8.6 face very high levels of total risk, because both business and financial risks are high. These individual risks are compounded and hence must be multiplied not added to arrive at the total risk. Therefore, investors should demand very high returns from these types of businesses. Companies which follow this strategy are characterized by their spectacular success or equally spectacular failure. For example, high borrowings in a business with a volatile market can cause total collapse if a combination of rising interest rates and declining demand occur together, as happened for furniture and electrical retailers in the UK during 1989.

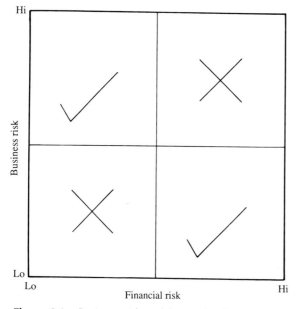

Figure 8.6 *Business risk and financial risk*

Although high total risk can be detrimental to the company the combination of low financial and low business risk is equally not rewarding for investors and can have adverse effects on the value of the company. Since risk and return are correlated positively, low total risk will by definition produce low returns. Companies in the bottom left hand box of Figure 8.6 often produce returns so far below the average for their industry that many investors would prefer to put their money into a building society.

These companies can however be very attractive to potential acquirers. A number of mergers and acquisitions in recent years have been motivated by the perceived potential for value enhancement given by these companies. It is possible to achieve this by increasing financial risk; e.g. borrowing to increase the return obtained by shareholders. This is considered in more detail later.

Companies should attempt to achieve a balance between business and financial risk and it is evident that the more successful companies are those in the top left and bottom right quadrant of the matrix, which appropriately combine high and low risk strategies.

Therefore, if the business strategy of the company is seen as high risk, the company should adopt a conservative, prudent financing strategy so as to ensure that the combined total risk is acceptable. Alternatively, if the company is well diversified and has a good balanced portfolio of relatively low risk potential projects, it can try to increase the overall return available for investors by adopting a more aggressive way of financing the business. This requires an understanding of the way in which the cost of capital is calculated for the company.

Cost of capital

This section of the book has so far discussed investment decisions, capital investment budgeting and the various methods of evaluating projects in order to achieve the long term objectives of the company. The net present value method, the internal rate of return method and the discounted payback method all depend on knowing what is the required rate of return for the project and the company. The overall rate of return for the company should be adjusted for risk so that the risk adjusted return required from a project can be calculated. The first stage is to establish the cost of capital for the company.

Whatever the financial objective of the company, if the company is to survive in the long-term, it *must* achieve a return in excess of the cost of funds invested in the company.

The cost of capital is the rate of return the company has to pay to the various investors of funds in the company. The various sources of funds to the company are, in general terms, equity and debt. Profits after taxation, less the dividends paid out to the shareholders, are funds that belong to the shareholders which have been 're-invested' in the company and are therefore included in the category of equity. These costs of equity and costs of debts are the rates of returns that need to be offered to these two groups of investors in order to attract funds from them.

(a) The cost of debt

Borrowing £1,000 from a lender at an interest rate of 10 per cent over the next 5 years, the cost of debt (i.e. interest) is simply £100 p.a. However for businesses, interest payments are normally deductible as an expense for tax purposes, and consequently if tax rates are 30 per cent, the after-tax cost is £70 p.a, which is a cost of debt after tax of 7 per cent. It should be remembered that the company must have taxable profits against which this interest expense can be offset as, otherwise, the company will have to bear the gross before-tax cost of debt. The cost of debt should always be lower than the return demanded by equity investors, not least because of the tax advantage given to interest costs.

The more fundamental reason is due to the risk associated with each type of investment. Lenders have a prior claim on the cash flow of the company and can often also take specific security on certain assets, which can be realized to repay the loan if the company gets into financial trouble. This reduces their perception of risk, although their return is also normally restricted as they do not participate in any excess returns achieved by the company; all of which are available to the equity investors.

(b) Cost of equity

Equity shareholders invest in the company in one of two ways:

(i)   From a new issue of shares
(ii) From retained earnings.

Retained earnings can be seen as funds which are due to the shareholders but have been retained in the organization on their behalf. They therefore have the same equity cost as a new issue of shares. Shareholders expect their returns from the company in the form of dividends, which are paid out to them, or capital gains, which are generated by an increase in the value of their investments, as a result of profits being retained within the company and re-invested successfully. The relative weightings given by the shareholders to each of these possible returns (i.e. dividends and capital gains) are affected by the reinvestment strategy and stage of development of the company. If the company is growing rapidly and has lots of opportunities for new investments, the rational investor will not expect a high dividends and capital gains) are affected by the reinvestment strategy and stage will buy the share hoping for a capital gain. Alternatively if the business has matured and the company is now producing high cash inflows but has limited new investment ideas, the investor should consider the share as a potential source of dividend income with limited prospects of capital gains.

(c) Weighted average cost of capital

It is therefore quite practical to work out, for any company, the demanded return on equity and the post-tax cost of debt, but this still does not give the effective cost of capital if the business uses a mixture of these sources of funds. However, as long as a stable mix of funding is assumed, it is possible to calculated an overall cost of funding for the business by using an appropriately weighted average of the individual costs of capital. Thus, if a company has an equity base of £100 million with outstanding debts of £50m, the individual costs of capital are respectively for equity 12 per cent and for debt 6 per cent after tax; the weighted average cost of capital (WACC) is:

$$\text{WACC} = \frac{100 \times 12\% + 50 \times 6\%}{150} = \underline{\underline{10\%}}$$

This WACC represents the minimum overall return which is needed if the business is to be able to satisfy the expectations of its sources of capital. It is therefore the minimum cut-off rate which can be applied to the 'average' project, but the business may wish to add a premium for any additional risk involved on a specific project. Equally some projects will have a risk profile below the average for the company as a whole and can therefore be financially evaluated using a lower discount rate than the WACC.

Allowing for risk in project evaluation

The easiest and most common method of allowing for risk is by adjusting the discount rate applied to the future cash flows arising from the project. By this method a premium can be added to the average required discount rate as a safety margin to compensate for the enhanced risk of the project. This acknowledges that if the same discount rate is applied to all proposed capital projects, no distinction would be made between high and low risk projects.

However, another way of allowing for risk can be by using the payback evaluation technique in either its simple, crude form or preferably, by calculating the discounted payback for the projects. The company can set a maximum period for the project to repay its original investment and this also reflects the risk profile of the project. The maximum acceptable period needs to be set in the context of the particular industry; e.g. manufacturers of high fashion goods may set a payback target of 12–18 months whereas producers of heavy capital equipment may accept a payback in excess of five years.

A further approach in allowing for risk in project evaluation is to carry out sensitivity analysis in the project cash flows. Sensitivity analyses, or 'what–ifs', involve evaluating the impact on the financial returns from the project if certain key variables changed from those forecast in the base evaluation. The sensitivity of the overall returns from the project to relatively small changes in one, or a few, key variables helps managers to understand the risk profile of the project. If these variables are also non-controllable, the level of risk may be unacceptably high and the project is rejected. Sensitivity analysis is considered again, in more detail, in Chapter 9.

Questions

1   One of the difficult tasks in evaluating long-term investment projects is allowing for risk. How would you allow for risk in a conglomerate organization such as GEC?

2   Jumbo Tyres plc have two projects proposed with the following cash flows:

	Project X	Project Y
Year 0	(130,000)	(200,000)
Year 1	(400,000)	(100,000)
Year 2	90,000	130,000
Year 3	200,000	150,000
Year 4	480,000	150,000

The company considers ROI and NPV in evaluating projects. At a discount rate of 12 per cent which project should be accepted? How would you allow for inflation if all the above cash flows were at today's prices and inflation is forecast to be 5 per cent p.a. for the next five years?

3   Discuss how you would try to identify an appropriate discount rate for the Channel Tunnel project.

4   It is rumoured that GEC use a 25 per cent cutoff rate for all investment projects undertaken by its various divisions. Discuss the benefits and disadvantages of this approach.

Short-term decision-making

Overview

Short-term decisions have to be taken in the context of much greater constraints on the business (e.g. in terms of the level of fixed, committed, period costs). However, short-term decisions are essential to the achievement of the long-term business objectives and consequently the short-term plans must form an integrated part of long-term planning. The benefits of budgeting, as short-term planning is normally known, are similar to other types of financial planning.

First, it highlights the financial implications of the operational planning decisions which all businesses take and enables the managers to accept these implications before implementing the plan.

Second, it enables the actual outcome to be evaluated against the expected out-turn as the budget period unfolds and allows modifying decisions to be made, as necessary, in the light of the very latest information.

The budgeting process is iterative and should be neither 'top-down' nor 'bottom-up', but a combination of both. Budgets should be agreed with the managers who have to achieve them and not be imposed on them. However, a budget is not a forecast, which is normally simply a quantification of the expected outcome. Budget targets should be achievable if the process is to have a positive motivational impact on line managers. In large organizations, detailed segmented operating budgets should be prepared but, for all businesses, the budget process should end up with an agreed, acceptable set of future financial statements for the business as a whole.

The only certainty about budgets is that they will be wrong, because the assumptions will contain errors and some of the expected interrelationships will not produce their anticipated outcomes. Thus a key part of the process is to produce contingency plans by using sensitivity analysis. Many businesses now take this one stage further by continually updating the budget via a rolling forecast system.

In order to avoid some of the inevitable game-playing in the budgeting process business can use zero base budgeting.

Introduction

The previous chapter examined the issues involved in long-term decisions and the strategic planning process which is required to achieve the objectives of the company. As stated in that discussion short-term planning must be properly integrated into this long-term process, but there are significant differences caused by the time variations and these are considered at the start of this chapter. Short-term planning, which is referred to throughout this chapter as budgeting, is then placed in the context of the strategic planning process and the benefits of budgeting are considered.

The budgeting process is explained in detail, in order to illustrate the stages involved and the way in which, once again, the process is continued and iterative. This is further illustrated by discussing the rationale of using sensitivity analysis and flexible budgeting before examining the role of zero base budgeting within organizations.

Briefly at the end of the chapter the financing implications of budgets are discussed but, as before, the detailed specific issues regarding raising funds for the business are regarded as outside the scope of this book.

Differences between the short and long-term

Throughout this book great emphasis has been made of concentrating resources on analysing those cash flow items which will change as a result of management decisions, i.e. the relevant costs. Not surprisingly, this represents one of the major differences in financial decision-making between the short and long-term. As discussed in Chapter 8, in the long term the business has the potential to re-allocate resources, acquire additional resources, divest from unattractive areas of the business, and generally remove most of the constraints which are stopping the organization from achieving its long-term objectives; at least, in terms of the long-term business plan.

In the short term, this decision-making freedom is much reduced and managers are more constrained by the impact of past decisions.

Thus it may be much more difficult to increase the total level of available resources or even to reallocate certain resources to other areas where the financial returns seem more attractive. It may even be impossible to improve the financial performance of the business in the short term by closing down parts which are making losses; not necessarily because the decision cannot be taken and implemented, but due to the lack of real savings which would be generated in the short term. Consequently in short-term decision analysis, although the key issue is, as always, identifying relevant costs, there is a greater emphasis on segmenting costs between fixed and variable, committed and discretionary, product and period, etc. In this short-term time-scale, there will be no change in fixed, committed, period costs as the result of most decisions and, hence they can be excluded from the decision evaluation process. The input–output relationships which exist in the business are likely to be more stable over the short term and, therefore, there is a good opportunity to use standard costing both as a planning technique and as a control mechanism.

However, there is another difference caused by this restricted time focus which has a particular impact on the planning function. Long-term planning can set objectives which relate to the mission or goals of the business and the resulting strategy should indicate how the business is to achieve these objectives over the long term. Obviously, short-term planning should start the business along the road towards these objectives, but there is a potential conflict between this assistance for the long term and achieving an acceptable level of performance in the short term. Some degree of compromise is almost inevitable, but it is vitally important that a balance is maintained so that the budget does not become overly concentrated on maximizing the short-term performance of the business, to the detriment of the longer term. A long-term plan is not merely the addition of a number of one year short-term budgets! In order to avoid this, the position of budgeting within the long-term planning process must be clearly understood.

Position of budgets within the long-term planning process

Budgets are the translation of an organization's long-term goals into short-term plans and are, therefore, an essential component of any strategic planning process. This can be seen diagrammatically in Figure 9.1, which shows how the budget interprets the short-term strategy and turns this into detailed operational tactics for the various parts of the business. It also highlights how the budget can be regarded as being at 'the sharp end' of the planning cycle in that this is the part that is acually implemented. The best textbook strategy in the world can only be proved in the market-place and this has to be done through the implementation of the short-term budget.

It is therefore important that the objectives of the budget fit properly into the longer-term strategic aims and objectives of the business, as previously stated. It is even more important that the relative success of the long-term strategy can be monitored as quickly as possible, so that any necessary modifications can be made before the potential to redress the situation has been lost. Thus the budget objectives should contain key early indicators of the likely success of any medium to long-term critical success factors, if the overall corporate objectives are to be achieved. If for example, the long-term plan hinges upon the successful launch and development of a new product, the budget monitoring process should highlight the short-term performance of a new product, as it is launched, against the level of initial performance required for the achievement of the longer-term success of the plan.

It may be possible to start this monitoring and feedback process at an even earlier stage if the long-term plan included provision for the development of the new product prior to its marketing launch. In this case, the initial budget can set short-term objectives for various stages of the development and testing process for the critical new product, and performance can be monitored against the achievement of these specific short-term targets. It is most likely, if a new product is behind schedule in terms of being ready for its targeted launch date or is relatively unsuccessful in its initial period of sales, that it will suddenly, without major

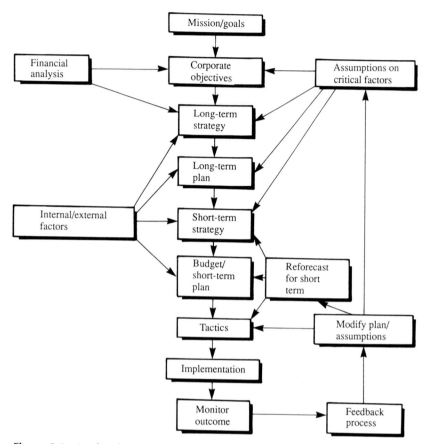

Figure 9.1   *Updated planning model*

subsequent changes to marketing strategies, blossom and achieve all of the previously established long-term objectives, which have been included in the long-term plans of the business.

This need highlights another important component in a good budgeting process, which is operating within an overall long-term business plan. The detailed budgets which are eventually produced should be split between maintenance and development activities. A maintenance activity can be defined as anything which is carried out to keep the business where it is at present or moving along an existing well-established strategic path, such as marketing support to maintain the position of an existing product. This definition is not meant to imply that these activities are not important but, in many cases, their impact is principally felt immediately or relatively quickly. With development activities, this is often not the case. A development activity can be defined as anything which attempts to change the business in the longer term or to move the business into a different strategic path. Thus the launch of a major new product would clearly be a development activity but, interestingly, so would the implementation of a decision to disinvest from a major part of the existing business. These longer-term development decisions should be properly financially evaluated using the appropriate technique to take account of all the relevant cash flows which are forecast to result from the decision. The most appropriate technique for decisions with long-term impacts is clearly one form of the discounted cash flow analysis technique and the decision should be included as part of the capital investment budget process, which was considered in Chapter 8. The short-term portion of these decisions will be included in the budget period, which is produced out of the long-term plan, but this budget may not include the major benefits of the development activity.

Clearly the successful implementation of development activity-type decisions is of critical importance to the overall success of the long-term plan, but this brings back the problem of conflicting time-scales and the use of short-term decision techniques while implementing budgets. Within the budgetary period, development activities tend, almost by definition, to require discretionary expenditure to be incurred whereas much of the expenditure on maintenance activities will be either already committed or of an engineered type where managers can exercise little real discretion. This means that, if managers want to alter the outcome of the budget during its implementation, they have a greater apparent degree of freedom to affect the level of development activities. However, if the business is to achieve the long-term objectives, this apparent level of discretion has to be restricted; particularly as the problem is frequently exacerbated because the immediate financial impact of many development activities is adverse due to the normal need to incur expenditure in advance of receiving the financial benefits. This is made even worse when this advance development expenditure is required on items which are not considered as assets for accounting purposes, for example the development marketing needed to build a successful brand. If the short-term financial performance of the business is judged by comparisons of actual levels of accounting profits or ROI to budgeted levels, managers may be tempted to compensate for any under-performance in the maintenance-type activities of the business by reducing expenditure on these critical development activities.

If the budget is properly analysed and specific objectives are included for both areas, this type of cross-subsidization or resource transfer cannot be done without reference back to the long-term plan so that appropriate modifications can be agreed in these objectives. This segmentation of objectives and close integration of budgets within the long-term planning process prove that budgeting is not merely an extension of last year's actual results, even if the extension tries to take account of inflation estimates and some forthcoming cost and selling price changes. The budget should be much more comprehensive than that and this implies that it will be more expensive to implement; we have always argued that management accounting procedures should be justified using a cost/benefit analysis and budgeting is no exception. The expense incurred in implementing a good budgeting system must be financially justified by evaluating the benefits which can be achieved from such a system. This is especially true if the budget is to be broken down into 'task' related segments which is what is required to split fully development and maintenance activities, as is discussed later in this chapter.

Benefits of budgeting

It is, first of all, important to clarify that all businesses plan, but not all businesses produce budgets. Budgets can be defined as the financial quantification of the operational plans of the business, and therefore budgets can be produced in the absence of a long-term, strategic plan. The benefits of budgeting are reduced in the absence of longer-term objectives but the same type of benefits can be achieved as for the long-term plan.

First, the budget provides a basis for accepting the financial implications of the operational planning decisions proposed by the business. If the potential outcome of these plans is unacceptable for any reason, the budget should be re-run until an acceptable compromise is reached. Given the short-term nature of budgets, it may be impossible to remove a sufficient number of operating constraints affecting the business so as to enable all the desired objectives to be achieved. Consequently, the managers must establish a hierarchy, or priority list, of objectives which establishes how the best compromise can be achieved. In the light of the previous points, it is important that this priority list also strikes the desired balance between short-term performance and investing to achieve the critical long-term objectives.

The financial implications should not be considered solely in terms of profitability because the cash usage or generation may also be of great significance. The cash needs of the business should be forecast and may prove to be a more critical constraint than the achievement of the budgeted level of profits. It has already been stated that businesses cease trading because they run out of money rather than through making accounting losses; a common reason for running out of money is failing to forecast properly the cash requirements of future plans. This can result in the ludicrous position of a growing, profitable company collapsing because it has inadequate or inappropriate funding – this is normally described as 'overtrading'.

The second major benefit of budgeting is that the budget provides a reference base against which the actual outcome can be evaluated as the budget period unfolds. If the actual results start to diverge from those expected, decisions can quickly be taken to try to modify actions which will put the business performance back into line with the budget. The budget is inevitably based on a wide range of assumptions about the external environment and several of these will prove to be inaccurate, even in the relatively short-term planning periods required for budgeting. Consequently, it may prove impossible to restore the business on to plan and the budget should have been adequately analysed so that it is relatively easy for managers to identify the most appropriate alternative course of action, given the actual environment in which the business is operating. Therefore, the regular and rapid monitoring of actual performance against the budget is an integral part of a good budgeting system. This exercise of financial control should also distinguish between divergences from the plan which are controllable by the managers and those over which they can exercise no control. As is discussed in more detail in Part Four, managers should only be held responsible for things over which they can exercise control, but this does not mean that other changes do not affect the relative performance of the business or that they should be ignored in the financial control process. What is required is that the budgeting system splits these items and accepts that the relative economic performance of the business is not necessarily the same as the relative managerial performance of the people running the business. In an unforeseen economic boom, almost any group of managers should have no trouble in beating the budget, whereas in the depths of a recession the best possible management team will lose less money than the rest.

These over-riding benefits of a budget system can be usefully broken down into more detailed advantages, which are easily remembered as the 4C's: namely coordination, communication, commitment and control.

Coordination of activities

A well integrated budgeting process will ensure that all the segments of the budget fit together in a properly coordinated fashion. The first part of this is checking that the overall objectives of the short-term plan are consistent with the objectives of the long-term plan, as has already been mentioned. However, the major need for coordination is across the various areas of the business, which are all trying to develop and then implement their own parts of the budget. If the sales and marketing budget is not internally consistent with the operating (e.g. production or service) areas of the business, the salesforce may find themselves taking increased orders which cannot be fulfilled due to a lack of capacity within the operating areas. A very common coordination problem relates to different interpretations of the planned timing of events. For example, if the launch of a new product is included in the budget, the research and development managers may be planning that this will happen towards the end of the year whereas the marketing department have included sales from the beginning of the budget period. The coordinating role of the budget should make sure that everybody involved knows the timetable for all such events and, equally important, understands what their role in the process is and how many other people are depending on them to deliver on time.

Communication of information

This communication among the inter-related areas of the business is another major benefit of a good budgetary process. It makes managers aware of the plans of the business as a whole and of the other parts of the business. In some organizations, the planning process is possibly the only occasion on which managers at several levels within the business communicate across function or divisional boundaries. The process of communication leads inevitably to the involvement of the managers in the development of their budgets and their interfaces with other areas of the business. As they become more involved and realize the extent of their ability to influence the relative achievement of the objectives of the company, there is often a considerable benefit due to a very positive impact on the motivation of managers.

Commitment of managers

This positive motivational effect can show up in an increased level of commitment, by individuals and groups of managers, towards achieving or even exceeding their budgeted objectives. Indeed it has often been proved that if people understand why they are doing something, particularly if they realize that it is important to many other people, they will be prepared to accept tougher objectives than if they are simply given a task to do without any explanation as to how it fits into the overall scheme of things. This increased commitment also makes managers more willing to be judged by their level of attainment against the objectives which they have set for themselves, and this makes it easier to exercise budgetary control.

Control of the business

As already mentioned, budgets can be used as a reference base against which to judge actual performance as the business moves through the budget period. If the managers have not been involved in the development of their own budgets and consequently are not positively motivated towards achieving the budget, this process of control through monitoring against budgets can become very negative. Indeed, in some organizations the budgeting process is seen by managers as a necessary evil, which distracts them from their main task of managing the business and towards which task the budget makes no positive contribution whatsoever. Another negative type of reaction is for managers to regard the budget as an opportunity to indulge in some very subtle game-playing, in order to end up with a set of budgetary objectives which are very easy to beat. These managers hope that, by beating these managerial performance parameters, their positions within the organization are enhanced. This game-playing can take the form of padding forecast expenditure levels so that actual expenditures are below this level, without the manager having to try to manage the area more effectively or efficiently. In organizations, particularly those which use cash expenditure budgets, the process can become absurd because, having padded one year's budget, the manager has to spend the budget by the end of the year or else next year's allocation will be cut. This would be unacceptable if the culture of the organization considered the seniority of its managers as being indicated by the relative size of the expenditure budget which they controlled. Consequently managers may bring forward expenditure from the following year by ordering early and paying early as well; remember the system is controlled by cash, so the payment must be made by the end of the existing budget. In many cases, these payments can be made before the products (whether goods or services) have been received! Obviously, these managers are building up bigger problems for themselves in the future, but they are successfully playing the game at present.

The causes of this clear example of poor financial control are partly the lack of commitment of the managers, but mainly the wrong use of a financial control system. In many cases where budgeting systems are not being successfully used, the financial control system is being used as a method of apportioning blame for the adverse performance of the business. Thus an adverse variance against plan is automatically seen be managers as something to be avoided at all costs; hence, game-playing takes place when the budgets are being set. Alternatively, managers spend a large amount of their time trying to spread the blame onto someone else or arguing about the costs charged against their particular areas of responsibility by the accounting department. These disputes can become particularly vehement if there is a mismatch between the managerial authority actually exercised by the budgeting system. Many managers argue aggesssively that they are held responsible for adverse variances against budgets over which they can exercise no control at all. When this is linked into their pay levels through bonuses, etc., it is hardly surprising that the end result is a demotivated, cynical, game-player! The financial control system should be used as a learning process, which tries to improve future decisions as a result of analysing the outcome of past events. Managerial performance evaluation can be partially based on the achievement of budgetary objectives, but these must be controllable, as mentioned earlier and developed in detail in Chapter 11.

If this emphasis on financial control as a learning process is maintained, it is clear that a good budgeting system can produce significant benefits for the organization. It is now time to consider the budgeting process in detail.

The budgeting process

The starting point

A major benefit of budgeting is ensuring that the operational plans of the business are internally consistent and are also based on a coordinated, consistent view of the outside world. This means checking that internal resources are properly matched, and that the plans of each area are mutually compatible with each other and with the overall corporate plan. Several iterations around the budgeting cycle may be needed to achieve this consistency and therefore the budgeting process can be regarded as circular, as is demonstrated in Figure 9.2.

Due to its essentially circular nature, it is not absolutely critical where the planning process is started, but it is possible to waste a considerable amount of management time and effort if planning is not started at the most logical point.

In long-term planning, the logical starting point is with the formation of the goals and objectives of the business which fit in with the established mission statement. Although there may be existing constraints which are impeding the business at present, it is quite practical to plan that, over the period of the long-term plan, these impediments to the achievement of the corporate objectives will be removed or, at least, that their impact will be significantly reduced. Since, when preparing a short-term plan, many of these resource constraints cannot be removed or avoided, the logical starting point for the budgeting process is at a key immovable constraining factor.

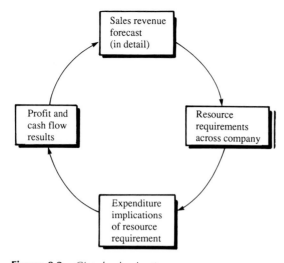

Figure 9.2 *Circular budgeting process*

For many companies, this will be total sales revenues because it is impossible to improve significantly the sales performance of the business with the existing products, channels of distribution and salesforce resources, etc., and yet, altering these constraints will take more time than is allowed by the time-scale of the budget. Sales revenues can obviously be adjusted by changing unit selling prices which will affect projected sales volumes, depending on the forecast price elasticity of demand, and part of the budgeting process should be to select the optimum mix of selling price and expected volume. This need not necessarily be the combination which maximizes the total contribution towards fixed costs, as is discussed later in this section.

In some cases, the critical constraint on the level of activity may not be the ability of the business to sell all of its potential output. The company may be constrained by its productive capacity, as in the example of the continuous process operation which is already working twenty-four hours per day, seven days per week and only closing down for essential maintenance work. If the lead time required to increase this capacity is greater than the budget period, this should be regarded as the prime constraint. The budgeting process should start by assessing this area, as all other areas will have to match their level of activity with this constrained volume of output. Alternatively the business may find it very difficult to recruit skilled employees and one of the long-term strategies may be to introduce a training programme to reduce the impact of this constraint. Even so, for the duration of the budget period, the lack of skilled personnel may be the critical constraint. Once again, the process should start by analysing the level of available resources in this area and deciding on the optimum deployment of the resources.

If profit maximization is the only budget objective, the optimum solution is to maximize the contribution generated from each unit of this critical constraint; thus, the financial measures used would be contribution per machine hour or contribution per skilled labour hour, in the above examples. However, as mentioned earlier, budgets normally have a set of objectives rather than a single profit target. This is done to ensure the required balance between the short term and the long term, and this set of objectives may include non-financial targets, such as growth in market share or launching a new product, which avoid an exclusively short-term focus.

For example, the soft-drink manufacturer discussed in Chapter 6 had established a long-term objective of achieving a 30 per cent share of some specific segments of the UK market within five years. Unfortunately, two short-term constraints existed, which were that the existing production facilities were inadequate to supply such a level of demand and the current channels of distribution did not give the company access to a large enough proportion of the market to make the objective attainable. If the business concentrated on the short term only, it could set its selling prices at a level which would generate only sufficient demand which could be supplied from the existing production capacity. However, if the business is to achieve the long-term objective, the short-term plan must start to remove the two key constraints and therefore investments should be planned for increasing production capacity and developing improved channels of distribution. The short-term impact of these activities, both in terms of profit and cash flows, is likely to be adverse but this should not deter the managers from implementing decisions which help to achieve sound, well-thought-out long-term objectives.

Top-down or bottom-up

This aspect of encouraging or motivating managers to act in certain ways has, throughout the book, been developed as the role of management accounting; but, the desired way of acting has consistently been argued as being in line with the overall corporate objective. This enables us to deal very quickly with the frequently asked question of whether the budgeting process should start from the top and work down the organization or start at the bottom and be passed up the hierarchy. If managers are to acquire the desired level of commitment to the budget, the objectives cannot simply be imposed from above. However, if managers are allowed to develop the objectives for their areas completely independently, their resulting departmental budgets are unlikely to be properly coordinated to achieve the desired corporate objective.

Budgets therefore should be neither top-down nor bottom-up, but must be a combination of the two and the budgetary process should reflect this desired balance. Thus the process may start with the development and communication of budgetary objectives by senior managers; but the practicality of these objectives can only be validated by the departmental managers, who will ultimately implement the plan. If inconsistencies are subsequently identified in the objectives or if it is found that these objectives cannot be achieved with the existing available resources and in the current external business environment, the problem, and preferably a suggested solution, should be referred back to senior managers for a decision as to how to resolve the conflict. In practice, this iterative process up and down the organizational structure is quite frequent during the period when the budget is being prepared and, as a consequence, many companies have built this referral procedure into the formal budgeting process.

However, issues regarding the organizational sequence of budgeting are not restricted to the setting of objectives and often arise in terms of the preparation of individual area budgets. For example, should the sales budget be built up by the field salesforce using their knowledge of individual customers or should it be developed by the marketing department from their understanding of market trends and forecasts of the market shares for the products sold by the particular business. Once again, the obvious answer is that both sources of a sales plan should be used and the differences should be discussed and reconciled, so that the best sales plan is produced using the combined skills and knowledge of the managers within the business. The separate areas of the budget should not be regarded as being 'owned' by groups of managers, so that they can preclude other managers from voicing their opinions and views. Equally these outside opinions and views must be supported by evidence, if the managers putting them forward expect to be taken seriously; comments from a production or administration director purely to the effect that the sales and marketing department are not selling enough are distinctly unhelpful, but unfortunately far too common!

Segmented budgets

So far we have referred to 'the' budgeting process but have also mentioned various specific elements of the budget, e.g. the sales budget. In order to classify this, it may be useful to discuss the various ways in which the budget should be broken down. The overall budget, or 'master' budget as it is often called, is prepared for the business as a whole, but this is really a synthesis of a number of segmented budgets, which must all be properly integrated and coordinated if the short-term plan is to have any practical relevance and value.

The first method of segmentation is that the overall business may be broken down into operating divisions which are more readily able to focus on particular products and/or markets. As already stated, the success of any business plan can only really be proven by selling products in the marketplace and, consequently, a good way of analysing the plan is by product and market focus. Another way of segmenting the budget is by operational area of the business, so that these budgets can focus on particular types of activities and the alternative courses of action which can be selected in this particular area. Thus a sales and marketing plan would be developed, and this would feed into a production plan which would then feed into separate budgets for the buying area, the personnel department for recruitment and training, the engineering area for increased or modified production requirements, etc.

These functional plans will often be prepared on the same or a similar format, to the focused product/market segmentation as is used for the sales planning exercise. However, these separated functional budgets should then be consolidated in order to ensure that adequate total resources are available in the area to support all the company's short-term plans. Equally, the segmented plans are also consolidated to provide the overall budget for the organization and this budget is compared to the objectives. If unacceptable, the process may have to start again until an acceptable compromise is reached, and this process epitomizes the budgeting cycle.

The budgeting cycle

In some companies the budgeting process is characterized by, and indeed dominated by, the budgeting cycle which is a phrase frequently used to depict the period of time during which the budget is prepared. Unfortunately this period is sometimes regarded as the only period of the year when managers are supposed to be thinking about planning ahead. Consequently, once the budget is completed it is immediately consigned to the bottom drawer of the filing cabinet, and is not brought out again until the next budgeting cycle starts when the document is brought out, dusted off and updated. This is obviously the wrong attitude to budgeting, as to be of real practical value the budget should be an action based plan which is regularly monitored and updated so that it is continuously referred to as the year unfolds. However, there still does need to be 'a budgeting cycle' if the plan is to be completed before the start of the period to which the budget relates.

The budget time-table is normally subject to a few practical constraints imposed internally by the business. For example, the completion date is normally fixed by the timing of the review meeting held to approve the overall budget for the total business. This meeting may be held quite close to the start of the actual year but this runs a risk that, if the proposed budget is unacceptable, the business may start the next fiscal period without an agreed budget. Consequently, there is normally some allowance for final readjustments should they prove necessary, but there are other practical reasons for the budget approval to be given some time before the start of the period. Once approved, the segmented and detailed budgets have to be communicated throughout the organization, and the detailed numbers have to be built into the accounting system so that management accounting comparisons can be made in the normal way. All this takes time!

However, there is also a very practical reason for not starting the budgeting cycle too early. Budgets are based on a whole range of assumptions about the state of the external and internal environment which will exist during the budget period. The further ahead that manager are forced to look to make these assumptions, the less accurate they will be and consequently the assumptions should be made as late as possible. Unfortunately, the rest of the budgeting cycle is very largely dependent on these assumptions and hence very little preparatory work can be done until the basic assumptions have been established. This does not mean that these assumptions cannot be modified in the light of updated information and indeed they should, as is discussed later, but it does explain why the budgeting cycle is often compressed into a relatively short portion of the year and this consequently creates an intensive workload for those involved.

Another timing problem is caused by the essentially sequential nature of the process and this is exacerbated by the probable need to iterate the sequence several times before arriving at a satisfactory conclusion. In a large group, where the organizational structure introduces another time-consuming sequence of seg-mented budgeting decisions, the time pressure can become considerable and there is a real danger that the quality of the analysis suffers as a result. Managers can get into a mechanistic way of simply filling in the budget forms sent round to them without necessarily really thinking about proposing changes to the way they should do things in the future.

If we take a business where the sales forecast is the short-term key constraint, the sequence can be illustrated in a simple way. Marketing managers will develop a forecast for the movements in market volumes and will propose pricing strategies for the business which should achieve the agreed objectives for market share, etc. They will also prepare a budget for the marketing support (e.g. advertising and promotion), which is needed to achieve this short-term objective and to move the business towards any longer-term objectives which have been agreed. This sales forecast is validated by the sales managers, who will build up a sales forecast from individual customers or groups of customers, given the assumptions made by the marketing department on selling prices, etc.

The sales volume forecast is the most relevant output for the operating (i.e. production or service) area of the business, as this dictates its own planning and determines its resource requirements. Any potential resourcing constraints must be removed, if possible in the short term (e.g. working overtime, new shift patterns, more resources), or the sales plan will have to be modified to fit with what can be resourced.

The adjusted, integrated output plan from the operating area forms the input information for the budgets of the purchasing and personnel areas for resourcing the necessary inputs in terms of raw materials, energy, skilled labour, etc. It should be noted that the necessary lead times for these various resources will differ and consequently a time sequenced action plan (datal plan) is as important as a financial budget to ensure that resources are available when required (e.g. labour must be hired in time for any required training to be carried out before they are needed to supplement production levels).

As already mentioned, if the budget becomes inconsistent as this process is implemented, it is vitally important that the inconsistency is removed; even if this means going back to the beginning by reforecasting sales and then repeating the whole process. This need for consistency and the use of money as the common business language, which makes all these various resources directly comparable, have been the main reasons for the degree of control often exercised by financial managers over the budget process. This involvement should be in a coordinating role rather than as 'the imposer' of the financial budget, because of their knowledge of the 'common language'.

The end result of the budgeting cycle should be an action based short-term plan, which produces the best mix of results that can be achieved given the constraints under which the business will be operating during the budget period. In financial terms, these results can be depicted by the normal set of financial documents, which should cover the period of the budget, i.e. a profit and loss account and balance sheet together with a cash flow forecast.

The cash cycle

The need to forecast the cash flow implications of the budget has already been mentioned and the projected cash flow statement is, for many businesses, at least as important as the profit and loss account. In order to produce this forecast as accurately and as meaningfully as possible, the managers need to develop a model of the specific cash flow cycle which operates in the business at present. This existing cash cycle then needs to be modified to take account of any proposed changes in the way the company intends to do business in the future, as well as to allow for any changes in the scale of activity of the business.

This is illustrated in Figure 9.3 which shows how cash goes out to pay wages, suppliers and operating and sales expenses, before more cash is received from customers following a sale. The 'operating cash cycle' of the business is defined as the number of days between the cash leaving the business to pay for the goods and services and it being received back from customers as a result of these specific goods and services being sold. This operating cycle period indicates the growth in financing needed for additional working capital if sales levels are expected to increase during the budget period.

However, even more importantly, this operating cycle should highlight the impact of any proposed changes to the method of operations which have been incorporated in the budget. For example, one fast moving consumer goods company planned to change its customer base quite significantly and to focus its attention on larger chains of retailers, whereas previously it had concentrated on smaller independent retailers. Its budget included the increased sales revenues, and the improved efficiencies due to the larger order sizes and economies of scale in the processing areas, but its operating cash cycle was not altered. Hence its predicted financing need was based on the existing model using the increased level of activity expected in the budget period. The company experienced tremendous liquidity problems when the actual operating cash cycle turned out to be significantly increased due to administrative delays and simply slower payments from the new larger, more powerful customers.

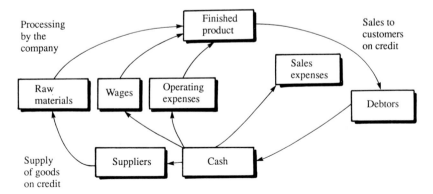

Figure 9.3 *Cash circulation process*

New product launch

It may be useful to bring together the discussion on the budgeting cycle by considering how a budget, which incorporates a new product launch, would be put together. This is illustrated diagrammatically in Figure 9.4, which highlights the sort of iterations which need to be superimposed on the sequential process.

This process can be applied to a large number of companies but is derived from one particular company which wished to grow but also wanted to continue its existing record of annually increasing profits. The market research department was given a task to identify growth opportunities which utilized the existing competitive advantages of the business. These were strong channels of distribution and good production skills in the particular process technologies used in existing products. This type of brief is a good way to focus the 'tasks' previously mentioned, which are important elements of budgeting. It thus becomes possible to achieve the balance between improving the short-term performance of the organization by working the existing business harder and making positive moves towards the longer-term objectives. A diagrammatic way of highlighting the proposed growth strategies which are included in the business plan is by using the Ansoff matrix shown as Figure 9.5.

The main strategic thrust of each of the four different ways of expanding the business is shown on the matrix. By including specific tasks, relating to increasing market share or entering new markets, in the budget objectives, this can be used

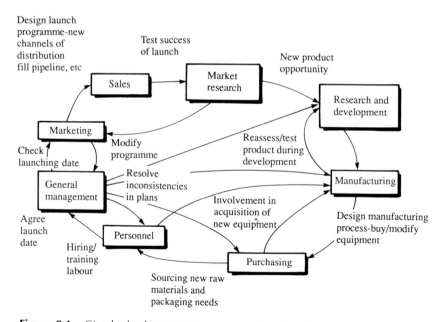

Figure 9.4   *Circular budget process: new product launch plan*

PRODUCTS

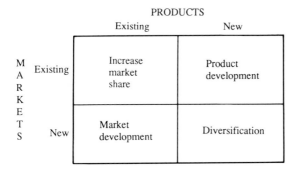

Figure 9.5   *Ansoff matrix*

as a clear way of stopping managers from concentrating exclusively on the short term.

Returning to the new product example shown in Figure 9.4, the market research department identified a particular new product opportunity aimed at a specific segment of the company's existing market. This product specification was passed to the research and development department which had to allocate resources to developing a product with the required performance, which could be produced at a cost which enabled the target selling price to be achieved. As part of this process, the operating areas of the business were involved in deciding how the product should be produced. In this case, this involved buying some new equipment and modifying some existing equipment. Purchasing needed this information in order to source the required information and they were involved at an early stage so that suitable sources for new raw materials and packaging could be identified. Personnel had to set up training programmes for this new process and had to decide whether existing employees could be redeployed or new people would have to be recruited.

All these issues had to be resolved before a launch date could be agreed and the sales and marketing department had to design the launch programme for the new product. When the costings had become firm, the selling price was reviewed against the original target established by the market research. For this product this created an additional problem because the production process was subject to a steep learning curve, which meant that the cost level reduced with volume produced. Of course, the volume demanded was affected by the selling price chosen and so, yet another iterative loop had to be evaluated as shown in Figure 9.6.

Clearly all the areas of the business had inputs to this budgeting cycle and, unless all these inputs are correctly coordinated, the new product could generate into a fiasco. Unfortunately that happened in this case study; the new product was launched before adequate stocks had been produced because there was a delay in getting production levels up to plan and costs were also significantly above their targeted level, at which the financial justification had been carried out.

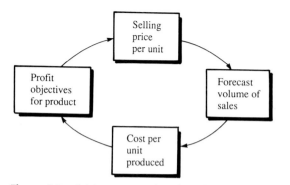

Figure 9.6 *Pricing strategy in a learning curve environment*

Calendarizing and sensitizing the budget

This example leads to two other aspects of budgeting which are important. Budgets are normally prepared for a year but the financial control process will obviously be much more frequent. Consequently the annual budget has to be broken down into shorter segments, against which actual performance can be compared. In some cases, this will not create a problem because the budget will have been built up on a period by period basis, and this detailed level can be incorporated into the accounting system. However, for many companies, calendarizing (i.e. the breaking down of the budget across the year) can create problems when it is not done properly. The simplest way is obviously to divide the total budget evenly across the year and, very occasionally, this method may be satisfactory. This will not be true if the budget includes significant changes which will take place part-way through the year or where the business is growing rapidly. A graph of sales for a growth company is shown as Figure 9.7 and this illustrates the potential problem.

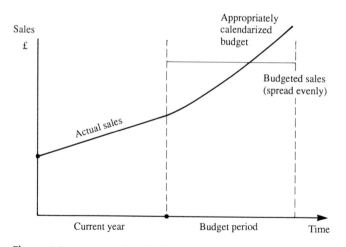

Figure 9.7 *Impact of calendarization*

If sales are rising rapidly and the budget is based on continued growth, it should be clear that the sales in the budget period need calendarizing as indicated. Unfortunately many companies still ignore this obvious point and spread budgeted sales evenly across the period.

Comparisons of actual results to budget are now going to be meaningless on a period-by-period basis and a major benefit of the exercise has been destroyed. This problem can be dramatically increased when the same logic is applied to cost levels for a growth company if there is, for example, a need to build substantial stocks prior to the sales levels increasing.

The other important aspect of budgeting is the need to allow for the inevitable errors that will occur within any budget. If the benefit of a budget was significantly reduced as soon as any basic assumption were proved to be wrong, there would be little point in starting the budgeting process. The budget must be developed in a robust way and plans should be outlined which cope with the range of key variables which can reasonably be foreseen. Thus the managers should use sensitivity analysis, as discussed in Chapter 8, to calculate the impact of changes in major variables and critical interrelationships incorporated in the budget.

The simplistic way of doing this is to change all major items by 10 per cent in both directions and compare the impact of each item on the outcome of the short-term plans. Not surprisingly, this mechanistic approach indicates that the biggest items have the biggest impact on the achievement or non-achievement of the budget. However, not all items are subject to the same degree of error in forecasting, and a much better way of carrying out sensitivity analysis is to use the manager's expertise and judgement to predict the likely range of levels for all major items. By using these ranges, which are specific to the items concerned, a much more meaningful assessment of the impact of forecasting errors can be incorporated. This enables managers to concentrate on producing contingency plans for the most likely situations which have large impacts on the future performance of the business.

Rolling forecasts and flexible budgeting

The use of sensitivity analysis clearly allows managers to plan for a range of possible situations, which differ from the final agreed budget, and these contingency plans can rapidly be implemented should the need arise. Also the actual results can be compared to the predicted outcome of the sensitivity analysis, rather than being compared back to the now out-dated and falsely-based budget.

A budget therefore is not a static document, but it is very difficult to use something which is continually changing as a meaningful reference base as the year unfolds. This is like trying to hit a constantly moving target but, equally, short-term decisions should be based on the best, most up-to-date information available and not on estimates made at the time of the annual budgeting cycle. Many companies try to reconcile these issues by preparing a budget, which is then not changed, and using regularly updated *forecasts* to take account of changing circumstances. This adds another dimension to the planning cycle; actual results are compared to the predicted outcomes, i.e. budgets or forecasts, and these actual results are used to prepare updated forecasts for the remaining budget period (this additional stage is, in fact, included in Figure 9.1). In some companies, the comparison is made as a two-stage process. The first updated forecast is compared to the original budget and all the proposed changes (remembering that a forecast is a forward-looking document) are evaluated and explained. The actual results are then compared, not to the budget, but to the updated forecast, and any further changes between the latest expected results and what actually happened are explained in detail.

For subsequent forecasts, the comparison is made back to the previous forecast and not to the original budget. Consequently, the actual results are always being compared to the latest expected out-turn and deviations which require explanation should be relatively small. However, many managers are concerned that this type of process, in fact, reduces financial control rather than enhances it, due to the fundamental differences between budgets and forecasts.

A *budget* is an agreed, financially quantified plan of actions and policies, which is to be implemented in a specified time period in order to achieve the corporate objectives. The budget is agreed against a set of assumptions regarding the external environment and the overall long-term plan of the business. By comparison, a *forecast* is the latest prediction of the results of the business using the most up-to-date information available on the internal and external environment. Thus it does not have to be an agreed plan, and may not necessarily be aiming to achieve the original set of objectives incorporated in the budget.

This gives rise to a concern that operating managers may agree to a tough set of budget objectives, knowing that they can adjust their forecasts over the succeeding months to a more realistic set of objectives. At the end of the year, these managers may claim to have achieved the objectives of the latest forecast, but the business could have fallen well short of its original objectives. Such a problem can be overcome if the financial review process pays proper attention to these divergences from the budget, which would be highlighted in the updated forecast submitted during the year. In many companies, these updated forecasts are not subjected to the same rigorous scrutiny which is applied during the formal budget cycle.

If desired, the process of comparison can be done as a single stage so that the original budget retains visibility throughout the year. Unfortunately, if the updated forecast is to have any relevance as a learning process, it should be used as a basis of comparison for the actual results so that future forecasts can be improved. This often leads to the actual results being compared against both the original budget and the updated forecast, and this may be done both for the current period and for the cumulative year-to-date figures. Not surprisingly, such a multiplicity of comparisons can create confusion and there is a better solution which has been adopted by a wide range of businesses.

A principal concern of using budgets as the primary basis of comparison is that the basic assumptions included have been found to be incorrect and that, as a consequence, the budgeted results are no longer relevant to such an exercise. If the budget could be modified to adjust for the impact of these incorrect assumptions, this adjusted budget would serve as a more relevant basis for the subsequent financial control process, as the actual results are recorded. This can partially be done by 'flexing' the budget, which takes account of the actual levels of sales volumes which occur and incorporates the planned impact of these sales level into the budget. In other words, the flexible budget shows how the short-term plan would have looked if the sales volumes had been correctly predicted. It is possible to adjust, or flex, the budget for other predictive errors but this is much less common in practice; companies prefer to build these other changes into the updated forecasts.

There is still a further complication of the budgeting process which has led to yet another development of these updated forecasts. As mentioned earlier, the budgeting cycle tends to be compressed into a relatively short period close to the end of the current accounting period, i.e. as near to the start of the budget period as possible. Thus as the actual year progresses, the business reaches a period of the year where the existing budget has almost completely been replaced by actual events and yet the new budget has not been agreed. In planning terms, the business is heading into a void and managers will find it difficult to make the right decisions without appropriate reference points and sign posts, which are provided by these short-term plans. (It should be remembered that the business should still have the objectives of the continuing long-term plan, which can provide a more general guide to the most desirable choices from those available.)

Managers can avoid this planning vacuum if each updated forecast is always extended by one period. This means that as the first period of the budget becomes actual, a forecast is made for a full year ahead, thus forecasting for the first period of the following year. This process is repeated each period, so that the updated forecast always looks a year ahead, and consequently managers always have an adequate short-term plan to refer to as they face new decisions. Some companies use a variation of this technique by not forecasting into the next year until the second half of the current year, and then only forecasting the first half of that year. Their objectives is to avoid the problems of only having a very short time horizon to their plans but they do not wish to increase the work-load excessively.

This increasing work-load is obviously the major problem of such a sophisticated *rolling forecast* system, as it is practically impossible to produce a full budget every month! Most companies using this system fully understand this and hence have developed some very good methods of focusing managerial attention on the key areas which are likely to change during the year. This enables the rolling forecasts to be produced without an uneconomic cost being incurred and, if these forecasts are well done, the budgeting cycle can be compressed still further because a lot of the basic analysis and assumptions has already been reviewed in previous forecasts. A criticism of this process is that it takes managers' attention away from the main budgeting cycle and these forecasts, which have not necessarily been agreed as delivering an acceptable end result, acquire a credibility within the organization which is out of proportion to their accuracy and to the effort which went into their preparation. This area is discussed in more detail in Part Four.

Zero base budgeting

Even with a very sophisticated budgeting system, incorporating rolling forecasts and flexing, there is an inevitable tendency, after several years, for next year's budget to be based on the current year's actual figures. Indeed many companies see this as a way of ensuring that some level of 'management task' is incorporated into the budget. This is achieved by setting the budget level at this year's level plus an allowance for inflation but minus an expected improvement in efficiency due to 'management tasking'. The problem is that this type of budgeting system has two major deficiencies.

First, it creates an implicit acceptance of the current way of doing things and can stifle really innovative changes. Thus improvements are likely to be small incremental evolutionary steps, rather than large revolutionary strides. This can make it more difficult for the business to make progress towards any dramatic long-term strategic objectives. For example, if your overseas competitor has a significant cost advantage in manufacturing and can also develop new products in three years compared to your five–six years, as was the case for many British companies, a 50 per cent p.a. management task included in the budget is not likely to transform your competitive position. This is particularly true if the same competitor is improving its own efficiency at over 10 per cent p.a.!

Second, the use of the existing cost level as the basis for generating future acceptable levels encourages the 'game-playing' which was mentioned earlier. If managers know that next year's budget will be a reduction, in real terms, from this year's actual expenditure, there is a clear incentive to keep this year's expenditure as high as possible without exceeding this year's budgets. There is another form of game-playing which is carried out at the time of agreeing the budget, and this is to get agreement that certain items of expenditure were not included in the current year. Therefore next year's budget should be increased to take allowance of this new area of expenditure. If this increased cost actually replaces another existing cost area, a key objective if the game-playing is to avoid having that area reduced by a compensating amount. A third form of game-playing can be done either at the time of preparing the budget or during the actual year as comparisons are made against budget. This is a sophisticated game, which relies on a good understanding of the particular accounting policies and practices applied by the business, as it revolves around re-classifying actual items of expenditure to different areas from their allocation in the budget.

For example, the manufacturing director may have an expenditure problem within the maintenance area which looks as if it will substantially overspend against budget. One possible decision would be to stop maintenance activity but this could have the disastrous effect of stopping production in the factory. Another possibility is to reclassify some major pieces of preventative maintenance as capital improvements so that they are not regarded as revenue items and therefore would not be charged against this year's maintenance budget. A capital improvement is added to the asset value on the balance sheet and depreciated over the remaining life of the asset. Another way of affecting particular perceptions of performance is to move items of expenditure from an area regarded as controllable to one which is non-controllable by the particular manager. This could be done, for example, in the marketing area where product advertising would normally be regarded as controllable by the marketing manager. However, many companies have a budget for general corporate advertising and public relations, which is not chargeable to individual products or even groups of product, Clearly, if a marketing manager can get some items of expenditure re-classified as corporate rather than product, the reported performance against budgets of the product can be changed significantly.

This time, effort, ingenuity and consequent cost which go into game-playing are very substantial in many companies and it is this behaviour which leads to the perception of the management accountant acting in the role of policeman within this type of organization. Fortunately there is at least one way out of these problems.

If the budget is developed from an assumption of no existing resources (zero base), all resources have to be justified. This forces managers to go back to basics and the particular proposed method of operation has to be compared with the alternative options, using the concept of opportunity cost. Thus the logic of producing certain components internally would be compared with the cost of buying them in from an outside supplier, or producing them by a different type of process. In the sales area, the existence of the field salesforce would be ignored and the optimum way of achieving the particular sales objectives would be evaluated. This might not include any field salesforce or its size might change significantly.

An obvious problem of this far-reaching planning review process is the massive amount of management time needed to carry it out properly, and the potential disruption which it causes to the business while it is going on. Therefore the most popular way of implementing a zero base budgeting process is to do one area of the business each year on a rolling basis, so that every area is examined every five years or so. The objective is to avoid the worst type of the problems indicated above which tend to build up over time.

Financing the plan

The importance of including a cash flow forecast as part of the budget outputs has already been mentioned. One obvious reason for doing this is to enable the company to recognize, as early as possible, the potential needs for additional funding which may result from the proposed actions incorporated in the plans. In Chapter 2 the significance of appropriately matching the sources and uses of funds was discussed and therefore the cash flow forecast should indicate not only the amount of funds which may be needed, but also the time-scale for which these funds may need to be invested in the company.

In the case of increasing the level of investment in many types of fixed assets, the long-term nature is easily identifiable and the company should organize appropriate long-term or even permanent sources of funding for this need. However, permanent funding, i.e. equity or very long-term replaceable debt, should be used for some parts of the working capital employed within the business. It may sound strange to suggest that permanent funding should be used for debtors or stocks, when the individual items involved will be turned into cash in, at most, a matter of weeks. However, these individual items will normally be replaced immediately and therefore, as long as the business continues to trade at the same level and in the same way, the funds will continue to be required in the business. Indeed, if the plan includes an expectation of expansion, additional funds may need to be invested on a permanent basis in order to finance the additionally required working capital.

On top of this base level of funding of working capital, the business may have a need for seasonally fluctuating financing for working capital. This would provide financing for increased levels of stock-holding prior to the peak sales period of the year, and for any delay in collecting payments from customers as a result of this maximum rate of sale. Using the same matching principle for sources and uses of funds, it is clear that this variable demand for funds should be satisfied by the variable source of finance, such as can be provided by an overdraft facility from a bank. In this way the company only has to pay for these funds when it uses them in the business, and this reduces the total costs incurred through interest payments even though the percentage rate charged on the facility may be slightly higher than on a longer-term fixed facility.

Another type of funding need for most businesses relates back to Chapters 7 and 8 dealing with long-term investment projects. Most such projects are characterized by a need to spend money in advance of the returns being received and hence, as mentioned in these chapters, these projects create a financing requirement. However, the financial returns from the project should more than repay this investment over the life of the project, if a valid method of financial evaluation has been used. This indicates that the funding is not needed permanently but, equally, the need is for a longer period than for seasonal working capital fluctuations. As a result, a medium term type of funding may be required to provide for the investment

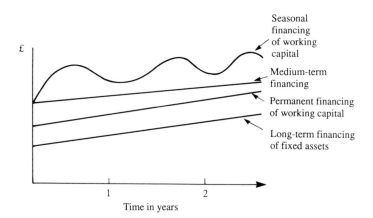

Figure 9.8   *Finance needs and timescales*

projects proposed in the long-term plans and those portions included in the budgets.

A diagrammatic representation of these various categories of financing need is shown in Figure 9.8 and it is important that the business has identified a suitable mix of sources of finance for this planning requirement. In reality, these identified funds should be able to cope with any foreseeable fluctuations which may arise out of the contingency plans, which have been prepared as part of the sensitivity analysis referred to earlier in this chapter. Assessing whether a source of funding is suitable involves not only matching the time-scales but also involves ensuring that the financial risk is compatible with the business risk of the company, as discussed in Chapter 8. This is to ensure that the whole of the effort put into the planning process considered in this part of the book is not put in jeopardy due to selecting the wrong method of financing for any particular part of the business. Ensuring that the overall business strategy is a success is considered in the next chapter, which deals with the specific issues associated with strategic decisions.

Questions

1 You have recently joined a newly established software consultancy as financial controller. How would you approach, step by step, the compilation of a budget for next year?

2 A number of large companies start their budgeting process for any year a number of months ahead of the budget year. If you are the controller of JBA plc, an airline whose budget for 1993 requires planning from January 1992, what are the problems you envisage and how would you overcome these?

3 Due to the Gulf crisis and the recession, your company's cost structure as planned for the 1991 budget is now vastly different. What action do you propose?

10

Information requirements of strategic decisions

Overview

Strategic decisions are of critical importance to the organization and hence the best possible information should be supplied to the makers of these decisions. A strategic decision will have a potentially significant impact on the success of the existing business strategy. This business strategy must be established and evaluated in the context of the external environment and consequently strategic management accounting needs a similar external focus which is not present in most traditional management accounting systems.

Traditional management accounting systems also have problems dealing with strategic decisions because they are usually designed to cope with routine, regular operational reporting issues which focus on subdivisions of the business. Unfortunately, strategic decisions tend to be unique, irregular, multi-functional and to make significant differences to the subsequent performances of the separate responsibility centres which they affect. A good strategic management accounting system has to be flexible enough to cope with these factors. It should also take into account the dynamic changes which can take place in the external environment, thus upsetting the comparison of the actual outcome to that originally forecast in the pre-decision evaluation.

Many strategic decisions involve expenditure on marketing activities which are designed to have a long economic life, such as the development of a new brand. Strategic management accounting must differentiate its treatment between this long-term development expenditure and the short-term maintenance type activities. This requires the appropriate use of long-term cash flow based decision techniques rather then relying on accounting presentations. Similar problems can be experienced in other areas of the business, such as evaluating and controlling research and development.

Much of the material for this chapter is taken from the forthcoming book *Strategic Management Accounting* by K Ward, to be published by Butterworth-Heinemann.

Introduction

In the previous chapters of Part Three we have considered a variety of techniques for dealing with a wide range of different types of financial decisions. However, a certain category of business decisions can be regarded as being more important than any others. Strategic decisions, which can have significant impacts on the overall success of the existing business strategy, should be regarded as of critical importance to the organization. As a consequence, the business should ensure that the best available relevant information is provided to the strategic decision-makers. However, such a laudable aim can have severe implications for the management accounting information which is required within the business. In this chapter we attempt to distinguish these particular information aspects of those strategic decisions which have financial impacts.

An initial step in this process is to define what is meant by a 'strategic decision' and how this type of decision is different to the multitude of other business decisions which are regularly taken by managers. The simplest and most logical definition of a strategic decision is, as stated above, any decision which has a significant impact on the success of the existing business strategy, but even this definition requires further clarification. What is meant by 'business strategy' is nowadays the subject of very many long and very complicated textbooks; we will use a relatively simple working definition of business strategy and the even more important concept of strategic management. Having established this, the decisions affecting this business strategy can be considered in more detail, and the common characteristics, if there are any, brought together.

In fact, as will be seen later, the tremendously wide range of potential strategic decisions raises a number of significant problems for most traditionally orientated management accounting systems. These problems are considered and related to particular examples of financially orientated strategic decisions, before considering potential solutions through examining a major strategic decision for a company.

This case study involves the launch of a major new product and these kind of marketing issues form a large proportion of strategic decisions for many companies. Consequently, the key issues involved in evaluating marketing investment issues are considered separately. The strategic decisions affecting the other major functional areas of the business are also considered in this chapter.

Strategic management

Strategic management can be regarded as an integrated management approach which draws together all the individual elements involved in planning, implementing and controlling a business strategy. A fundamental aspect of any business strategy is the development of a series of specific actions which will serve to bridge the gap between where the business is today and where its goals and objectives state that it wants to be in the future. Setting goals and objectives for the organization is a pre-requisite of business planning, as discussed in Chapter 8. However, these goals and objectives must be established in the context of the external business environment in which the company is currently operating and that it expects to encounter during the time-scale of the strategic plan.

This immediately highlights that the supporting financial analysis must cover the key aspects of this external environment as well as including the internal financial interrelationships within the business. Most traditional management accounting systems focus almost exclusively on the internal operations of the organization; strategic management accounting requires a much greater emphasis on understanding and evaluating factors external to the organization.

The business strategy will normally also have a reasonably long time-scale for the fulfilment of the more generally expressed goals of the organization. This does not mean that all strategic decisions are long-term in their impact. Indeed, the success of the launch of any new business strategy should be established as quickly as possible by setting up short-term financial indicators which can be readily monitored. This early financial control process should avoid continuing for longer than necessary with a strategy which is an obvious failure. Although the strategy has long-term implications, the business will also need to make short-term financial decisions to adjust, correct or fundamentally change the strategy as it unfolds. Inevitably strategic decisions are a combination of both short-term and long-term decisions, and one of the most difficult aspects of many strategic decisions can be balancing the short-term and long-term implications of the decision.

This also indicates that business strategy involves far more than developing a corporate plan as it is a continuous process of planning, implementing and controlling the business strategy. Hence the phrase 'strategic management' is used to indicate a management style which should be adopted by the company. Unless this is achieved, managers can become overly focused on the day-to-day problems and pressures of running the business. Hence their decisions tend to be guided by an excessive concentration on the short-term impacts. Every so often, possibly annually, these same managers are supposed to stand back from the business and to think 'strategically'. In other words it is time to prepare another strategic plan. So they forget about running the business for a while, during which time they consider the long-term prospects for the business and evaluate what is happening in the external environment. Not surprisingly the output of this kind of strategic planning process is often a long, noble sounding document which is rapidly filed by all operating managers in the bottom right drawer of their desks or filing cabinets. The next time it sees the light of day is when it is, once again, time to change into a strategic planning role.

Unfortunately, this problem is often particularly true for financial managers within the organization. Management accountants in many businesses still spend a very high proportion of their time producing historic reports explaining what has already happened or providing financial inputs to regular short-term operational decisions with almost no strategic significance whatsoever. Occasionally, when there is some spare time available, they may attempt to update the strategic plan and consider whether the base assumptions regarding the external environment, competitor reactions, etc., are still valid. The concept of strategic management as a continuous process of planning, implementing and controlling a business strategy is designed to counter this danger of separating strategic or business planning from the day-to-day operation of the company. If it is to be of real value to the business, the strategy must be considered at all major decisions and the plan updated automatically as part of the normal management accounting process.

For many large organizations it is also important that business strategies are developed at the appropriate levels in the organization. Thus an overall corporate strategy is needed for the business in total with separate but linked competitive strategies for each sub-division of the business which is competing in different markets with different products. This is discussed in more detail early in Chapter 11, and the hierarchy of strategies and objectives is illustrated in Figure 11.2.

In Chapter 1 we distinguished management accounting from the other areas of involvement of financial managers, which were defined as financial accounting and financial management or corporate finance. One of the differences which was highlighted was that management accounting is not involved with externally reporting financial information, whereas financial accounting's primary role is to do this, and financial management is often required to provide lending or investing financial institutions with supporting financial information. It is true that the role of management accounting is concentrated on providing supporting information to internal decision-makers, but it is important that this is not taken to mean that management accountants are not interested in, or can ignore, the wishes of key external influences on the company. Nowhere is this more clearly illustrated than in the area of strategic decisions.

When formulating a business strategy, senior managers will be trying to balance the requirements and desires of a wide range of key stakeholders. One obvious important group of stakeholders are the owners (in most organizations, the shareholders) of the business but, as is indicated in Figure 10.1, there are other parties with a valid claim to be considered when business strategy is being selected. The relative power of each group is very important and this may change significantly over time or because of the particular strategic issue which is dominant at any particular time. For example, if the business strategy involves a reduction in the product range being produced and sold or in the location of major plants etc., the employees are likely to be a very interested and influential group of stakeholders.

Alternatively, if the strategy is to go for a period of rapid expansion, the employees may be very happy, but the prospective providers of the financing of this growth (i.e. either shareholders or lenders such as banks) will now become very interested in the future prospects for the business. Clearly managers should be taking account of the interests of all these stakeholders when they are deciding on the long-term strategy of the business and in the continuous implementation and updating of that strategy. Management accounting has a substantial role to play in this process by providing the relevant decision support information. In this context, 'relevant' has to include information on the needs and wishes of the appropriate key groups of stakeholders who are likely to be affected by each strategic decision. Consequently, the strategic role of management accounting requires a very good understanding of the external and internal potential impact of forthcoming decisions, and of the reactions of affected parties.

In many cases these stakeholders' requirements are in conflict with each other

Figure 10.1 *Stakeholders impacting on business strategies*

and managers have to decide which is the most appropriate choice to make in the overall best interests of the business and all the stakeholders. As has already been discussed, it is ideal if goal congruence can be achieved whereby everybody is aiming to achieve the same set of objectives. This is particularly important for the managers themselves, who are of course one important group of stakeholders. A common area for causing problems between managers and shareholders can be in the relative risk profile of the selected business strategy. Throughout the book we have regularly referred to the need for a positive correlation between risk and the expected financial return for any potential investment. However, this basic theory depends on the assumption that all stakeholders demand the same level of increased return for accepting an identical increase in risk. In practice the perceived change in risk may not be the same to each interested group and consequently different incremental returns may be demanded.

Most shareholders in companies will have spread their investment risk across several companies by having a well-spread portfolio of investments. Consequently if any single company performs badly, or even goes out of business, the loss is reduced as a proportion of their total investment base. Thus these well diversified shareholders may be quite happy for an individual company to engage in a high risk business strategy, since if it succeeds they will receive a good financial return through an increasing share price or rising stream of dividends. However, other groups of stakeholders, such as managers and other employees, will find it much more difficult to diversify their risks and consequently the impact of business failure

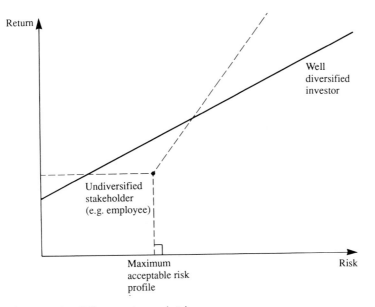

Figure 10.2   *Different views of risk*

will be much greater. Also the potential benefit to these stakeholders accruing from the success of any high risk strategy may be much smaller, and so they have a greater downside risk but with lower upside potential. This conflicting view of risk and return can be considered diagrammatically as shown in Figure 10.2.

When evaluating strategic decisions, the most important stakeholders must be considered and their relative risk/return profile taken into account. Very few traditional management accounting systems take these types of factors into account.

Problems of traditional management accounting systems

There are several problems associated with strategic decisions and the design of traditional management accounting systems. By definition, a strategic decision is likely to have a significant impact on the success of the existing business strategy. The evaluation of this forthcoming decision should logically, therefore, be carried out in the context of the existing business strategy and its original or updated objectives. This requires a linkage in the accounting information system between the objectives and the strategies used to achieve them.

Most accounting systems emphasize the size or value of decisions as the criterion which signals the need for most financial evaluation, rather than using the strategic importance of the decision. Also the accounting system often measures and reflects the effect of a strategic change rather than evaluating the cause of the change. For example, an apparently minor reduction in the research and development budget could lead to a delay in the development of a major new product. In most accounting systems this would only be highlighted when the actual sales levels were running significantly below those in the strategic plan, due to the late launch of the new product. By this time it is very difficult and normally very expensive to correct the strategic error. However, if the management accounting system was focused on key strategic issues, one of which would have been the launch of the new product, the proposed reduction in R & D expenditures would have been evaluated in terms of its potential impact on the business strategy.

Accounting systems should therefore consider the sensitivity of the overall plan to particular key decisions, and these very important decisions should be subjected to the greatest level of financial evaluation. In many cases the very large value decisions do not have the greatest strategic impact or range of potential outcomes. Another major related problem of most management accounting systems is that they are designed to cope well with regular reporting requirements which are of most value in supporting more routine, operational decisions. By their very nature strategic decisions tend to be 'one-off' type decisions and frequently deal with situations which the company has never faced before.

This increases the complexity of processing the relevant financial data as there may be unknown interactions and multiple alternatives which need to be evaluated. However, it also introduces an even more fundamental issue of how to collect this required financial data, given the non-repetitive nature of strategic decisions. If the management accounting system is too rigidly designed, it may be very difficult to gather financial data in the appropriate formats and within the necessary timescales to support the strategic decision-making process. It is important that the design of the information system takes account of the need to access the base data for a wide range of different types of decision, which must be evaluated using different elements of the costs and revenues collected and recorded automatically. This area is considered in more detail in Chapters 11 and 12.

Decisions regarding the introduction of new products or the abandonment of existing products should clearly be classified as having strategic relevance. Their evaluations also need very different types of financial information which would not normally be included in the regular, operationally biased financial reporting systems. In the case of a potential new product, the financial evaluation should include the incremental costs and sales revenues which would result from the new product and the evaluation should be done over the appropriate economic life of the product. Incremental costs and sales revenues should take account of any changes caused to the sales levels of existing products plus any variations to the general cost levels of the business, such as the need to increase sales and distribution resources. If the prospective decision involves stopping the production and sale of any particular area of activity, the relevant financial evaluation is also based on the changes in costs and revenues, but now the relevant costs are those that would be saved as a direct consequence of the decision. Clearly in neither case can the relevant costs be collected as an automatic part of any historic accounting system when the information needed relates to future costs and revenues which are specific to particular potential courses of action.

The overall impacts of strategic decisions tend to be long-term even if the decision can be implemented quickly, e.g. a decision to close down a particular product can be taken and implemented rapidly but the lost sales revenues will affect the results of all future accounting periods. This means that the long-term financial evaluation techniques discussed in Chapter 7 and 8 are appropriate and thus all the caveats discussed in these chapters should be borne in mind. However, a further complicating issue of strategic decisions is that they normally affect more than one area of the business. For example, a new product launch involves research and development, sales and marketing, operations, accounting and finance, information technology and even personnel if new employees are needed. In most companies a large part of the internal accounting system is designed on a functional basis due to the need to provide regular historic reports of expenditure by department, etc. Thus the need to collect data from a wide range of the functional areas within the business can, once again, complicate the provision of good financial support for major strategic decisions.

Not only is collecting the data difficult but the decision now crosses over several responsibility centres and hence will affect several managers. Naturally there is no problem with who actually takes the decision, as important strategic decisions are taken at the most senior levels of the company. However, if this decision has significant impacts in several areas of the business, it is important that the evaluation of performance is considered carefully. A strategic decision to close down a product line may be economically sensible but it significantly affects the ability of several managers across the company to achieve previously established and agreed targets. These lower level measures of performance should be modified in the light of the changed strategy which is now being implemented. This is a major area of weakness for many management accounting systems. In some cases no adjustment at all is made to the existing targets. In our example of the discontinued product, this would probably significantly demotivate the salesforce as their ability to achieve their sales revenue or contribution targets is greatly diminished. Alternatively, some companies would simply remove all the sales revenue for the discontinued line from the salesforce targets and use the revised totals as new targets. This is potentially equally dangerous because the salesforce should be able to re-allocate their resources to sell greater volumes of the remaining range of products; this effect should have been considered and included in the financial evaluation which led to the abandonment decision. Thus the basis of the decision should provide the input for the required changes to the evaluation system, but it must be remembered that these represent best *estimates* of the outcome of the decision.

The implementation of the decision still needs to be monitored and controlled and this is also more complicated for strategic decisions than for more regular operational decisions. The success of the strategic decision is frequently dependent on the external environment and any unexpected changes in this environment can result in major changes to the actual outcome of the strategic decision. Evaluating the success of past decisions against a set of moving targets can be extremely misleading unless the management accounting system is capable of adjusting for the changes in the external environment. This would mean that a revised expected outcome could be established and the actual results could be compared to this much more relevant benchmark. However, in Chapter 1 the primary value of financial monitoring systems was highlighted as being as a learning process which enables better decisions to be made in the future. This area is discussed in more detail in Chapter 11. The benefits of learning from previous decisions are easy to see in the case of regular monthly monitoring of an on-going production process but, as already indicated, most strategic decisions are unique and therefore will not be repeated. The value of a monitoring and evaluation process is consequently not generated by the specific nature of the decision in question, but must be seen in the context of improving future similar important questions. Obviously once the business has closed down a particular division it cannot close it down again but it can learn from the subsequent evaluation of such a decision. Issues regarding the provision and analysis of the financial information used and the accuracy of the financial evaluation of the impact of the closure decision can be highlighted through a monitoring process, as well as considering how well the consultation and decision process worked. Thus the monitoring system for strategic decisions should be designed to improve the future strategic decision-making process, rather than simply to pass judgment on the particular decision which is being monitored. The emphasis must be on 'why' the decision went well or badly, rather than concentrating on the actual outcome and using the monitoring system to appor- tion blame.

Case study

A recent practical example may make these issues much clearer. For confidentiality reasons the identity of the company and the actual product concerned cannot be revealed but this should not affect the points which are being illustrated. The business concerned was a major food products division of a large consumer goods multinational. One of its product ranges was in the fast growing convenience cook-in sauce market but major competitors has recently entered the market with a much improved quality product, presented very well in clear glass jars which emphasized the quality of the product.

Not surprisingly these competitors were charging a premium price for their products but, during the launch periods, these prices were being heavily supported by consumer promotions. Also very heavy media (mainly television) advertising for the new brands was taking place and initial market research results indicated that the new products were selling very well with good consumer reaction and strong repurchasing after the initial trial. The case study company was very keen to take a share in this new segment of the market which was forecast to be the dominant element of the whole convenience sauce market in a few years time; indeed the research department had already been working on a similar high quality range of products. However, the business had no expertise in producing such a range of cooked products in glass jars and did not, at that time, possess either the necessary technology or the production facilities.

It was decided that the opportunity to launch a suitable range of new products should be properly evaluated before a decision was taken. At this stage it is important to place such a potential decision in the context of the existing divisional and group strategies, so that the criteria on which the financial evaluation was to be judged can be understood. The group was quite large (market capitalization of over £1 billion) and had manufacturing and marketing businesses around the world. However, relative to its major global competitors it was not that big and its shares were very widely held with no-one controlling a large block of voting power. Also some of its main brands, which were genuinely household names, were now quite mature products with relatively limited future growth potential. As a consequence the group was highly profitable and generated very good cash flow from these mature brands. The particular division fitted this picture of the group very neatly with a range of strong food brands, most of which were now in mature slow growth markets.

The group was very keen to identify new higher growth related markets where its proven levels of expertise should give it a relative competitive advantage. At the same time it was concerned to maintain and, indeed, grow profitability as it was probable that any short-term downturn in profit would have caused a reduction in the share price and have left it open to a potential take-over bid. There had been several rumours circulating in the stock-market regarding the possibility of a corporate raider launching a take-over bid in order to split the group up and sell off the individual branded businesses.

The divisional managers were therefore aware that growth was a key objective but that this growth must not place in jeopardy their profit generating capability in the short term while the new product was developing its share of the market. In the recent past most of the investments made by the business had either been in extensions to existing ranges of products or in efficiency improvements to the existing manufacturing facilities, both of which increased profitability and produced a positive cash flow very quickly. Hence new investments were justified using the payback criterion discussed in Chapter 7 and by evaluating the impact on the division's return on investment in the third year of the investment. These criteria are quite common for mature, stable companies, but they do not provide a good guide for assessing the financial return from a long-term growth product being launched into a very competitive market.

The financial managers had to devise new financial evaluation criteria and this was done while the base data were being compiled. As this was a new product in a very new and fast growing sector of the market, the business could not rely on any historic data extracted from its core businesses. Detailed forecasts of all sales revenues and costs had to be developed. This required the involvement of managers from all areas of the business and it necessitated them re-allocating resources away from previously planned projects – no business has an unlimited supply of resources and all decisions involve some form of priority setting and resource allocation choice.

In some areas the costs could be predicted with a high degree of accuracy due to the existing expertise within the business or work already done on the project (such as in the area of raw material formulations where R & D had already carried out a range of development trials). However, the potential sales revenues of the new products were more difficult to predict with any degree of accuracy as they depended upon the rate of growth of this segment of the market together with the overall growth of the market and the relative market share achieved by the new product launched by the division. The marketing department developed a model to predict the total market size and the rate of growth of this new segment. Relative market share was developed using both a top-down approach and a bottom-up forecast. In other words, share was predicted by assessing the potential to gain consumers by using market research and assessing the expected impact of the marketing activities which were planned. Also the sales potential was assessed by the salesforce by considering the distribution which could be obtained for the new product with key multiple retailers and the rate of sale which could be achieved through these outlets.

These forecasts were not in reality independent because, as is shown in Figure 10.3, the potential sales levels for such a product are a function of the product awareness and propensity to consume created by the launch advertising and promotions and the distribution effectiveness achieved in the retailers which enables willing purchasers to sample the product. The remaining key elements are the combination of price and quality which will determine the level of repurchase, which must be high if the launch expenditure for this type of product is to be financially worthwhile. Repurchase levels are driven by the proportion of trialists who buy again and the frequency with which they subsequently use the product.

The complexity of these relationships should now be clearly apparent, as should the infinite possibilities for achieving any desired level of market share. The financial evaluation really needed to know what possible combination of attributes was most cost effective. For example was it more beneficial to achieve a 20 per cent level of awareness with a rate of distribution of 80 per cent or the other way around; assuming that each alternative required the same investment. Indeed the evaluation should have been based on making the optimal investment in marketing and this is discussed in more detail later in the chapter. In practice for a company with a strong history of launching and developing branded products in this type of market, it should have been possible to develop a logical model which predicted the most important interrelationships among the key variables

However, not all the variables were internally controlled because the response of competitors to the threat of such a new product launch could have taken various forms. They could have virtually ignored the new product because the rapid growth of the markets enabled them to expand their own sales as quickly as they needed

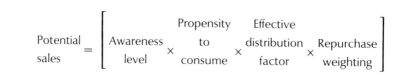

Figure 10.3 *Potential sales levels*

to. Alternatively, they could have responded aggressively by increasing the level of their marketing activity to reduce the effectiveness of our division's own level of launch activity (there is a well developed marketing concept which relates effectiveness to the 'share of voice' generated by any particular product). A third reaction could have been to reduce their selling prices either to attract more consumers or to give retailers a better profit margin so as to discourage them from stocking the newer product. Once again the financial evaluation needed to incorporate the estimated impact of the most likely response from competitors. As the range of possibilities is so great the evaluation should highlight the most critical items and this can be done by using sensitivity analysis techniques. All that is involved with these techniques is simply varying each significant variable by a small amount (say ± 10 per cent) and monitoring the potential impact of the change on the overall financial return from the project.

So far the evaluation has concentrated on forecasting sales revenue levels, but it is actually changes in profit and cash flows which are relevant to justifying the launch of a new product. Some costs were quite easy to predict and were under the control of the business, but others were less easy. In this case the problem caused by the form of packaging was quite difficult because this would have required a considerable capital investment in new plant and machinery and such an investment would have been high risk. If the new product had not succeeded, the division would have wasted its investment as it had no other use for this relatively specialized equipment. Even if the product was successful, the on-going rate of sales was very uncertain, and so, how large did the new plant need to be to cope with the output required? An alternative solution was to defer the installation of the production plant until the product had been successfully launched and the required eventual output could be estimated more accurately, thus reducing the risk of wasting a large capital injection into fixed assets. This could be achieved if the business used an external contract packer who already had expertise in this type of packaging presentation.

However, this external contractor would demand a profit margin over its costs and there would also be increased costs incurred in doubling handling the products, extra transportation and quality control involvement so as to ensure that the initial image of the new products did not suffer. In the actual case these additional costs meant that no profits would be achieved from sales made during the external contract packing phase of the project. Once the division had installed its own production plant (planned for the third year of operation) the projected profit margins improved substantially and the project started to look attractive.

The business was thus able to collect all the information required by involving a wide range of managers from all areas of the division but the financial managers needed to select the most appropriate method of evaluation. Given that this was a long-term investment project which was expected to grow for a number of years after launch, they decided to use the most powerful long-term financial decision technique, discounted cash flow. Unfortunately the impact of the contract packing in the early years distorted the financial evaluation and made the overall project seem relatively unattractive in the short term. However, the extra costs of the contract packing were incurred as a way of reducing the risk involved in committing to a very high level of investment in fixed assets before the success of the product was guaranteed. Therefore this part of the project expenditure could be evaluated separately based on reducing the risk and deferring the capital expenditure: effectively the net extra cost is being paid as an insurance premium and should be regarded as such.

Once the insurance element has been separately justified the project can be evaluated as if the in-house plant was operational at the start of the project and the higher margin was therefore achieved. This made the project look more attractive financially, but more importantly it enabled the managers to focus on each decision separately rather than being confused by looking at the overall effect of the total project. As stated, a model of the key variables needed to be developed and this was done. The results of this model indicated that the most significant impact on the financial evaluation was generated by changing the rate of growth forecast for the segment of the market.

This sensitivity analysis result showed the key risk of the project because there was little that the division could do to influence this parameter. If the expected growth in the market was not realized then the investment was not financially justifiable. However, this reinforced the value of deferring the major capital investment in new plant and machinery by using outside contract packers. It also emphasized the need to set up a system for monitoring, as early as practical, the growth in the sector and any indication that this rate of growth was declining or that the market would not ultimately achieve the projected sales levels. If the main investment could be deferred until the risk of the market not achieving adequate size was substantially reduced, then the overall risk of the project was considerably reduced.

As stated earlier in the chapter, strategic decisions require a combination of inputs, analysis and monitoring techniques. The important role of the management accountant should be clear if the correct decisions are to be taken, using the relevant supporting financial information.

Marketing investment decisions

The above case study involved the development and launch of a major new product for the business and this project would clearly involve a high degree of expenditure on marketing in order to create awareness and to build brand loyalty. The financial return for this type of marketing investment will be received over many years through the higher sales revenues generated by the successful brand. Consequently the financial evaluation of such long-term marketing activities must be carried out over the economic life of the asset, as would be the case with other more tangible investment projects. So far we have deliberately used the terms 'investment' and 'asset' in the contexts of marketing acitivities to highlight that this is how such expenditure should be regarded.

Clearly not all marketing expenditure can be viewed as a long-term investment and the total expenditure must be classified into development and maintenance activities. Companies are quite capable of doing this split for expenditure on tangible assets. Maintenance costs are written off in that period's profit and loss account, while development expenditure is treated as a capital improvement and its cost is spread over the remaining life of the asset. If strategic decisions are to be properly evaluated marketing expenditure should be similarly split so that activities with longer-term benefits are appropriately matched with these benefits. One of the major strengths of using discounted cash flow analysis is that this technique automatically achieves this by including, at the appropriate value, all the cash flows which are relevant to the decision. Hence arbitrary accounting procedures, such as decisions to write-off all marketing expenditure immediately, do not distort the decision process if it is soundly based on discounted cash flows.

For most companies, the increasingly competitive environment makes control of marketing activities a vital area for the continued success of the business. Consequently, marketing investments should be treated like any other investment and be rigorously financially justified. This requires forecast of incremental cash flows which result from the marketing expenditure and these must be considered over the life of the investment. Instituting this discipline into the justification of marketing decisions can also help by forcing managers to consider the period over which particular activities will continue to generate increased sales levels. These forecasts of economic lives can be evaluated in the context of the type of marketing expenditure and the stage of development of the product concerned. The concept of the product life-cycle has been well developed for many years and, as illustrated in Figure 10.4, shows how the sales of a product develop over time. This life-cycle can be broken into various phases as shown. These different stages of development are very useful in strategic planning because the strategy of the business will need to be modified to fit each stage. Also the probable size and time-scale of the benefits

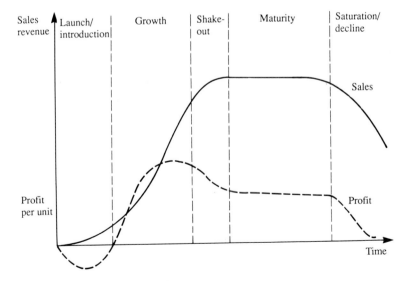

Figure 10.4 *Product life-cycles*

of any specific marketing initiative will change as the product moves through its life-cycle. For example, it may be easier to increase market share significantly while the market is growing rapidly because competitors may be growing very quickly anyway and they may be fully utilizing their productive capacity. Attempting to gain the same relative increase in market share in a very mature market is likely to result in a fierce competitive reaction. If the market is no longer expanding, any market share gains must be balanced by a competitor's losses in sales volumes and these will normally be strongly resisted through price cutting, or increased marketing support. Indeed it is this competitive pressure caused by over-capacity which causes the normally sharp decline in the profit per unit sold during the shake-out phase at the end of the growth period.

Other types of strategic decision

It is also important that the managers of the business modify the way in which they try to control the business financially in each stage of development. This is considered in more detail in Chapters 11 and 12, but here we will concentrate on the most common types of strategic decisions which are encountered at each stage of development.

The launch or introduction stage of the product life-cycle is obviously primarily concerned with developing, testing and successfully launching a new product into the market. Therefore the financial evaluations need to take into account the prospective long-term financial returns from this type of strategic decision. This requires a great degree of long-range forecasting for many new products and if the products are particularly innovatory and previously untried it may be very difficult to obtain a meaningful future sales forecast. In some cases therefore, there is no point in trying to develop a full discounted cash flow forecast as a detailed control mechanism, even though an approximate evaluation needs to be carried out to justify the initial commitment of resources.

An example may make this clearer. Another large multinational with interests in the food industry was considering the sales potential for a new type of artificial meat product utilizing a similar technology to that employed in nylon spinning. The initial research expenditure was required to develop the technology to a point where a good quality meat substitute was produced. This work was to be attempted before it would be possible to decide on how this new concept should be launched into the market, e.g. as cold meats, cooked meats, canned pie fillings, etc. Consequently it was very difficult, prior to any initial research work, to produce a detailed long-term cash flow forecast incorporating future sales revenues and cost estimates for the as yet unknown products. Indeed, to attempt to do so would have introduced a very spurious degree of accuracy into any sophisticated discounted cash flow analysis. It was, however, possible to evaluate the potential benefits of the project by assessing the total processed meat products market which was currently available and computing the financial return which could be achieved by taking a very small share of this market, such as could be achieved by developing a single successful product.

This return was more than adequate to justify the initial research into product development but could not be used to monitor the success of the project, as it was far too vague and distant. The project was controlled and monitored by establishing physical development milestones (i.e. specific achievements) which had to be achieved before the next phase of development funding was released. In other words, if the project was progressing satisfactorily additional funding was made available, but if no progress was being achieved the whole project was to be fundamentally reviewed. This financial control process is based upon the logic that the business can only exercise control before funds are committed to the project. It is at this stage that managers can genuinely exercise their discretion over whether to release additional funds to go on to the next stage of the project, and most research projects need to be controlled on this type of phased basis. If this is not done for a major project and all the funding is regarded as committed immediately, the business has completely lost effective financial control of the project. It could find that the managers running the project return five years later to say that they have now spent the £10 million which they were allocated but, unfortunately, the project has not worked! Surprisingly and worryingly, many companies still effectively use this type of control system by using a comparison of actual expenditure against budgeted expenditure as their only financial control mechanism. In other words, as long as the managers did not spend more than their £10 million budget, it does not appear to matter whether they actually achieved anything.

Once the product has been more specifically defined so that its target market and position within that market are known, it becomes practical to develop a much more detailed long-term cash flow forecast. Indeed it can be very strongly argued that, if this is still not possible, the product is probably not clearly enough specified to be worth the investment of further large amounts of money. This phase of investment tends to involve large expenditures on tangible fixed assets, such as plant and machinery, and large sums may need to be tied up in working capital, i.e. as stocks of raw materials and finished goods and as outstanding balances due from customers. However, there are also likely to be sizable expenditures needed for marketing so as to create awareness and to develop a brand image, etc. All of these investments must be financially evaluated prior to their commitment and the obvious financial technique is, as previously discussed, discounted cash flow evaluation. During this growth phase one critical area for financial monitoring is the rate of growth of the market as this was one essential element in the original justification. Part of the marketing expenditure should be directed to making the overall market grow, while most of the remainder should be attempting to increase the market share of the particular product range. As far as possible these marketing activities should be evaluated separately as it may be necessary to consider modifying expenditure levels as the life-cycle develops. It is important to understand whether it is the overall rate of market growth which is diverging from expectations or whether the expected level of market share is not being achieved. Clearly any corrective action which can be taken will differ considerably depending upon the specific cause.

Inevitably the rate of market growth will slow down as the market reaches maturity. It is vitally important that the business is able to predict this change to a stable mature product as soon as possible, and this should be highlighted by the financial monitoring system. This change to a mature product requires a fundamental alteration in the strategy of the business with regard to this particular product. No longer should the business be seeking to justify new large-scale investments in increasing output levels to cope with regularly increasing customer demand. Also the marketing strategy should change dramatically. Expenditure designed to make the market grow is no longer a sound financial investment and, as argued above, in a mature, stable market it is much more difficult to justify financially marketing investments designed to increase market share at the direct expense of competitor's existing sales volumes. Consequently, marketing expenditure should now primarily be targeted at maintaining the product's existing market share. These types of marketing activity clearly cannot be regarded as development investments as they have a short-term focus and impact.

At this stage of development the business strategy is now concentrated on producing a positive cash flow so as to recover the substantial previous investments made in developing, launching and building the existing product. Hence most imvestment decisions will now be designed to improve the efficiency of operations, e.g. cost reduction strategies, etc., rather than trying to grow the sales of this product. Of course, the business may decide to use the strong cash flow being produced by this mature product by investing in development or growth of other products at earlier stages in their life-cycles.

For a mature stable product the financial control system can concentrate on shorter-term financial results because there is not such an emphasis on investment for the future. Thus return on investment type measures can now be used, although some of the caveats referred to earlier in the book (particularly Chapter 8) should be remembered.

Eventually the product will move out of the stability in sales which is the hallmark of the maturity phase and a downward trend will become apparent. This is caused by the market becoming saturated or the product being replaced by a newer, more improved way of satisfying customer needs. Sales volumes and profits per unit both tend to decline rapidly during this final phase which ends with the death of the product. Clearly the business strategy should now be to minimize any investment in the product and even maintenance type activities need to be carefully justified financially. This includes marketing maintenance, as it may no longer be worthwhile to retain the previous high market share which was a critical success factor during the mature, cash producing stage. It also includes maintenance of plant and machinery and a key area now becomes the question of whether to reinvest the depreciation being charged each year on existing equipment. During the earlier phases it would normally have been an automatic assumption that the business would, at least, reinvest so as to maintain the existing productive capacity of the product. However, once it becomes certain that the product is in a long-term decline phase, this is no longer unquestioned and the financial return from reinvesting must be evaluated. Indeed, a key financial control parameter at this stage is to concentrate on the short-term cash flows of the product because the critical strategic decision is to choose when to stop producing the product altogether. This should be done as soon as the net cash flows turn negative and appear likely to stay that way: there is no point in investing in a dying product!

These different phases of development do therefore indicate the need for significantly different systems of financial evaluation and control, which should be tailored to match the critical strategic decisions facing the business at each stage. These issues of financial control are discussed in more detail in Part Four, but some debate exists about the relevance of using product life-cycles in this way. The counter arguments are based on the premise that not all products follow a life-cycle. This premise is caused by a misunderstanding of the difference between products and brands: it is a perfectly valid statement that all products follow a life-cycle but this is not necessarily true for brands. A brand can, after all, be transferred from a declining product to the new replacement product which may be entering its growth phase. This distinction between products and brands is considered in more depth in Chapter 13.

Questions

1 Why do traditional management accounting systems have problems coping with many types of strategic decision?

2 'Investment decisions in intangible assets are more difficult to evaluate using management accounting techniques.' Discuss.

3 Business strategies change over time. What impact should this have on the management accounting system used in the company?

4 'Management accounting is essentially internally focused, while strategic decisions are externally orientated.' Is this statement valid, and how can the apparent conflict be resolved?

Part Four

Control

11

The requirements of financial control systems

Overview

As a major role of management is taking decisions, financial control systems must be designed to act as decision support systems and the quality of these decisions can be improved by good financial information. Thus their role is much more than merely explaining the financial impact of past events and they should be fully integrated into the analysis, planning and control process advocated throughout this book. The historic explanatory process is still important as analysing and learning from the past can improve managers' ability to anticipate and hence control the future.

Financial information systems can also play an important behavioural role within a business both by communicating the overall financial plan objectives and indicating how specific managerial objectives are linked into these larger corporate goals. Thus such a system has a powerful motivational potential, which may turn out to be either positive or negative. If the individual managerial objectives are well defined and are seen to help to achieve the overall plan, managers should be positively motivated and the regular monitoring process should assist this by ensuring that all the parts of the business are still moving towards the agreed targets. Ensuring that all these sub-objectives are in line with the overall corporate objectives is not easy, but achieving and maintaining this goal congruence is a key role for a good financial control system. If managers are judged against performance standards over which they have no effective control or which are not, in reality, in line with the overall corporate objectives, there is a real danger of significantly demotivating managers. The financial control system must also, therefore, distinguish between evaluating economic decisions which affect the financial performance of the business and evaluating managerial performance, which should be based on those areas where the manager can genuinely exercise some degree of control.

Further, the control system has to be able to separate efficiency and effectiveness measures and to report each appropriately. Efficiency measures are most relevant where there is a direct measurable relationship between the level of inputs and the level of outputs expected, such as is the case in many engineering relationships. As a result, the relative efficiency of the performance in this area can be assessed by comparing the actual level of output with that expected under the predictable relationship. However, although the efficiency of any particular area may be high, this type of financial evaluation says nothing about the relevance of these efficiently produced outputs to the specific objectives of the business. Hence a measure of the effectiveness of the business performance is also needed which should indicate how well the objectives are being achieved and whether any changes are needed in the future to bring the business back into line with its financial plans.

A good way of providing this type of relevant financial information, particularly in a large company, is to break the business down into smaller responsibility centres. Each responsibility centre is set specific objectives and an appropriate method of financial evaluation is devised to reflect the relative financial independence of this area of the business. Breaking the business down and providing tailored financial information to each area dramatically increases the required output from any financial control system. Fortunately this workload has been reduced by the advent of more and more sophisticated computer systems, which have drastically altered the cost of providing financial decision support, so that now the opportunity cost of not having the information can outweigh the cost of supplying it.

Supplying this tailored financial information requires a clear understanding of when it is needed and how the information, as opposed to the raw data, should be presented and to whom. Designing financial information systems can be easily summarized, therefore, as supplying the right information to the right people at the right time. As with most things, saying it is much easier than doing it in practice!

Introduction

The main objective of this part of the book is to explain and then to illustrate the key requirements of a financial control system as it should be designed, implemented and operated within the overall management accounting process. Financial control must be exercised in the context of our analysis, planning and control model, as illustrated in Figure 11.1, if it is to assist in achieving the corporate goals and objectives. In the initial discussion on financial planning in Chapter 1 it was stated that the only certainty in any financial plan or budget is that the outcome will differ from that planned. The assumptions made in the plan may be incorrect regarding either the external environment or in the internal results which will be achieved upon implementation of the plan. A control system is necessary to enable the business to respond to these unexpected events by making decisions which either put the business back on track to achieve its original objectives or direct it towards appropriately redefined objectives if those originally conceived at the planning stage have now become irrelevant.

The planning process itself has major advantages for a business but it cannot ensure that its goals and objectives are achieved without a well designed monitoring and action based financial control system. Through the development of a financial plan, as discussed in Part Three, the business should have become aware of the financial implications of its operating plans, and consciously accepted these outcomes; if any of the forecast financial results were unacceptable, the plan should have been modified until an acceptable compromise was achieved. For example,

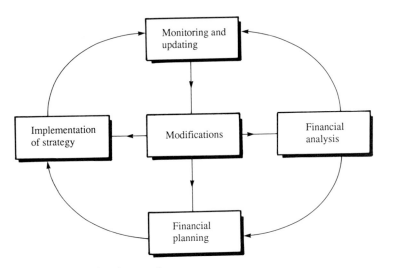

Figure 11.1   *Role of control process*

the financial plan should highlight the financial requirements of the proposed strategy so that the business can ensure that adequate funding is available not only to meet the base plan but also to meet any contingencies which may occur during the implementation of the plan. This is done by using the sensitivity analysis techniques discussed in Chapter 8, which reflect the implications of any forced changes in the plans due to different external circumstances. If this sensitivity analysis indicates that lack of suitable financing may be a constraint on its successful implementation, the plan should be modified to remove this potential constraint before the problem actually arises. The same is true for all the other alternative situations which are highlighted by the sensitivity analysis of the basic plan. The objective for the business is to produce a range of contingency plans, which can be quickly and effectively implemented as soon as the relevant set of circumstances are recognized.

Thus a monitoring system is obviously essential in order to enable these contingency plans to be initiated as required. This can be done by identifying key changes in the external environment from those originally forecast in the plan and prompting the right managers to make the corresponding changes to their future plans.

However, no business, no matter how sophisticated its planning and forecasting techniques, can foresee and evaluate every potential combination of possible external circumstances and changes in internal relationships which will occur during the planning period. Consequently, the financial control system must also be capable of identifying and analysing the impact of new and completely unexpected situations. It should aim to provide the best possible financial information to the managers who may need to modify the future objectives of the business in the light of these new circumstances. Indeed, this monitoring process should really be viewed as an integral part of the continuous function already described as financial analysis; our analysis, planning and control model emphasizes this continuous iterative nature of management accounting.

One key element of this integrated role of financial control is that the whole process must be regarded as one of learning from the past so as to make better decisions in the future. Financial control must not be used in a negative way simply to apportion blame for past mistakes, as this will have the wrong impact on the managers involved in the process, as is discussed in detail early in this chapter. A good system of monitoring and analysing the actual results compared to those expected in the financial plan can provide the necessary feedback which enables better plans to be prepared next time as well as allowing the current plans to be modified appropriately. This emphasis on the financial control system as a learning process also indicates that resources should not be unnecessarily wasted on a very detailed analysis and explanation of an extraordinary non-recurring event. Learning from the past is possible only if similar events are likely to reoccur in the future.

However, if a major function of financial control is to assist in the achievement of goals and objectives of the business, the process must consist of much more than merely monitoring and analysing. Decisions may need to be taken which will change the business strategies and tactics being employed or even alter the previously established goals and objectives. Thus the financial control system must be designed as a decision support system and there is no point in producing vast quantities of financial information if it cannot be used in any of the decisions facing the business. By definition, decisions affect the future not the past, but most financial analysis relates only to the past. This reinforces the need to regard this historic financial analysis as a learning process to improve the ability of managers to predict what will happen in the future. Managers who can anticipate and predict future events are much more in control of their businesses than others, e.g. competitors, who merely react to what has just happened. The accuracy of this anticipation and prediction should be greatly improved if the financial control system is properly used to learn from similar happenings in the past.

This raises a further key element in designing a financial control system: decisions are taken by people, not organizations. It is therefore vital that the necessary control information is provided to the manager who can take any required decisions. The necessary information itself depends on the type of decision which can be taken by the manager and therefore the control system must be tailored so that the 'right' information is provided. This could be done, and unfortunately is in many management accounting systems, by providing all the available information that could be needed for any decision. The supporting logic seems to be that if this is done, there is no danger of the manager who actually needs a particular piece of information being without it: everybody receives all the available information!

As well as being a very expensive system to operate due to the sheer volumes of reporting involved, it is also a very inefficient system of financial control. All managers receive a great mass of financial reports, most of which have absolutely nothing to do with their areas of operation and responsibility. However, all of it needs to be perused, if not studied in depth, because buried within the irrelevant data may be something which is very important and requires their immediate attention. Not surprisingly, it may not get immediate, or even rapid, attention due to the time taken to find this critically relevant piece of financial analysis. In other words, to be of real value as a decision support system, the financial control process must supply the *right* information to the *right* managers at the *right* time, and each of these areas is considered is detail in the next chapter. Such a saturation style system of financial control is also inefficient and ineffective because the financial information needed by managers changes significantly depending upon the type of decision being considered, as discussed in Chapter 6. Thus, providing all managers with the same stereotyped financial analytical information may lead to some completely falsely justified decisions, which are actually against the best interests of the business.

Communication and motivation

As stated above, business decisions are a critical element in any financial control system and these business decisions are taken by managers, either individually or in groups, on behalf of the total organization. This can cause a potential problem throughout the financial planning and control process because the corporate goals and objectives are established for this total organization, and they are normally expressed in terms of specific *activities* which are to be carried out, whereas the financial control process can only be implemented by *people*. It is therefore essential that these overall business objectives are broken down into appropriate segments which can be directly applied to the functional and operational areas of the business, which are managed by these decision-makers who are responsible for and involved in the financial control process.

Thus, each area of the business should have its own clearly defined objectives and targets, which fit into the overall business goals and objectives. A hierarchical system of objectives and strategies is shown in Figure 11.2. These sub-objectives and their relationship to the total business plan must be clearly communicated to the relevant managers who will be held responsible for implementing this part of the plan. This does not mean just telling them, however specifically, what they have to do, but requires that senior management ensures that all levels of the organization understand what the overall plan is trying to achieve and where their particular role fits in. If all managers realize *why* what they have each been asked to do is important, there is normally a dramatic improvement in their motivation to achieve these individual objectives. Also, once this has been done, it is possible to design the financial control system so that they are held 'accountable' for the achievement of the key elements of the plan which are under their control.

It is critical that during this breaking down of the plan, there is a strong linkage between authority and accountability because it is tremendously demotivating for managers to be held accountable for something over which they can exercise no control. This means that the managers must be given the authority to make and implement decisions as necessary to achieve the particular objectives set for their

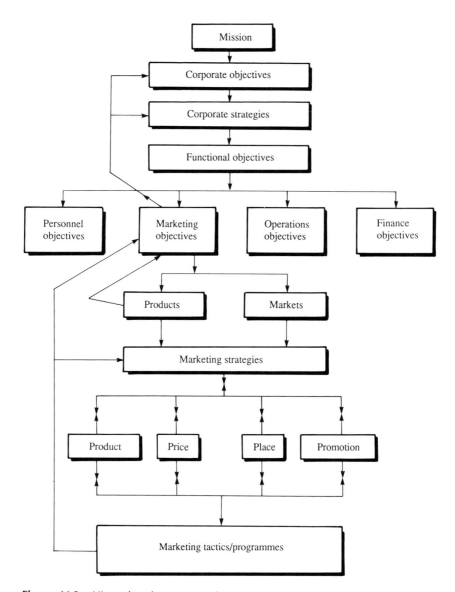

Figure 11.2   *Hierarchy of corporate objectives and strategies*

areas of the business. It also means that these managerial objectives should not include items which can arbitrarily change from those planned as a result of external circumstances and so make it impossible for the manager to achieve the planned objectives, without any fault on the manager's part.

An example of this could be in the manufacturing area of a particular business where an agreed objective was to keep the unit production costs down to £10 per unit. If the plan included a bought-in raw material component at a cost of £5 per unit out of the total of £10, but the actual cost for this raw material alone was £12, it is clearly impossible for the manager to achieve the original total cost objective of £10 no matter how efficiently the rest of the manufacturing area is run, as is shown in Figure 11.3.

To hold the production manager personally responsible for the excessive cost of the bought-in raw material if there is no degree of control over raw material prices within the manufacturing area is illogical and can dramatically reduce the benefit to the business of the whole financial control process. However, such a significant change in raw material prices does have a substantial economic impact of the financial results of the business and cannot therefore be ignored in the design of a financial control system.

What is needed is for the system to distinguish clearly between an economic measure of performance and an assessment of the particular managerial performance involved. In our manufacturing area example, the economic measure of performance must include the actual raw material prices which are being suffered by the business, and the financial control system will consequently show a financial performance which is considerably worse than was planned. The objective of the control system should be to highlight the problem as early and quickly as possible, and also to indicate ways in which the adverse impact can be minimized. In the same way, all

Unit cost breakdown

£s per unit

	Planned levels	Actual levels	Unit variance from plan
Bought-in raw material	5	12	(7)
Other raw materials	1	1	—
	6	13	(7)
Labour	2	1	1
Energy	2	4	(2)
Total production costs	10	18	(8)
Other overheads, etc.	10	13	(3)
Total cost	20	31	(11)
Contribution	10	(1)	(11)
Selling price	30	30	—

Figure 11.3 *Manufacturing cost example*

potential opportunities should be noted and ways of exploiting or enhancing their future benefit pointed out. Thus in most normal financial decisions, the business is trying to select the option which has the maximum economic benefit, even if the impact of this 'best' alternative is simply to make a smaller loss than under all the other choices.

Selecting this most attractive economic option requires a clear understanding of the overall corporate goals and objectives so that the 'best' fit with these overall objectives can be achieved. However, these economic decisions are made by individual managers, and therefore the ideal financial control system must motivate these individual managers to want to choose the alternative which is in the best interests of the overall business. Returning to our manufacturing area example may make this clearer. As the raw material cost of the product has increased dramatically, the manufacturing manager should be motivated to reduce all the other associated costs wherever practical and to use as little of the now expensive raw material as possible. In most cases, the business would expect the manager to be controlling manufacturing costs effectively anyway and there may be limited new savings available. However, there may be alternative ways of producing this particular product which utilize other raw materials or require more labour but, consequently, less of the original bought-in raw material. When the raw material was forecast to cost £5 per unit these alternatives may not have been cost effective, but with the sudden jump to the actual £12 cost, a different method of manufacturing may be economically beneficial.

Unless the managerial performance evaluation of this manufacturing manager is properly established, there may be no personal motivation to implement such a change and the business could miss out on a way of reducing the adverse financial impact of the cost increase. Suppose, for example, that the manager was judged principally on the usage of labour as being one area definitely under direct 'managerial control'. If the comparison of actual usage was made against budget or planned levels of usage, there is a strong personal disincentive for the manager to change the method of production to one which uses more labour but less raw material, even though such a change may be economically to the advantage of the business. An increase in labour usage against a fixed plan would make the manager's performance look worse unless this performance took into account the benefit of the real savings achieved for the business by using less raw material. Unfortunately, even including this does not automatically solve the problem, because against the original plan the cost of the raw material has increased significantly. The real economic saving is achieved against the updated actual opportunity cost of the raw material, not against the now obsolete much lower planned cost, as is shown in Figure 11.4. Companies should not expect their managers to behave altruistically, particularly in those cases where very great emphasis is placed by the company on the achievement of individual management targets. The company must consequently take great care that these managerial performance measures are in line with the overall objectives of the business and, if these overall objectives are modified due to changed circumstances, the managerial performance measures must also be reviewed and modified if necessary. This concept, which is known as goal congruence, is very difficult to achieve throughout any business, particularly

It is possible to halve the bought-in raw material needed by more careful processing, but this more than doubles the labour time required. As shown below this is not economically justified at the planned cost levels:

Cost per unit

	Plan production method	Alternative method
Bought-in raw material	5	2.50
Other raw materials	1	1.00
	6	3.50
Labour	2	5.00
Energy	2	2.00
Total production cost	£10	£10.50

However, when compared using the new actual cost for the bought-in raw material the situation is dramatically different:

	Plan production method	Alternative method
Actual raw material costs:		
Bought-in raw material	12	6
Other raw materials	1	1
	13	7
Labour	2	5
Energy	2	2
Total production cost	£17	£14

Note: If the lower labour actual costs shown in Figure 11.3 could be maintained, the saving would be even greater, and the actual total cost increase would be dramatically reduced. However, the manager may not want to change to this new alternative method, if the managerial performance evaluation is not changed accordingly.

Figure 11.4 *Alternative method of production*

where the external environment is very dynamic and subject to rapid and unpredictable changes. However, if managerial performance measures become dysfunctional (i.e. they are against the best interests of the overall group), the business will have very great difficulty in controlling and maintaining the motivation of the managers affected.

Quite frequently this problem can be exacerbated by an excessive concentration on individual performance targets with a consequently inadequate communication of the initial overall business objectives and the interrelationships linking the two sets of performance criteria. For example, in the sales area of a business, targets are often simply expressed in terms of sales revenue levels, which may relate to a specific growth rate over the previous year. This objective is normally linked to the overall business plan by a series of implicit assumptions, which may no longer be realistic as the planning period unfolds. Once again returning to our manufacturing example, the sales area may have been set a specific target in terms of the sales revenue of our particular product which they were expected to sell in the forthcoming year. The sales managers would have developed their specific plans to achieve this objective against the base assumptions of the £5 cost for bought-in raw materials. Thus forecast selling prices for the product and for competitive products would have been developed and predicted levels of customer demand established to see how the target could be achieved.

This simplistic sales revenue target may no longer, given the dramatic increase in the total cost of the product, be achievable or, even more importantly, the business may not want to achieve it, as shown in Figure 11.3. The sales managers may see competitors increasing their prices or reducing their promotional and salesforce activity as they change their strategy in line with the new cost levels being incurred. If our sales managers are strongly motivated only to achieve and exceed their individual sales revenue targets, they may push for increased sales activity levels on this product, while maintaining the originally planned level of unit selling prices. These original selling prices may now generate a loss, or an unacceptably low profit contribution, on every unit sold and, if sales levels are increased above those set in the business plan, the situation becomes increasingly financially disastrous for the overall business.

In economic terms, the business clearly needs to rethink its strategy for this product given the unexpected and dramatic change in the external environment. The new strategy will need to take into account the potential and actual reactions both of competitors and customers to the large cost increases being incurred in producing the product. A good financial control system should play a major role in providing and analysing this updated financial information so as to assist the decision-makers in selecting the optimum new strategy. However, some of these inputs will need to be provided by various managers within the functional areas of the business, including the sales and marketing area. These managers should obviously understand why such updated information is important but the sales managers may still be very demotivated if the result of their revised inputs is a substantial selling price increase which makes it impossible for them to achieve their previously set management performance target. (This would be caused by the necessary increase in selling prices leading to a reduction in the volume of customer demand so that the total value of sales revenues achieved was reduced; but at least these reduced sales levels would be made at an acceptable profit.)

One obvious cause of the problem in this example is the assumed planning linkage between increasing sales revenues (set as the target for sales managers) and an increase in the overall profitability of the business (a normal business objective). This linkage may have been true with the original planning assumptions but could be subsequently destroyed by the external real changes in the environment, which means that managers are being encouraged to act against the best interests of the business. As far as possible the company should avoid introducing the possibility of this type of conflict, but the financial control system must be designed so as to highlight these conflicts whenever they occur and the business must adjust the management target to remove them immediately.

This can also cause demotivation among managers because no-one likes to be judged against a target which is consistently being moved, particularly if the movements themselves seem arbitrary and uncoordinated. One helpful element in avoiding this problem is the previously mentioned good communication of both individual targets and overall business objectives, with the emphasis being placed on the linkage between the two. However, additional important elements are the way in which the business is broken down into areas for financial control purposes and the selection of the most appropriate critical success factor for each of these areas of the business as the main element of the managerial performance criteria. This means highlighting the key issues which the business wants managers to concentrate on out of all the things over which they exercise control. These key controllable issues should be used as the managerial performance measures for each area, and should ensure that managers are properly motivated to act both in teams and as individuals in the best interests of the overall business.

Efficiency versus effectiveness measures

It is critical that the business sets managers objectives which motivate individuals or groups of managers to try to achieve the overall corporate objectives and the simplest way of doing this may appear to have all managers judged by how well the total business succeeds in meeting these objectives. The benefits in simplicity are more than outweighed by the complete absence of matching the idea of controllability to this assessment of managerial performance or taking into account the personal contribution to the total achievement of the business. Even for the chief executive of the business, such an overall performance criterion is inadequate on its own. The overall business performance is likely to be significantly affected by the actual external environment, relative to that forecast in the plan, and not even chief executives can be totally in control of these external factors, although they may be held somewhat responsible for the accuracy of their forecasting of this external environment.

Therefore for all managers, their performance should be assessed against measures over which they have a high level of control and where the successful achievement is important to the overall success of the business. This will encourage and motivate managers to perform well in their respective areas but the business must still distinguish between efficient performance and effective performance. Efficient performance can be defined as achieving a very high level of output for any given level of inputs and its measurement obviously requires an expected relationship between inputs and outputs.

Thus, if a standard or expected level of performance can be established and included in the financial plan, the efficiency of the actual performance can be assessed against this relative standard, usually by comparing the actual inputs used against the standard allowance for the actual outputs achieved. To be of value this input-output relationship must be very predictable, as is frequently the case in many physical engineering relationships. Consequently this type of cost is normally referred to as an 'engineering cost', and the degree of efficiency of the manager responsible for the area can be monitored quite closely as long as the physical input–output relationship remains unchanged. A change could be caused by an alteration in the way of doing things, such as producing the product by using a different mix of raw materials and labour than was forecast at the time of the plan or budget. Where the budget can be analysed into such stable engineering relationships, standard costs can be developed and used, as discussed in Chapter 3, and the control applications of these are illustrated in more detail in Chapter 12. However, if the financial control system concentrates exclusively on the efficiency of managerial performance, there is a grave risk that this performance may become ineffective.

An old and classic example of this can be given from manufacturing in the automobile industry where there are a large number of engineering style relationships and the use of standard costs has been well developed for many years. If manufacturing managers are judged solely by the efficiency of their operations, they will be highly motivated to out-perform against the standard levels established for each planning period. This is fine as long as the requirements of the overall business do not change due to major upheavals or developments in the external environment. Thus the most efficient form of manufacturing may be to make only one model of car and to produce it in one colour (i.e. a black model T Ford). As long as the market only wants a cheap form of motorized transport this will be a very successful strategy. However, if a new competitor starts to offer the potential customer a wider range of models in a range of colours, this emphasis on manufacturing efficiency which had been so successful could prove to be disastrous. Thus General Motors was able to overtake Ford Motor Company in terms of market share and profitability and remained ahead for over 50 years, despite a massive investment in new models from Ford in the following years. This single error in strategy nearly bankrupted the company at the time.

Effective performance can therefore be contrasted with efficiency and can be defined as significantly helping to achieve the overall corporate objectives. In the car example, these corporate objectives for Ford would undoubtedly have included maintaining dominant market share and company profitability, both of which were undermined by continuing for too long with an efficient but outdated product line. In today's market-place a similar excessive emphasis on efficiency can lead to decreases in the quality of output as cost reductions take priority. This can have similarly disastrous impacts on market share and profitability, particularly if the customer has come to expect a very high quality product because that is what is being delivered by the competition (the automobile industry could still be used as the example, but the initiating competition would now be characterized as the Japanese manufacturers).

Incorporating effectiveness in terms of achieving quality targets is not, therefore, necessarily easy in financial terms for the separate areas of the business. However, it often can be done by identifying additional specific objectives which, if achieved in each area, will significantly contribute to the related overall corporate objective which has been established in the plan. For example, nowadays in the automobile industry, manufacturers would normally establish overall qualitative objectives for each new model launch which must be achieved if the model is to earn its targeted financial rate of return. Such an overall objective might be to achieve the 'best in class' rating against all equivalent cars from current competitors and this rating would include a comprehensive assessment of performance, styling, level of fittings, quality and reliability, as well as price. These assessments can then be broken down into specific objectives for the various areas of the business and the manufacturing area might be given specific targets to reduce the level of faults and repairs needed on cars after they have been delivered to customers, as well as the level of internally identified problems which required reworking prior to delivery. This type of objective would reduce the total managerial emphasis on simply making the product as cheaply as possible whatever the quality of resulting output. It should be replaced with a much more realistic balance between producing the high level of quality which is demanded by the customer in the market-place and achieving this as cost effectively as possible.

A positive outcome would be for the manufacturing management to analyse and propose alternative methods of production which either reduce costs without detrimentally affecting quality or possibly improve a key area of quality substantially in exchange for a relatively small increase in cost. Senior management can then decide if the trade-off is worthwhile; occasionally, the ideal and easily approved option is identified and proposed which generates an increase in quality combined with a reduction in manufacturing costs. The financial control system must be capable of incorporating these more qualitative measures of effectiveness as well as the more mathematical efficiency measures, if it is to assist in improving future decision-making. Thus the way in which the business is broken down into responsibility areas and how the specific objectives for these areas are inter-related is an important part of designing a financial control system. The inevitable changes in the external environment from those incorporated in the plan must also be taken into account or the financial control system may rapidly become irrelevant.

Where an efficiency control measure is being used, such changes can normally be made relatively easily and objectively. This can be done by 'flexing the budget', as explained in Chapter 9, so that the impact of the changed circumstances is reflected in the expected levels of the inputs to be used. The actual inputs used can then still be compared to a relevant 'standard' measure to achieve a view of the efficiency of performance. Even if there has been a fundamental change in the physical input to output relationship due to a revised method of operation, it is normally possible to define a new, stable input–output relationship and to use this new standard to measure and control the efficiency of this area of the business. The changes from the original plan can be financially quantified and shown separately in the financial reporting system to highlight that they should not be included in an assessment of managerial performance but that they do affect the economic performance of the business.

Many businesses now do this by calculating the total impact of these externally caused variations from the plan and calling it a 'revision variance', thus effectively setting a revised expected financial outcome for the plan in the light of the updated assessment of these external factors. Other businesses prefer not to alter the financial plan once it has been prepared, and thus use rolling forecasts, which are prepared regularly throughout the period, as the means of incorporating these changes to the expected results for the business. The important issue for a good financial control system is that senior management receive a valid presentation of the position of and the prospects for the business, which separates out changes from their earlier expectations into those which are externally caused and those which relate to good or bad internal managerial performance.

By using efficiency measures, the monitoring of stable input to output relationships can be made quite straightforward through using a thorough system of variance analysis, which is illustrated in Chapter 12 and was also discussed in Chapter 9. In these areas there is little room for managerial discretion as the level of inputs needed or outputs produced is largely controlled by the defined physical relationship, and a relatively small improvement in this ratio may represent a very good managerial performance. However, in other areas where no such definable relationship exists or where managers may be able to change completely such a relationship by altering the way the business operates, the manager can be said to exercise considerable discretion. Thus 'discretionary costs' are separated from engineering costs, and discretionary costs are usually defined as those which can be altered by the particular manager's decisions rather than being predetermined by an uncontrollable relationship. A clear understanding of the level of discretion which can be exercised by individual managers is fundamental to the design of a financial control system, because the segmentation of the business must be closely correlated to the discretionary authority of the various groups of managers.

Reconsidering an example given in Chapter 1 will make this much clearer before we go on to consider this segmentation of the business into the various possible types of responsibility centres. Managers can only be regarded as having discretionary authority over costs if they are capable of making decisions which genuinely change the level of the costs. So, it is important for all businesses to understand which managers have this discretion over their varying types of costs. Consider the costs incurred by the field salesforce of a particular company, which are set out in Figure 11.5. At first sight it may appear that each area sales manager has a considerable level of discretion over these costs as any managerial decision could affect each line item. However, a more detailed inspection would reveal that some of them will be dictated by corporate policy decisions which the area sales manager cannot individually alter, e.g. salaries, etc., training and types of car given to salesforce

	£000s
Salaries, including NI, pension contributions etc.	2,000
Commissions	1,000
Car leasing expenses	300
Petrol and servicing	300
Accommodation and subsistence	800
Entertaining	300
Training	300
Customer samples and promotional material	500
External support costs	1,000
Total field salesforce costs	£6,500

Note: Salesforce consists of 80 direct sales people, plus 20 support administrative and managerial staff.

Figure 11.5 *Field salesforce costs*

personnel. Other costs such as car running expenses, accommodation and subsistence, and customer entertaining, are largely dictated by the physical area covered by the sales person and by the nature of the business; again, the discretion of the area sales managers is very restricted. The real discretionary level of authority of the area managers is consequently over the number of sales people employed in each area. The total cost of each sales person can be largely treated as a physically derived input–output model where the manager can have little impact. A good manager may improve the efficient utilization of this physically derived cost slightly, but the major impact should be in the effectiveness of exercising their discretion over how many people to use in each area.

Where managerial discretion can be exercised is the only place where true managerial responsibility is located, and the financial reporting system must be designed to reflect this. Thus, if in the above example, the area sales managers do not have control over the number of people in each area as this is decided centrally, then the financial reporting system should not hold the area sales managers responsible for the field salesforce costs, except to the degree that they can achieve efficiency type improvements relative to the standard cost set by the company.

Responsibility centres

If the financial control system is to provide meaningful information to the right managers in time for it to be useful in their future decisions, most organizations must be broken down into appropriate sub-divisions, which are relevant to the operational decisions being taken by the business. Thus this break-down of the financial plan and corresponding design of the financial control system must be logically structured. A major focus of this exercise is to allow each responsibility centre to operate as a relatively self-contained area of the business, with specific sub-objectives and strategies which have been derived from and fit into the overall objectives of the business.

For this to work in practical terms, each responsibility centre needs to have control over its own inputs and to have some kind of output, even though all these outputs may be internally used as inputs by the rest of the business (e.g. an internal service function such as the personnel department could be treated as a responsibility centre for financial control purposes). Also the responsibility centre must have a manager, or group of managers, who exercise discretionary authority over its level of activity, unless its performance is only to be measured at the efficiency level. There is also the vitally important need to identify for the responsibility centre specific objectives, which are capable of being monitored, and which are completely in accordance with the overall objectives of the business. For most commercially-orientated organizations a major overall business objective relates to a financial target which may be expressed as a return on investment percentage, profit objective or take some other form such as growth in sales revenue, etc.

As stated earlier, it is much easier to achieve goal congruence if responsible managers are judged on exactly the same criteria as is established for the business as a whole, but such a simplistic system is impractical. However, it may be possible to establish compatible financial objectives for the sub-divisions of the business, which are expressed in similar terms to those for the whole business and also maintain the integrity of the goal congruence concept. The level of relevant financial objective clearly depends upon the level of discretionary control which can be exercised by the managers responsible for each sub-division. Several such generic levels of sub-division have been developed and are widely used by businesses as ways of instituting financial control throughout their organizations.

Responsibility centres can be established in two principal ways:

1   Divisionally by reference to business units supplying specific markets, customer groups, channels of distribution or products.
2   Functionally by area and type of managerial responsibility; e.g. production, operations, distribution, sales and marketing, research and development.

In our earlier definition of a responsibility centre it was stated that there must be some kind of measurable financial output but that this could be completely internal to the business as a whole (such as where the distribution department provides a service to the business as a whole and charges for this service). If this is the case there needs to be a system of setting these charges among the various levels of responsibility centres. This process is known as 'transfer pricing' and can raise many problems if not carefully designed and implemented; these problems are considered later in the chapter and illustrated in Chapter 12. As a consequence of some of these problems caused by establishing responsibility centres which only have outputs to other internally based responsibility centres, some companies have focused their main attention on responsibility centres which have external customers.

These are often described as strategic business units (SBUs), as an SBU is defined as having control of its own resources and making sales to external customers. SBUs are normally responsible for a specific product group or market segment, and therefore many of the resources involved are specific to this responsibility centre which helps tremendously in the financial control process. As previously stated all responsibility centres will have qualitative objectives which are needed to assist in establishing the effectiveness of its operation, as opposed to its efficiency. However, the level at which the financial objectives can be set will depend upon the level of discretionary control exercised within the division. No sub-division of any large group can really be considered as exercising complete discretion over its own financial affairs, as this includes how it raises long-term capital, including shareholders' equity. By definition, a business which has complete discretion over raising new funds from its own shareholders is an independent business and not a sub-division of another. Thus finance is often the main link of the responsibility centre back to the centre of the group, particularly where the business is operationally independent.

However, even without complete financial freedom the managers of the responsibility centre may have discretion over the assets employed in their section of the business and have flexibility in setting selling prices and controlling operating costs. This enables the responsibility centre to be controlled as an investment centre, in which the managers are held accountable for the profits achieved relative to the investment tied up in the business. At another level, managers may control selling prices and operating costs, and hence the profit levels of their business, but not have the freedom to make major investment decisions as these are still controlled centrally. This type of sub-division can be financially controlled as a profit centre, with managers being held accountable for the absolute financial return generated but not for the relative return on investment.

A variation on the profit centre concept is where the responsibility centre does not have complete control over its costs, and this is often caused where some services are supplied centrally by the group on a mandatory basis. It is, of course, unfair to hold managers responsible for costs over which they exercise no control and these arbitrary, centralized costs should be excluded from the divisional assessment of managerial performances. (It must be remembered that some of these costs may be very relevant to the assessment of the economic performance of the division.) Such a responsibility centre can most logically be controlled as a contribution centre, where its controllable sales revenues less its controllable level of expenses generate a financial contribution towards the overall other costs of the group. Using this level of financial control is normally preferable to getting involved in the problems of sophisticated cost apportionment systems, which were discussed in Part Two and Chapter 6.

If the responsibility centre does not control many of its costs it cannot be treated as a profit or contribution centre, but it may control the level of sales revenue which it generates. One method of financial control which can be applied is to treat this as a revenue centre, but the implicit assumption involved, which is that increasing sales revenue is automatically a good thing, must be remembered. Where there is no discretionary control over sales revenue, the simplest form of financial control is to consider this responsibility area as a cost expense centre.

This gives us four main types of divisional and functional responsibility centre, each of which is now considered in detail:

1 Investment centres.
2 Profit and contribution centres.
3 Revenue centres.
4 Cost (or expense) centre.

Investment centres

The importance to the overall business of putting any profit which it achieves into the context of the financial investment needed to generate that profit has been highlighted throughout the book. An absolute profit level of £1 million may sound impressive but as an annual return on an investment of £1 billion, it is considerably less than satisfactory! Not surprisingly, if this is a very important way of judging the financial performance of the total business, it seems the most compatible way of assessing the financial performance of the sub-divisions; provided that the management do exercise control, not only over the profit level but also over the level of investment in their division.

An investment centre's management should therefore concentrate not just on increasing the absolute profit made by their division but on improving its level of profitability (i.e. level of profit per £ of investment). This could, of course, be achieved by reducing the investment required even if this led to a lower absolute profit level being achieved. The basic equation for an investment centre is quite simple, as shown in Figure 11.6, if return on investment is used, but return on investment

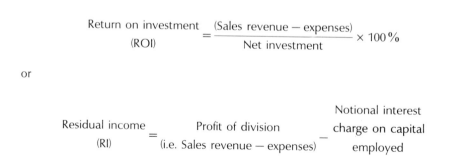

$$\text{Return on investment (ROI)} = \frac{(\text{Sales revenue} - \text{expenses})}{\text{Net investment}} \times 100\%$$

or

$$\text{Residual income (RI)} = \text{Profit of division (i.e. Sales revenue} - \text{expenses)} - \text{Notional interest charge on capital employed}$$

Figure 11.6 *Investment centres: financial performance measures*

(ROI) calculations suffer from a number of problems, as discussed in Chapter 2 and 7.

The simpler problems associated with using ROI as an assessment of financial performance are the normal accounting problems of measurement; in this case measuring both the profit and the investment of the division. There are many problems associated with measuring profits and investment for the whole of the business where, at least, the limits of the business are clearly defined. In the case of a division of a larger business, these problems are obviously likely to increase. Consequently, investment centres are normally restricted to relatively self-contained divisions which can be, and are, run as independent operating entities. Many large companies will only therefore control SBUs as investment centres as the problems of defining the boundaries of such an externally focused division tend to be fewer. However, the more fundamental problems associated with ROI as a financial performance measure remain, even if the accounting measurement issues are resolved satisfactorily.

ROI is a financial ratio which is normally expressed as a percentage and it therefore suffers the same problems as all financial ratios: managers may concentrate on managing the ratio rather than managing the business. As stated above, the ROI of a division may be improved even though profit declines, as long as the investment is decreased by a proportionately greater amount. This may be in line with the stated corporate objectives of the total business, but it may still not be in accordance with the long-term growth objectives of the company, i.e. the company may wish to improve its profitability and grow in size, rather than shrink. Indeed, an infinite return on investment can be achieved by producing a £1 profit on a zero net investment, but such a return will not finance a high rate of absolute growth! Thus companies using ROI as a financial performance measure should incorporate some other financial, non-financial, or even qualitative measures which will focus managers' attention on the specifically desired improvements in profitability.

One way of achieving some reduction in managerial game-playing is by using the residual income (RI) measure as the yardstick of relative financial performance. As shown in Figure 11.6, RI is an absolute value rather than a financial ratio which alleviates some of the problems, but more importantly RI is calculated by deducting a risk-related expected return from the divisional profits. In a division which is achieving a high level of ROI on its existing investment base there may be a reluctance on the part of management to invest new funds at a lower rate of return than is currently being achieved. This can be against the best interests of the group as a whole and can make the role of central management much more difficult. As mentioned above, for many largely decentralized businesses the major role which is still carried out at the centre is that of fund raising. The central management obviously wish to invest these funds in the most advantageous way possible and this usually means allocating them to the division offering the best financial return for the relative risk involved. (We must always remember that risk and return are positively correlated, so that if the perceived level of risk increases the desired return must be commensurately increased, as shown in Figure 11.7.)

Unfortunately for these group managers the highest potential financial return within the group may be in the division which does not want to undertake the

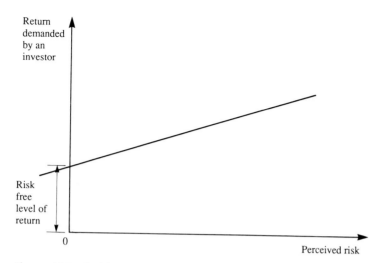

Figure 11.7 *Risk/return relationship*

Divisions	A	B	C	Total
Actual profit	£5m	£3m	£2m	£10m
Actual investment	£10m	£20m	£20m	£50m
Current ROI	50%	15%	10%	20%
Prospective ROI on new investment of £10m	30%	12%	15%	

Note: All new investments are assessed as having the same risk level.

Comments

The group would obviously wish to invest the £10m in Division A as this would yield the highest return to the group.

However, A's management may not even propose this prospective investment as it would reduce their overall ROI to 40 per cent from its current level of 50 per cent. Conversely C's management would be keen to invest at 15 per cent because this would improve their overall ROI.

Figure 11.8 *Problems of allocation of resources using ROI*

investment as it would reduce the overall ROI, hence reducing its perceived level of financial performance. This is numerically illustrated in Figure 11.8, where it is clear that there can be a conflict between the best economic interests of the group and the perceived managerial performance of a particular division.

If the group changes its method of financial control to RI rather than ROI, the situation could be dramatically altered, as shown in Figure 11.9. By charging each division a notional rate of interest on all the group's funds invested in that division, the divisional RI can be regarded as an economic profit after paying for the group's

Divisions	A	B	C	Total
Actual profit	£5m	£3m	£2m	£10m
Less: Interest charge on investment at 20%	£2m	£4m	£4m	£10m
Actual residual income	£3m	(£1m)	(£2m)	—
Impact of new investment – prospective profits	£3m	£1.2m	£1.5m	N/A
Less: Interest charge on £10m @ 20%	£2m	£2.0m	£2.0m	
Incremental residual income	£1m	(£0.8m)	(£0.5m)	

Comments

1 Using a 20% notional interest charge shows that only Division A is currently achieving a positive residual income.

2 More importantly, it also shows that by investing the incremental £10m, A's RI is increased by £1m, whereas B and C show a substantial negative RI on their potential new investments. A's management should, under this system, want to invest in the new project whereas C's now should not: thus restoring goal congruence with the group's objectives.

Figure 11.9 *Impact of using RI instead of ROI*

Division A is currently achieving a ROI of 50 per cent as shown. Its managers have identified an opportunity to sell and leaseback its freehold land and buildings, which will further enhance the divisional ROI to 90 per cent. This is because the deal removes £5m of assets from its balance sheet, but only reduces its profit by £500,000, being the leasing costs involved.

Division A	Current position	After sale and leaseback
Profit	£5m	£4.5m
Investment	£10m	£5.0m
ROI	50%	90%

Comment

Clearly the deal would seem very attractive to A's managers but to the group the position may not be so clear. By disposing of such a major asset, the overall cost of the remaining funds to the group may have increased. The group has also given up the potential of capital appreciation on the land, and this is why the acquirer would be willing to provide such relatively cheap funds.

Impact of using RI

If a risk related notional interest charge was being applied by the group it might charge 10 per cent on the low risk freehold land and buildings and 30 per cent on the higher risk other assets of division A. This would give an average of 20 per cent for the total assets of £10m. Thus selling the land would have no impact on RI as shown:

	Current position		After sale and leaseback	
Profit		£5m		£4.5m
Notional interests	£10m @ 20%	2m	£5m @ 30%	1.5m
Residual income		£3m		£3m

Note: the figures used are purely illustrative, the additional risk premium would not be 20 per cent as shown here.

Figure 11.10 *ROI versus RI*

cost of capital. This is indeed how most companies set the notional interest rate; that is, at the risk adjusted cost of capital for the group. Some companies are now becoming quite sophisticated in using this approach by charging different notional rates for different risk classifications of assets. Thus, freehold land and buildings may be classified as low risk with a consequently lower attributable cost of funding, whereas group funds invested in fashion type stocks by a division would be charged at a higher risk related rate.

This process can also help to reduce the need for some of the game-playing by managers under the ROI system because the financing cost associated with the asset will bear a much closer resemblance to the alternative costs incurred by the managers who are trying to improve their divisional ROI. This is illustrated in Figure 11.10.

A good financial control system will, of course, compare the actual performance against the budgeted performance rather than last year's actual performance, and therefore some of the measurement problems associated with ROI can be removed. For example, the impact of the potential incremental investment by Division A should be included in their financial plan, and hence their expected ROI would be reduced below their previous year's achievements. Unfortunately, in practice, this process only serves to increase the problem, because frequently the divisional managers do not wish to submit a financial plan which indicates a declining level of financial performance.

None of these changes removes the final and often critical problem with using either ROI or RI as the financial control measure with investment centres. The nature of economic investments is that the financial return is received over a relatively long period of time. Both ROI and RI are short-term measures of performance and the level achieved in any particular year may not be particularly representative of the long-term return which will be achieved by the division. Also both are backward looking accounting measures dependent on the judgements needed to assess profits and investments whereas, as discussed in Chapters 7 and 8, long-term investment decisions should be based on forward looking, objectively based cash flow measures such as discounted cash flow. If these long-term investments are justified by one method and yet financially controlled using a completely different measurement, there may be a great deal of confusion created; but that is what is still done in most companies today.

Profit and contribution centres

If a responsibility centre does not have effective control over either these types of investment decisions, or the related funding decisions such as sale and leasebacks, debt factoring or invoice discounting, it cannot properly be controlled as an investment centre. However, the division may have discretionary power to control its absolute profits by changing selling prices and controlling all, or a large part of, its costs. Most large businesses try to break down their operations into these profit, or contribution, centres as far as possible because they believe it focuses the attention of divisional managers on the critical issue of profits. In order to achieve this, responsibility centres have to be identified which genuinely do have managerial control of both sides of the profit generating equation, i.e. sales revenues and costs.

The easiest such sub-divisions which can be identified are similar to the ideal investment centre, i.e. vertical sub-divisions of the overall business which have their own market and products and are run on a decentralized basis. For these, the problems of measuring sales revenues and costs can largely be overcome, but many groups wish to create much less self-contained responsibility sub-divisions as profit centres. If the problem is one of the responsibility centre not controlling all of its costs, this can be solved by judging the managerial performance at the contribution level before these non-controllable costs are included. These non-controllable costs should be included in the financial control system if they are relevant to the economic decisions affecting this particular responsibility centre.

Where the problem is exacerbated because the responsibility centre does not generate external sales revenues, the financial control system must again distinguish between economic and managerial measures of performance. It is possible to establish internal selling prices for goods and services transferred among internal divisions of the group, and this can enable many more parts of the group to be financially controlled as profit or contribution centres. However, an externally established selling price between willing seller and willing buyer in an open market may be difficult to replicate for many of these internal transfers. As far as practical, all transfer prices should be set by reference to the open market price and both parties to the transaction should be free to seek alternative customers or suppliers if they do not like the deal they have been offered. Clearly in many highly integrated, capital intensive industries such potential for short-term disruption to supplies to other parts of the group could be extremely expensive and the group may restrict this ability to go outside for short-term opportunistic sales or purchases. However, where such an outside market price exists it is often used for internal transactions; the clearest examples are several of the large vertically integrated oil companies which sell from their oil exploration companies to their own marketing and distribution companies at the Rotterdam quoted market price. Consequently the perceived profitability of the downstream marketing companies can be dramatically affected by changes in the spot oil market price even though most of its supplies may be delivered from the group's own oil production capabilities.

Such a system may be very good for assessing the economic performance of each area of the business, and for indicating where future investment funds should be allocated. However, it is not sensible as a basis for the assessment of relative managerial performance unless downstream managers are given the discretion to source oil products from outside and to enter into long-term fixed price supply contracts, or to take other suitable hedging strategies to reduce their exposure to fluctuations in their raw material costs. If the group is capable of supplying all its end market needs, it would be illogical for the overall company to undertake these sorts of actions but this reduces the discretionary control that can be exercised by the divisional managers. Their basis of financial evaluation should be correspondingly adapted. Economic decisions should be based on the opportunity cost concept, as discussed in Part Two and Chapter 6. The concept is relevant for all allocation of resources decisions, but managerial performance assessments should exclude non-controllable areas of the business from their evaluations. This particularly means areas where the lack of managerial control is caused by a decision of the group centre which restricts managerial discretion, even though this may be in the economic best interests of the group as a whole.

Thus this exclusion provision also extends to transfer prices which are imposed on either buying or selling division, or both, by the centre and where the division is restricted from selling to or buying from outside the group. This type of imposed transfer pricing system is most frequently encountered in respect of group services, particularly those supplied by the centre itself. The basis tends to be a glorified system of cost apportionment because the transfer prices are often set exactly to offset the costs incurred at the centre in performing the particular function. Consequently the price charged to each unit should be compared against the cost of the unit providing itself with the particular function directly in the cheapest way possible (i.e. by doing it internally or buying in the service from an outside supplier). If economies of scale are being achieved by performing the function centrally, the savings would be highlighted by such an economic comparison, but this does not reflect on the efficiency or effectiveness of divisional managements.

As long as we remember how managerial performance should be evaluated and apply this properly, the potential problems of this type of transfer pricing can be minimized. Managerial performance should always be assessed relative to some target such as the financial plan or budget, as an absolute performance is a meaningless concept. Consequently the transfer price actually charged for any internally delivered service will be compared against the charge forecasted in the plan, and it is only the difference between them which will affect the relative perception of managerial performance. It is therefore important that, if managers do not exercise any control over the transfer prices charged to them, there is no difference between the actual and planned charges with no corresponding impact on their perceived managerial performances. This can often be achieved in the design of the financial control system by, for example, treating the transfer price as a fixed cost for the duration of the budget period. If so, the transfer price can then be established by reference to the potentially important impact it can have on forthcoming economic decisions, from which it cannot be excluded. Setting the transfer price at the appropriate opportunity cost level helps to reduce this potential problem at the division level, but does not necessarily achieve this overall for a vertically integrated group.

In many such groups, the various vertical divisions are run as profit or investment centres and consequently each division tries to make a profit on its sales internally, as well as on any to external customers. By the time the final division sells a product to an outside customer, there may have been several elements of profit margin extracted by the various divisions involved in the transaction. This can complicate the overall financial analysis for this type of product and market because the group needs to know the total profit made on the sale to the outside customer. For instance, the final selling division may wish to drop the product completely because the profit margin which it achieves does not make the sale financially worthwhile. However, the transfer pricing system may hide the high profit margin made by one or more divisions at earlier stages in the transaction. A good financial control system needs to highlight the total profits earned by the group on the sale to the outside customer; after all it is not possible to make a 'real' profit by selling things to yourself! Not only does the group need to know this financial information to ensure that sound economic decisions are made, but it is also important if sales divisions are to be properly motivated to act in the best interests of the group. If confusing signals are sent to the final sales division by the transfer pricing system regarding the apparent profitability of any particular product, the sales division may make inappropriate decisions regarding the allocation of their resources to this product. The goal congruence concept must be remembered in setting transfer prices as well as in all other aspects of designing financial control systems.

Revenue centres

The sales and marketing areas of many businesses are considered to control the sales revenues of their products or markets but not to exercise managerial control over all the costs incurred by their areas of responsibility. In many cases, these areas are financially controlled as revenue centres, where the managers are held accountable for the achievement of the sales revenue targets included in the plan. Earlier in the chapter the real level of discretion exercised by sales managers with regard to their direct costs was discussed, and the concept of controlling them by reference to the effectiveness of utilizing the number of sales people in each area was proposed. This issue of monitoring financial effectiveness should raise a doubt as to the logic of targeting sales managers against sales revenue alone. If the number of sales people is increased, it is likely that sales revenues will also be increased unless complete market saturation has been reached. However, the more relevant financial evaluation hinges on whether the profit contribution generated by the incremental sales achieved is sufficient to justify the increased expenditure on sales resources.

What is really wanted in revenue driven activities is for profitable sales to be increased and for any unprofitable sales to be phased out. This will not be achieved by a concentration on a simple sales revenue value measure, but requires that the logic behind the sales revenue target is broken down and individual objectives are established for the various areas of the sales and marketing function. The sales revenue target is actually composed of assumed selling prices multiplied by forecast sales volumes and each of these is established as relative estimates against the predicted external environment. Thus, selling prices depend on expected competitive movements, inflation levels, rates of exchange, significant raw material and labour costs, etc., while sales volumes are calculated from the forecast size of the total market multiplied by the anticipated market share that will be achieved.

Each of these individual elements can be isolated and made the responsibility of managers in the appropriate area, e.g. selling prices might be given to brand or product managers. Unfortunately, such a specific apportionment of responsibility may well be counter-productive as all these areas are inextricably interlinked. Thus if selling prices are increased above the planned levels, the division may lose market share and sell lower volumes than expected. The overall impact on profit may be extremely adverse but the brand managers could argue that they exceeded their targets and hence performed well. Once again, the managerial performance target is wrongly specified. The division does not want them simply to increase selling prices, but to find the selling price which maximizes overall profitability when combined with all the other elements of the marketing mix.

It may be better for the division to use more specific non-financial measures to focus managerial attention at the lower levels on specific, controllable areas and to concentrate the financial measures only at the more consolidated level of the division where the financial interactions of these constituent elements can be properly integrated and taken into account. This is particularly true for the assessment of all economic decisions, because it is pointless to try to evaluate the financial justification of a 10 per cent decrease in selling prices by saying that it created an increase in sales volumes relative to last year. What is important is the net financial impact relative to what would have happened without the price decrease now, not what did happen in a potentially very different external environment last year!

Cost (or expense) centres

If a responsibility centre does not produce any valid externally or internally measurable sales revenue, there are very limited possible methods of exerting financial control over this area of the business. The obvious method is to compare the actual level of expenditure incurred with some pre-set of budgeted level and hence run the area as a cost, or expense, centre. Most companies call these areas 'cost centres', although in accounting terms what is compared in most cases are the expenses written off in any given accounting period.

In most cost centres, managers are in control of physical outputs rather than financial values. They often can exercise relatively limited discretion over their expenditure levels as well, as these can be linked by input–output relationships to the required output levels. It can therefore seem easy to set a budget of acceptable expenditure and then monitor managerial performance by comparing the actual levels back to this budget. This type of financial control system is very common and has led to many managers believing wholeheartedly that any level of overspend against budget is automatically bad while an underspend of favourable variance is obviously a sign of good managerial performance. Such strongly held attitudes can be extremely dangerous unless there is a counterbalancing inclusion of very clear non-financial objectives for these responsibility centres which ensure that managers understand and act in the best interests of the group as a whole.

The key issue is what does the group want to motivate these cost centre managers to do. The objective, clearly, is not just to spend their budget allocations. By spending these funds they should achieve specific physical outputs or other objectives which are important to the overall success of the business. A classic example of this is the research and development area of the business, where substantial funds may be spent. It may be easy for the responsible managers to underspend their budget by simply doing less work, but the consequence would be less output of new products on time. This delay could be critical to the success of the overall business plan, and the R&D managers must be properly motivated to act in accordance with this overall plan. Thus it may be better if they can accelerate the development of a key new product even if this means that they marginally overspend their budget. The financial control system should encourage the divisional managers to propose such alternative strategies to the group. They must not be allowed to sit back and argue that *they* beat their financial performance targets even though the impact on the group was disastrous.

This is particularly important as many cost centres provide support services to the other operational divisions which may be run as profit or investment centres. The level of effective support can have a dramatic impact on the ability of these operational divisions to achieve their financial targets. Once again the financial control system must avoid an excessive emphasis on reporting the efficiency of performance and highlight the effectiveness of this performance as well.

It should be clear that these different classifications of responsibility centres are not mutually exclusive, but more hierarchical in nature. Thus a division may be controlled as an investment centre but it may itself contain further sub-divisions which are financially controlled as contribution centres, revenue centres and cost centres. The most important aspect of these divisional financial control measures is that they must be carefully linked into the overall corporate objectives and modified in line with the updated version of the business plan. They are not ends in themselves and an excessive concentration on divisional managerial performance targets may mean that the overall business results are less good than they should be.

Impact of computers

This variety of divisional performance levels and the other complicated requirements of financial control systems indicate that there is a massive need for financial analysis and reporting in all modern business. The same base data are required in many different formats to support economic decisions and to provide the necessary financial evaluations of managerial performances. Financial control can only be implemented by managers at the appropriate level of the business and hence the necessary supporting information must be provided at each of these levels. This information is also required on a timely basis so that changes can be made as soon as possible, and in sufficient detail so that the managers involved can select correct alternative option.

However, this appropriate level of detail will differ depending on the level of management to whom it is presented. The individual budget holders will want detailed information on all costs charged to each cost code classification for which they are responsible, whereas their line manager will probably only want information on those areas which are not in line with budgets or updated forecasts. At the divisional management level, even more summarized information is required unless managers are to disappear beneath an avalanche of financial reports. At the overall group level of management it is important that information is provided on all key issues, otherwise the business can rapidly get totally out of control.

Various management techniques have been developed to help in this process and an early one was 'management by objectives' (MBO), which is based on the development of a series of sub-objectives for each area of the business which, if all achieved, would mean the business in total achieved its objectives. In other words most business planning systems employ a form of MBO. The reporting system required the monitoring of the achievement of these objectives, and this was fed back into the centre so that the overall plan could be updated. As businesses became larger and more complex, the volume of sub-objectives meant a massive volume of reports was needed and this became unworkable for many companies. In fact they did not need all this information anyway, because if the business was on the right course as planned no changes were necessary. Therefore information was only really required on areas where the plan was not being achieved and hence where modifying decisions might need to be made. This led to the technique known as 'management by exception' (MBE), which assumes that everything is on target unless it is reported not to be. This technique should massively reduce the financial reporting volumes, while still ensuring that all levels of management are provided with the decision support information which they require.

MBE can only be operated when the financial control system is properly integrated into the financial planning process. This integration enables the actual results of each area of the business to be compared against the relevant section of the analysed plan. Acceptable levels of variation between the actual results and the planned level have to be established (e.g. $\pm$ 5 per cent). If the variation is greater than this acceptable level, the deviation from plan is reported to the appropriate level of management who can take action to correct the problem or modify other areas of the plan.

All of these financial reporting requirements would create a massive clerical problem if they had to be produced manually. Fortunately the ever increasing processing power of computers and their steadily decreasing costs have revolutionized the potential for financial control systems. If the business implements a properly designed financial data-base, it is possible to produce individually tailored financial reports for all levels of management with very little extra cost and effort once the system has been implemented. Even without this ultimate computer solution, the ability of modern computer systems to process vast quantities of data very quickly means that almost all businesses can provide the required financial information to managers within short periods of time. This is provided the necessary base data have been fed into the computer system in the first place, and this now presents a problem for financial control systems which is considered in the next chapter.

There is another problem of financial control systems which requires careful consideration when designing related computer systems. Much of the financial information needed for good financial control is required on a regular basis, and the system can be designed to produce this information on the required regular time-scales. Indeed with today's computer systems much of this regular analysis can be done automatically by the computer, and exception reports can be provided where relevant together with regular financial performance indicators. (It must be remembered that the computer system is not exercising financial control over the business. It is merely providing the necessary regular financial analysis, so that the managers within the business can exercise *better* financial control.) In addition to this regularly required financial information, the business will also face a wide range of one-off, unexpected decisions. Financial information will also be required to support these decisions and yet it is not possible to specify in advance what information is needed as the decision itself is, as yet, unknown. The financial control system must have adequate flexibility to cope with these unexpected demands for information, without making it necessary to delay excessively the preparation and presentation of the regular reports.

If a comprehensive financial data-base has been developed, all the potentially necessary supporting information should be stored in the system, and producing the appropriate financial analysis should be quick and relatively painless. Unfortunately, many companies are finding that their very sophisticated and expensive financial information systems do not have the necessary flexibility or comprehensive nature to cope with the range of critical decisions which the businesses are now facing. Presumably nobody thought of these issues when the systems were being designed, and solving these problems after the event can be incredibly expensive and very traumatic. However, the cost and trauma may not be as great as can be faced by the business which tries to make a critical strategic decision without any financial supporting information.

Computers have not only had a dramatic impact on financial control systems through their ability to process large volumes of historic financial data, they have had an even greater impact in the area of financial planning. The processing power of modern computers has allowed planners to consider the financial impact of a wide range of potential external environments and competitive strategies (usually described as 'what-ifs'). This enables contingency plans to be developed to respond to the more important consequences of these sensitivity analysis derived alternative scenarios. Should this potential situation actually occur, the business can respond much more quickly because it already has a plan developed to cope with this eventuality. The development of this wide range of properly evaluated contingency plans has helped tremendously in the area of financial control, because the actual outcome of the contingency plan can be compared directly to its expected outcome. In the absence of this alternative plan, the actual outcome would have had to be compared back to the expectations of the original plan, which would have been based on a completely outdated forecast of the business environment.

The use of such contingency plans can enhance the role of financial control as a learning process, as the actual results can be used to improve the forecasting accuracy of the contingency planning in the future. However, the key task for all financial control systems is to provide managers with the financial information which they need to make the best possible decisions. In other words the right information must be supplied to the right managers at the right time, and these issues are considered in detail in Chapter 12.

Questions

1 'Management accounting can satisfy all possible needs for financial information by providing all managers with all the available financial reports.' Discuss.

2 How can financial control systems be used positively to enhance communication and motivation?

3 Financial control systems are often quite good at monitoring efficiency. How can they help in improving effectiveness?

4 The use of profit as part of the system for assessing managerial performance is very common. What are the essential pre-requisites for such a financial control system to be of value to the business?

5 'If a department within a company does not produce financially measurable output, there is no way that a sensible financial control system can be applied.' Discuss.

12

Financial control systems in practice

Overview

Financial control systems should be designed to act as decision support systems for managers and consequently they should be operated as such. This requires that the right managers are provided with the right information at the right time.

The 'right managers' means ensuring that the information is supplied to the people who can actually make decisions to correct problems and take advantage of opportunities. The financial control system should differentiate between the 'nice to know' information, which helps to inform all managers about how the business is performing, and the 'need to know' information which relates to each manager's particular area of responsibility within the business.

The 'right information' indicates that managers must be supplied with information and not raw data, which require them to carry out a great deal of analysis before they can be used to evaluate any prospective decision. Information can be defined as data which have been processed to add knowledge. This information must also be tailored to fit the prospective decisions which the managers may be facing. This immediately presents a major problem because all financial decisions should be based on an analysis of the future cash flow which will result from the decision. Financial control systems almost inevitably analyse past events and so the historic information must be kept as current as possible. Even more importantly, the financial analysis of these past events must be used to update the expected outcomes of future decisions, thus using the financial control system as a dynamic learning process not just an historical explanation.

This process will require a great deal of data to be processed and turned into tailored information reports. As far as possible, the raw data should be collected as automatic elements of the normal accounting process. This removes the need for extra clerical effort and also should ensure the integrity of all the financial reporting as the same base data will be used in all reports. Where this is impossible because the data needed do not get included in the historic accounting system, great care should be taken to ensure the accuracy of the data collected. This is particularly true where the people inputting the data are unconnected with its subsequent usage as part of the financial control process.

Whenever practical, the financial analysis should utilize input–output relationships which can assist tremendously in the analytical process. The use of standard costs and variance analysis is a good way of achieving this analytical framework, but the overall objective is to identify causal relationships in past events which will help in predicting the outcome of future decisions. The time and effort involved in carrying out this detailed financial analysis can be dramatically reduced by the sensible application of computer systems, particularly for repetitive, regular reporting requirements.

Computers can also be used to develop complex models and simulations of all, or parts of, the business, incorporating the historically analysed interrelationships. Such a model can enable the financial plan to be continually updated from the historic analysis to incorporate changes in the external environment or in internal causal factors.

The 'right time' relates to the essential features of providing the necessary financial supporting information to the decision-maker in time for it to be useful in making the decision. This can be dramatically assisted by the use of computers which speed up the financial analysis process considerably. However, it can also be helped by the way in which the information is presented, which can reduce the time required by the decision-maker to understand it and act on it. The time of providing information refers not only to the speed of provision but also to the frequency of reporting, and both should be justified on a cost/benefit evaluation. Increasing either the speed or the frequency of financial reporting normally increases the cost involved, and there should be an economic justification for doing so.

The frequency of reporting should be matched to the decision time-scale and the timing of each report then phased in accordance with the length of time needed for consideration by the decision-maker.

Financial control systems must be operated as an integrated element in the overall financial process of analysis, planning and control.

Introduction

Information control systems will have been designed to supply reliable financial information to managers who are responsible for implementing the existing business plan and to assist in updating this plan and developing the next. Consequently, this design should be tailored to meet the needs of the existing business and any planned changes intended for the future. Operating this type of information control system therefore requires that the relevance of the existing design is checked against the current external environment and business strategy. The investment in the existing financial control system and its operating costs should have been justified by carrying out a proper cost/benefit analysis, and if these benefits are no longer being obtained the system should be appropriately modified.

For many businesses, the external environment and competitive pressures can change very rapidly and frequently. Consequently the design of the financial control system should allow for the necessary flexibility in reporting levels and frequencies. This is particularly true where a major investment is being considered, such as the development of a computerized financial data-base, because such a large investment can normally only be financially justified if it is expected to have a reasonable period of economic usefulness. Should the new financial information system be considered out of date almost before it has been fully installed and made operational, the benefits actually obtained will not have justified the expenditure incurred. In several industries, information is now a critical source of competitive advantage and hence companies are investing ever greater sums in trying to obtain still better or faster information to give them such an edge in the market-place. This pressure makes it even more important that line managers are fully involved in specifying the outputs of these systems and in agreeing how the necessary base data will be input into the system. In too many cases the financial information system never operates properly in the way it was designed to do because the right managers were not consulted early enough in the design phase or motivated to make it happen when the system was implemented.

The need for positive motivation is frequently forgotten but in many modern integrated information systems it can be critical, particularly where the new system increases the workload for one area, which is itself not a recipient of any benefits from the system. The extra work involved in inputting more data into an information system often falls on the clerical areas of an organization, whereas the benefits of improved reporting are normally felt by operational managers, who may be far removed from the problems caused for these clerically based personnel. For example, it may be very important for sales and marketing managers to receive very detailed analyses of sales by products, customers, and geographic areas. This type of regular reporting can clearly assist in future planning and may indicate areas where a reallocation of marketing resources could significantly improve the business' overall performance. Indeed, this information could be further improved if the analysis were not restricted to sales revenue levels, but also showed the relative contributions being generated by different areas of the business. Further, these managers would probably like to be able to request ad-hoc reports which focused on particular groupings of products or customers, or both, at particular times, such as during promotional or heavy advertising campaigns.

All of this information can be readily produced from most sales information systems nowadays, provided that the necessary coding references have been input into the system. This can most logically be done at the time of inputting the order or the sales invoice, depending on the system design, and requires that extra codes are added to products and customers. These extra codes enable the individual sales invoices to be stored and grouped into almost any combination and then summarized into a suitable reporting format, with very little extra manual effort. However, there is an increased workload involved in adding a potentially large number of extra codes to each invoice entered into the system, and this workload falls on a clerical operator who is probably not even going to see the segmented analysis of sales which is produced as a result. Obviously if the initial coding is inaccurately done, the resulting analysis will be similarly misleading and could lead managers to make very bad decisions; the old adage of 'garbage in, garbage out' can always be applied to information systems.

This potential problem should be considered in the design and subsequent operation of the financial control system. Undoubtedly the best solution is to remove the need for any increased workload or to minimize its impact. This can be done by automatically collecting all the data required for subsequent analysis as part of the normal accounting process. In the above sales analysis example this can very largely be achieved, because in order to generate a sales invoice the base data relating to the customer and all the products sold must obviously be put into the system. Most computer-based systems hold all regularly required data in their files (known normally as master files) so that clerical time is saved by removing the need repeatedly to key in the same data relating, for example to the name and address of the customer. In order to access any specific item held on these master files, the operator inputs an appropriate code number which is unique to the record required, and all the necessary customer or product details are automatically filled in on the sales invoice. This not only reduces clerical effort but also reduces the level of errors, provided that the correct reference number is fed into the system! In order to forestall the possibility of inputting errors, such as the transposition of two numbers in the access code, most systems build in a check digit at the end of the code number which enables the system to verify that it is a valid reference code (the extra check digit might make the whole reference number divisible by 13).

If this type of information system has been designed, the analytical information requirements should be incorporated into the code number used as an integral part of the system. Thus the product code number could include fields which relate to product groups, product types and sizes, etc. while the customer code number would incorporate fields covering the type of customer by size, channel of distribution, area, etc. The only problem is that the greater the need for subsequent analysis becomes, the larger the reference code needed to contain all of the cross-referencing data. However, this problem can itself be reduced by using computer held cross-referencing tables which are accessed by the initially input code number, and the use of check digits reduces the possibility of input error. Using this type of solution is very good as a way of minimizing the additional clerical workload needed to obtain good analytical information because sales invoices are essential to collect cash from customers and to provide basic accounting controls for the business. However, in many cases such a design can restrict the flexibility of the business should it subsequently require information to be presented in a different format; if the newly required coding cross-reference has not been built in, it is impossible to achieve the required analysis automatically. One possible answer is to include every possible combination of factors in the initial design specification and thus incorporate all of them into the coding reference, but this can make the reference number unworkable from a clerical point of view (giving a 16 digit reference number to a product with a unit selling price of 2 pence may not be cost-effective). A more logical design is to allow a maximum number of coding references but make it easy to alter the use of each reference digit so that changes in information needs can easily be handled. This may mean that customer and product references are being changed regularly so that there is a cost incurred for this flexibility due to the consequent decrease in clerical efficiency.

Such conflicts and trade-offs highlight the need for involving line managers in the design of financial information systems, and these managers should include not only those who will receive the output reports but also those who will be responsible for the inputting of the necessary raw data.

The right managers

Decision support information is of no value unless it is provided to the managers who have the authority to make and implement any changes which are required as a result of the financial analysis and consequent reporting process. Therefore a key element in designing and operating financial control procedures is to link together the specific activities which need to be carried out, if the business is to achieve the overall planned objectives, with the appropriate responsible managers who can be held accountable for carrying out these activities. As discussed in the previous chapter, the combination of authority and accountability is essential if managers are to be positively motivated by the financial control process.

This linkage of authority and responsibility for achieving critical sub-objectives of the plan means that the necessary financial information must be supplied to those managers who *need* it as the basis for decision-making. In many organizations access to financial information is based on seniority and not on the decision-making aspects of a manager's role. This is very wrong and can lead to important decisions being made in the absence of sound supporting financial information, even though the required information is available elsewhere within the business. For example in the sales area, which we discussed earlier in the chapter, sales and marketing managers may need to make decisions to alter the positioning of certain products or the pricing strategy to certain key customers in response to sudden changes in the competitive environment. In order to make the most sensible changes in the context of the business' overall objectives, these managers need access to the best available financial information regarding the potential impact of the available options. Thus, if product profitability and customer profitability analyses have been carried out, this information should significantly assist in the evaluation. However, in many companies information on profitability levels is restricted to senior managers only, and brand managers or key account sales managers may be excluded from this level. They may be forced to make decisions without the required supporting information even though they may be held responsible for the outcome of the decisions, while the personnel director may have regular access to these segment profitability reports.

The financial control system should ensure that the official organization structure does not stop decision-makers receiving the information they need to support their areas of responsibility and authority. The business may also wish to communicate much of this financial information to other managers as it may help them to appreciate both how the business is performing and how the activities in their areas of authority may need to change in the future in response to changes elsewhere in the organization. However, this motivational and contingency planning information can, in some ways, be classified as nice to know, because the managers receiving it are unlikely to make immediate decisions to alter what they are doing now as a result. This nice to know information should be separated from the essential need to know information, and must not be allowed to interfere with the right managers obtaining all the information which they need to know.

The right information

This immediately raises the question of what constitutes essential information for all these critically important decision-makers, at their various levels within the business. Production managers need information on the relative costs of labour, raw materials, and energy used in their departments if they are to be capable of evaluating alternative methods of producing the required output levels specified in the plan. This could most simply be provided by giving them all the time-sheets for the employees and the pile of invoices for raw materials and energy. Very little extra clerical effort would be involved on the part of the management accounting area, but equally little useful information would have been supplied to the production managers. Decision-makers need financial information not raw, unprocessed data and a key role for the financial information system is to turn the base data into usable information. The difference between information and data is principally that data have to be analysed, processed and presented in a logical, structured format if they are to be of value in giving knowledge to the recipient. Thus information is data to which knowledge has been added and, as such, it can easily be absorbed by the relevant managers and used to support their forthcoming decisions.

If the specifically relevant information is to be supplied, this means that the operators of the financial control system have to be aware of the type of forthcoming decisions likely to face each group of managers. Even then, the solution is by no means easy because, as discussed in Chapter 6, all financial decisions should be evaluated by reference to the future changes in the cash flows resulting from those decisions. Financial control systems can only produce information based on processing historic accounting data, as no data will have been collected and recorded on possible *future* transactions flowing from *potential* decisions. The analysis of these historic transactions must attempt to identify and highlight the causal relationships involved, which will enable managers to predict more accurately what will happen in the future. This means that the information should be as up-to-date as it can be, because the predictive value is likely to be greater but, more importantly, it means that there is limited value in conducting incredibly detailed evaluations of one-off events which can never reoccur. The financial control system must be used as a dynamic learning process, where the analysis of past events is used to update the expected outcomes of the forthcoming future decisions on a continuous, iterative basis.

This also means that the financial reports should differentiate between continuing impacts which will definitely have an impact on future events and those situations which may or may not reoccur depending upon the external environment or management action. Thus if raw material prices have unexpectedly been increased by all available suppliers, this cost increase is likely to have a continuing effect on the future potential profitability of the business, and managers must consider how they intend to respond to this change in their external environment. The business could decide to increase selling prices to offset the cost increase or to change to a now lower cost substitute raw material, or make other changes to its strategy rather than simply accept the lower profit position. Similar decision alternatives are not likely to be evaluated if the production labour cost goes up in one period because of operating inefficiencies due to sickness, disruption or other one-off causes. Wherever possible these analyses can clearly be communicated by reference to well understood and proven input–output relationships. These physical relationships can be incorporated into standard costs and the differences (or variances, as they are called) between the actual cost incurred and the standard cost which *should* have been incurred can be analysed. As before, the financial control system should try to pinpoint the causal factors rather than simply produce a lot of numerical comparisons, which are of no value in forecasting future relationships.

An example will make this process much clearer. (The numbers in this example have deliberately been kept very simple as it is the concept of the analytical process which is important.) A small pottery makes a range of products but among its best sellers are large earthenware teapots which have a selling price in the pottery showrooms or to distributors of £10 each. The teapots are normally made in batches and the main raw material used is a very expensive form of clay. Five kilograms of clay are normally needed to make a batch of 100 teapots, and the labour required for this same-sized batch is expected to be 40 hours if the process works normally. The forecast costs for the next planning period are £50 per kg for clay and a total hourly labour cost of £10. The pottery uses a standard costing system for the major direct costs of clay and labour only but which also includes the expected wastage/reject level of 5 per cent. The current standard cost statement is shown in Figure 12.1.

As with all financial plans, actual events differ somewhat. The cost of clay increases above the original forecast to £60 per kg due to a long-term shortfall in supply to the market, and hence the price is now expected to stay at this new higher level. The pottery also receives a large rush order from one distributor for 300 teapots at a special price of £9 each, and so the workforce puts in a considerable amount of overtime to produce them as quickly as possible. Overtime premiums of 50 per cent are incurred, but also the level of wastage and rejects increases to 15 per cent from the standard level of 5 per cent as shown in Figure 12.1. The actual costs and outputs for the latest production period are given in Figure 12.2, but management are also considering a new strategic alternative; at present, they are having to turn away a number of similar large orders and sales could be expanded if a two-shift operation was instituted. They estimate that the shift premium involved would increase the hourly wage cost to £13 and wonder whether this is a financially sound idea.

The rush order was not expected when the financial plan was prepared and the original budget for the month envisaged producing 200 teapots. Figure 12.3 shows the overall comparison of the original budget to the actual results for the month, as extracted from Figure 12.2.

From Figure 12.3, it is clear that the dramatic change in the actual level of activity from that forecast in the budget makes this analysis meaningless; the very large favourable sales variance is more than offset by the larger adverse cost variances. Does this mean that expanding sales above budget is a bad idea? The

Standard cost of teapots

Production units

	Per 100 batch		Per unit
		Selling price	£10
Raw material cost:			
5 kg @ £50	£250		£2.5
Labour cost			
40 hours @ £10	£400		£4.0
Standard cost	£650		£6.5
		Wastage allowance @ 5% of selling price	£0.5 £7
Sales revenue			
£10 each × 95 saleable teapots	£950		——
Contribution to overheads and profit	£300		£3

Note: The pottery management accept that some pots will be substandard and unsaleable and that some wastage of raw materials will occur, and so the expected saleable output is 95 teapots out of every 100 produced. An alternative method would be to increase all the costs to calculate the standard cost of producing 100 saleable teapots.

Figure 12.1

simplest way to make the financial analysis more realistic is to adjust the budget to show what should have been the result of the actual level of activity. This is done in Figure 12.4, in which the standard costs reflect the fact that in order to have 475 saleable teapots, the pottery *should* have had to produce 500, and the costs for 500 are correspondingly included.

This analysis is becoming more useful because it highlights that if the standards had been achieved, the contribution would have totalled £1,500 rather than £600

Actual costs for month of September

Total teapots produced:	550
Saleable teapots produced and sold:	475

Actual clay used	27.5 kg
Cost of clay per kg	£60
Total cost of clay	£1,650
Labour hours worked of which 150 were overtime:	200
Total labour cost incurred	£2,750

Sales revenue generated
  comprising 175 teapots @ £10 and
  300 teapots @ £9, representing the special order
	£4,450

Figure 12.2

included in the original budget; this reflects the impact of the increase in sales which were all forecast to be profitable. Unfortunately for the business, the actual contribution is significantly lower at only £50. The difference is made up of variations in all areas as the sales revenue is lower than the flexed (i.e. altered to include the actual level of activity) budget while both the actual costs are

	Budget		Actual	Variance
	£		£	£
Sales revenues	1,900		4,450	2,550
Less costs:				
Raw materials	500	1,650		(1,150)
Labour	800	2,750		(1,950)
	1,300		4,400	(3,100)
Contribution	600		50	(550)

Figure 12.3   *Comparison of budget to actual*

	Flexed standards		Actuals	
	£	£	£	£
Sales revenues		4,750		4,450
Raw materials	1,250		1,650	
Labour costs	2,000		2,750	
		3,250		4,400
Contribution total:		1,500		50

Figure 12.4   *Comparison of actual costs to standard costs expected*

substantially higher. If managers are to be able to make any of the decisions which appear to be needed, the financial analysis needs to provide much more clear and specific information on each of these areas.

Sales variances

The variances from budget revenues are caused by two factors; the volume actually sold is different to that originally forecast and some of these sales have been made at different selling prices. For the business as a whole there will also be another probable cause of difference, which is that the actual sales mix will not be the same as that forecast in the budget. These two variances should be analysed separately and Figures 12.3 and 12.4 give the base data needed. If the budget had correctly forecast the volume which was sold, the sales revenue would have been included at £4,750 instead of the budgeted level of £1,900. This represents the extra sale of 285 teapots and the correspondingly expected extra production of 300 teapots to bring the total to 500. This difference of £2,850 is simply due to the sales volume difference but this does not explain the difference between the original budget and the actual sales revenue figure. The revised expectation of sales revenue is £4,750 but actual sales generated £300 less than this. This can only have been caused because the sales were made at lower selling prices than included in the standards and, in this case, we know this to be true because 300 units were sold at the special price of £9 each rather than the standard selling price of £10. This sales price variance of £300 allows us to account for the total difference between the original budget and the actual sales revenues, as shown in Figure 12.5.

	£
Favourable sales volume variance	2,850
Adverse sales price variance	(300)
Net sales variance	2,550

Figure 12.5 *Summary of sales variances*

This analysis indicates that managers should be interested in two further pieces of information; why did the expected contribution increase not follow from the growth in sales volumes and is it financially worthwhile to sell teapots at £9 each. In order to provide the first required information, it is necessary to look at costs of raw materials and labour separately, while for the second issue they must be considered together.

Raw material variances

As with sales revenues, the raw material cost difference can have two components; a price element and a usage (or volume) element. In other words, the business may have paid more or less than expected for the raw material and have been more or less efficient in its usage of the raw material. The usage level is obviously affected by the volume produced and so the allowance for the usage of clay must be increased proportionately; this flexing of the budget appears to account for an increase to £1,250 from the £500 included in the original budget. However, the pottery actually produced 550 teapots in the period and therefore the allowance should have been 27.5 kgs of clay at £50 per kg giving a total of £1,375. The gap between this figure and the flexed budget (i.e. £125) represents the raw material cost of the higher wastage rate incurred in the month, but even non-saleable teapots need clay to be made. The actual clay used was the same 27.5 kg and so no excess clay was used, but it cost significantly more than expected. The price difference of £10 per kg was suffered on all 27.5 kg used and so this explains the remaining variance of £275, as is shown by the summary in Figure 12.6.

These variances should flag up different potential actions to the responsible managers if they are presented in the correct way. The increased usage allowance due to the higher level of activity requires no action because it was entirely expected, and only represents an error in the forecast included in the plan. The volume forecasting process should be reviewed but this would be done anyway. The much more important element is the adverse price variance because this is likely to present a recurring problem to the business as the higher raw material cost will

	£
Increased usage allowance, i.e. activity variance	(750)
Adverse price variance	(275)
Adverse wastage/usage variance	(125)
Net raw material variance	(1,150)

Figure 12.6 *Summary of raw material variances*

recur in the future. This means that the impact on future profitability levels should be investigated, and this impact is clearly indicated by the variance analysis carried out. However, it can be further highlighted by restating the unit cost level incorporating this higher raw material cost.

The adverse wastage or usage variance shows the extra raw material cost incurred in producing the 50 teapots which cannot eventually be sold. The managers need to decide whether this was caused by the rush to increase output to meet the higher level of demand and whether it is better to return to a more orderly rate of production. Alternatively, it may indicate that the forecast rate of wastage is too low and that this higher level will continue even if production levels reduce to previously forecast levels.

Labour variances

The differences in labour costs can also be broken down into those caused by variations in the efficiency of the labour force and changes in the price (or labour rate) paid for the hours worked. As for raw materials, there is an increase in the expected cost of labour due to the higher volume produced and this accounts for £1,200 of the difference (i.e. 300 extra teapots at 40 hours per 100 and £10 per hour). However, due to the rush order we know that some of the time worked was paid for at overtime rates, which are higher than those forecast in the original budget. This gives rise to a price or labour rate variance which is calculated by multiplying the actual hours involved (i.e. 150) by the difference in the labour rate per hour for each of these overtime hours (i.e. £15–£10), giving a total adverse labour rate variance of £750.

These two variances total £1,950 which seems to explain the full difference shown in Figure 12.3 but there are still other factors to be examined. We also know that the wastage level was higher than originally forecast because 550 teapots had to be produced to get 475 saleable ones, rather than the expected production level of 500. This incurred an excess labour cost for producing the extra 50 teapots of £200 if the work was done at standard efficiencies and at the standard rate per hour. However, if the labour force worked at the standard rate to produce the actual 550 teapots, they would have utilized 550 × 40/100 hours in total, or 220 hours. In fact only 200 hours were worked in total and so the labour force worked more efficiently than expected. This generated a favourable efficiency variance of (220 − 200) hours × £10 per hour, or £200. The favourable efficiency variance thus exactly balances the adverse wastage variance. This highlights how the financial control system must analyse the reasons for deviations from the plan, rather than just arithmetically balancing the numbers. The impact of these variances and the resulting action required in each case is very different and they should not simply be ignored just because they balance each other out.

The labour variances can therefore be summarized as shown in Figure 12.7 and the managers can review them to decide what action should be taken to improve the position where possible. One of the important adverse variances is that caused by the higher labour rate paid while working overtime. Unlike the adverse raw material price variance, this variance will not automatically occur in the future, unless management decide to continue working at this increased output level. Most of the increased output requirements are caused by the large special orders for which discount prices are quoted and hence managers need a specific analysis of the profitability of these lower priced orders before making any decision to continue at this level.

The restated unit cost shown in Figure 12.8 shows that the position is not in fact as good as may have been believed when the first order was accepted. With the increased raw material cost and overtime working, the lower priced sales make no contribution to profits and the extra effort actually generates a loss. This is without including the additional wastage rate which has been experienced, which would make the position more gloomy still. Even if a price increase could be obtained so as to pass on the raw material cost increase, the net contribution would not be attractive due to the penalty premium payable by working overtime.

If managers wish to continue working at the higher level of activity, they need to evaluate other alternatives and one of these is the proposed two-shift operation.

	£
Increased usage allowance, i.e. activity variance	(1,200)
Adverse labour rate variance	(750)
Favourable labour efficiency variance	200
Adverse wastage/usage variance	(200)
Net labour variance	(1,950)

Figure 12.7 *Summary of labour variances*

Discounted selling price		£9.0
Adjusted actual raw material cost 5 kg @ £60 per 100	− £3.0	
Labour cost assuming overtime working 40 hours @ £15 per 100	− £6.0	
Wastage allowance @ 5%	− £0.5	
		£9.5
Net contribution		£(0.5)

Figure 12.8 *Restated unit cost per teapot*

This does reduce the extra labour cost because of its guaranteed regular nature to employees, who can plan their working hours further in advance as a result. However, the extra labour rate per hour of £3 (£13–£10) still has a significant impact on the profitability of promotion price sales, as shown in Figure 12.9. It therefore does not look logical to implement this strategy unless managers are confident that the increased sales can be achieved without the need to reduce selling prices below £10. Preferably these selling prices should be increased to recover the raw material cost increases which have been suffered by the business.

The financial control system should, as far as possible, establish, investigate and financially evaluate causal relationships within the business, and it is probable that one has been revealed by this variance analysis exercise. The workforce has been working under time pressure to produce the higher level of output needed and this has resulted in two impacts: the labour efficiency has been improved but the

Discounted selling price		£9.00
Adjusted raw material cost	− £3.00	
Labour cost using two shifts 40 hours × £13 per 100	− £5.20	
Wastage allowance @ 5%	− £0.50	
Total direct cost		£8.70
Net contribution		£0.30

Figure 12.9 *Impact of two-shift option*

wastage rate has also increased due to this faster rate of working. If these two effects are compared together, as in Figure 12.10, it becomes clear that the cost of the greater wastage more than outweighs the benefits of the higher efficiency. Managers should therefore reconsider their strategy of trying to produce more quickly and it may, in fact, be worthwhile to consider whether the previously established 5 per cent wastage level could be reduced in a cost effective way by decreasing the speed of working marginally.

The other variances which were caused by the change in activity level seem to be painting conflicting pictures, with the sales revenue being favourable and the cost variances adverse. This is, of course, exactly what should be expected and presenting these results separately does not help managers understand the impact quickly and easily. If sales volumes increase and nothing else changes, the business should expect to see an increase in the contribution to profit at the planned contribution rate. Thus combining these individual variances would show more meaningful information to managers, and most companies would analyse the impact of the volume changes by calculating a contribution variance as shown in Figure 12.11.

This question of how to present the information is very important as if the receiving managers cannot easily understand what is provided, then it obviously is of no value as part of their decision-making process. Appropriate forms of presentation can also reduce the necessary lead time for providing financial reports, if comprehension is made instantaneous, and this can reduce the cost of operating

---

Favourable labour efficiency variance

$$\text{i.e.} \quad \left\{ \begin{array}{c} \text{Standard} \\ \text{hours} \\ \text{allowed} \end{array} - \begin{array}{c} \text{Actual} \\ \text{hours} \end{array} \right\} \times \begin{array}{c} \text{Standard} \\ \text{rate} \\ \text{per hour} \end{array}$$

$$(220 - 200) \times £10 \qquad\qquad = £200$$

Adverse wastage level

Raw material excess wastage	£(125)
Labour excess wastage	£(200)
Net impact	
	£(125)

Figure 12.10 *Off-setting labour efficiency and increased wastage*

Volume contribution variance

$$\text{i.e.} \quad \left\{ \begin{array}{c} \text{Actual} \\ \text{equivalent} \\ \text{volume*} \end{array} - \begin{array}{c} \text{Standard} \\ \text{volume} \end{array} \times \begin{array}{c} \text{Standard} \\ \text{contribution} \end{array} \right\}$$

$$(500 - 200) \times £3 \qquad\qquad = £900$$

This represents the net impact of the three volume variances calculated earlier:

Sales volume variance — favourable	£2,850	Figure 12.5
Raw material volume variance — adverse	£(750)	Figure 12.6
Labour volume variance — adverse	£(1,200)	Figure 12.7
	£900	

* The actual equivalent volume represents the units which should have been produced to achieve 475 saleable units.

Figure 12.11 *Contribution variance calculation*

the financial control system. The format should consequently be tailored to the type of information being supplied, but should also take into account the preferences of the managers involved. Behavioural research has clearly shown that people can absorb similar information much more readily if it is provided in the manner most suited to the individual, e.g. some people prefer visual formats such as graphs, pie charts and histograms to tables of numbers. Where numbers have to be included, the presentation can highlight the key figures and express the inter-relationships included by the way in which the tables are drawn up. Managers can also be greatly assisted by the inclusion of brief narrative explanations and by the provision of summary tables, such as shown as Figure 12.12 for our pottery example.

The right time

To be of value, all this analytical information must be provided to the decision-makers at the right time so that it can be included in their evaluation. This includes the question of assimilating the information as mentioned above but also depends

	£
Budgeted contribution level	600
Favourable expected contribution variance due to increased level of activity	900
	1,500
Adverse sales price variance	(300)
	1,200

Adverse price variances:		
Raw material cost increase	(275)	
Labour rate due to overtime working	(750)	
	(1,025)	

Adverse wastage variances:		
Raw material excess wastage	(125)	
Labour excess wastage	(200)	
	(325)	

Favourable labour efficiency variance	200	
		(125)
		(1,150)
Actual contribution		£ 50

Figure 12.12   *Overall summary of variances*

upon the frequency of the decision process. Giving a daily report on a long-term project which is only reviewed by managers every three months is a waste of effort. Similarly only providing a quarterly cash reconciliation for a branch of a bank because the overall bank only produces quarterly accounts can be disastrous. Cash must be balanced at least daily and the information must be provided accordingly. Not only must the information be provided daily but it must be available before staff leave at the end of the day if proper financial control is to be exercised. Finding out the following day that several million pounds is missing can be expensive, particularly as the staff member involved may also be missing!

Therefore reports must be timely but, as previously mentioned, increasing the speed of production increases the cost, and so delivery of reports must be geared to management review and action. Producing a daily report on a real time basis is only of value if it is monitored continuously and used as the basis of subsequent rapid decisions. A good example also comes from financial services and involves any modern dealing room environment, whether foreign exchange, money market instruments, commodities, stocks and shares etc., are being traded. Managers responsible for these areas need very fast information on the impact of the latest trades which have been carried out and on external market movements. This information forms the basis of their future moves to balance their trading position or to take advantage of opportunities in the market. If the financial control process is not capable of providing such up-to-date information the organization will, at best, miss opportunities to trade profitably and, at worst, go bust.

Thus these are two overall questions regarding this question of timing of information: how fast and how often should the information be supplied? It should by now be clear that the answer has to be individually tailored to the requirements of the decision-maker, and so the financial control system has to be capable of providing similar information in tailored formats at different times to the various managers in the organization. Fortunately the report generating software now available for computers makes this relatively straightforward, but many companies still generate too many standardized reports which have to be used by all mangers. One clear differentiation in speed of supply should be between 'need to know' and 'nice to know' information, because the decision can be delayed or worse if the essential information is not available in time. Many companies try to cover part of this problem by releasing summary reports very quickly and then following up later with the more detailed analysis.

This may be valuable but runs a risk that the subsequent detailed analysis may not agree with the 'rough and ready' quick summary, or may highlight relevant facts which would have changed the decision taken based on the first report supplied. Such businesses might invest their efforts more productively in producing the required level of detailed analysis more quickly if it is really important to the decision-maker. Many businesses still suffer from the accountant's generic penchant for detail and neatness, which results in incredibly detailed analyses and complicated reconciliations. These often actually make the reports less useful and certainly less easy to understand as a result. Most decision-makers prefer information which helps them to be 'approximately right' rather than waiting to get the detailed report which shows them how 'precisely wrong' their latest decision was, because the information was supplied too late.

However, management accountants must always remember, when operating financial control systems, that their role is to provide decision support information and they should not try to supplant the decision-makers and take over their role. The key is to give the right information at the right time to the right people.

Questions

1 Financial control systems rely on the integrity of the basic financial data. How can the errors within these data be kept to a minimum?

2 In order to be fully effective, financial control systems must provide the right managers with the right information at the right time. For at least one of the following managers discuss what this would mean in practice:

(a) A branch manager for a large supermarket chain
(b) A production shift manager in a confectionery company
(c) A research manager in a pharmaceutical company
(d) The superintendent responsible for a major oil refinery
(e) The administration manager in a large accountancy practice.

3 In our pottery example, the actual situation was changed once again. The cost of clay has now fallen to £40 per kg but wage rates have been increased so that the hourly labour cost is now £12. It has been possible to increase selling prices to £11 each. Recompute, using these numbers, the cost per teapot, and explain the variances from the original standard cost.

4 A new customer enquires about another special order, but this is for a teapot using a finer quality clay. The labour input is expected to be unchanged but this clay costs £75 per kg and each batch of 100 would use 6 kg of clay. The order is for 500 teapots but the pottery wants to set the selling price so that its profit is the same as it would be making the original design. Calculate the required selling price for the finer quality teapot.

5 How can variance analysis be kept as cost effective as possible?

Part Five

The Way Ahead

Evolution of the 'new management accounting'

Overview

Management accounting in many companies has failed to keep up with developments in other areas of management practice and business strategy and, in particular, with changes in information technology. The reducing cost of information technology has meant that companies have had a dramatic opportunity to revolutionize the way in which they plan and control their organizations. Unfortunately most have responded by simply doing the same things more quickly.

Also, management accounting techniques have not been developed by many companies in line with the recent rapid changes in strategic thrusts used by these companies which have highlighted a variety of different critical success factors. If these new critical success factors, such as time, are not appropriately incorporated into the management accounting system, the value of the regular management reports can be reduced dramatically. These changes in strategy must be closely integrated into the internal accounting control system because, if they are not, some very damaging strategic decisions may be taken without the business realizing the long-term implications.

Strategic mis-decisions can adversely affect the new marketing positioning of the business or the new financial control issues raised by flexible manufacturing systems. Management accounting systems have to respond to the new critical success factors which are relevant to these new strategies. This cannot normally be achieved by continuing to rely on analytical procedures which were appropriate forty or more years ago.

The development of these new accounting systems should be evolutionary not revolutionary, or the whole business may spin completely out of control. Companies should select relatively low risk, quick improvements so that early implementation builds confidence, not a sense of foreboding. However, many businesses need to start changing very quickly before their management accounting systems become completely irrelevant.

Introduction

Throughout this book we have highlighted criticisms and deficiencies in the traditional approaches to management accounting and have indicated some ways in which its contribution to the overall success of the business can be improved. In this chapter we attempt not only to bring together these issues but also to develop a more coherent structured approach to management accounting in the modern business environment.

It is argued by some business commentators e.g. Johnson and Kaplan[1] 1987 and, more importantly, senior line managers in some large organizations that management accounting is outdated and largely irrelevant to the needs of the modern manager. This extreme view still casts the management accountant in the role of 'scorekeeper' or 'bean-counter', but with the added criticism that even the historic score is provided too late to be of any relevance. While we do not agree with this view, it has to be acknowledged that in many companies the rate of change in other areas has outpaced the development of management accounting systems and left them woefully outdated and inadequate.

The nature of management has changed dramatically in response to an increasingly competitive environment, where the speed and scale of changes seem to be ever increasing. This places greater emphasis on the manager's ability to make decisions more frequently and more quickly. The impact of these decisions is also magnified by the intensity of competitive pressures so that any wrong decision, which is not rapidly corrected, can have disastrous implications for the whole business. This ability to make rapid, frequent and correct decisions hinges on the quality and timeliness of the supporting information which may still be supplied through a set of monthly management accounts which are only produced at the end of the following month. This changing role can be compared analogously to the alterations in the roles fulfilled by other major providers of information, e.g. the newspaper industry. The function which newspapers originally fulfilled was to report factual events in a timely way, i.e. the following day in the case of daily newspapers. Nowadays this historic factual reporting role is inadequate to sustain their profitable continued existence because there are other much faster methods of communication. Thus even in a simple area of scorekeeping, such as reporting the football results, newspapers are no longer a prime source of the base information because interested parties will already have received the scores from radio, television, ceefax, telephone enquiry data-bases, etc. The role of the newspaper consequently developed into providing an analysis of the results with, for example, a detailed match report and commentary, but even this is now seen as inadequate. Most newspapers now devote most of their efforts to providing predictive analyses, rather than historic explanations, and see this as a way of maintaining their position in the increasingly competitive media industry.

Similar changes in emphasis can be seen as being needed for management accounting and the major frustration of line managers is caused by the knowledge that technology advances have created the potential for these changes to take place. Thus a key place to start this analysis is with the opportunities created by the developments in information technology. These developments require changes

---

[1]Johnson, H T and Kaplan, R S (1987) *Relevance Lost: The Rise and Fall of Management Accounting*, HBS Press, Boston, Mass.

in other aspects of management accounting because information can now be processed much more quickly; but it is essential that usable information is produced, not fast useless data. Also there is a strong tendency in many companies to use information as a key element of their competitive strategy and this requires the information to be produced more quickly. However, if speed in operations is a critical strategic issue, the system of control should reflect this and this can be done by using throughput accounting.

Linking financial control systems to the critical success factors of the business is one way of highlighting the need to link management accounting systems to the business strategy being implemented. One increasingly common strategy is to look at larger markets, at the globalization of brands, and this has severe repercussions for management accounting. The trend towards concentrating on brands and customers as the major assets of the business can also demand changes in management accounting techniques, because the historic concentration on products rather than brands or customers will provide misleading information unless the system is modified.

Changes in other areas of the business also require modifications in the supporting information systems, and this can most easily be illustrated by the impact of flexible manufacturing systems. All of these significant issues can have even greater adverse implications if the new information is not supplied in a format which is appropriate to the user's needs and wishes. There is still a significant communication gap in many companies between what the decision-makers want to receive and what is supplied by management accountants. This is a challenge which can, and should, be taken up very rapidly if management accounting is to make the very positive contribution of which it is capable, and which is being achieved by the leading exponents of the new approach to management accounting.

Information technology

In Part Four many issues relating to providing management information were discussed and the significant impact of developments in computer power was considered. The key issue of this technology revolution is the failure of most companies to achieve the massive potential benefits caused by the resultant reducing costs and increasing capabilities of modern machines. In far too many cases, the computer is simply used as a very fast mechanistic processor of data, with the fundamental system of financial control being applied in the same way as in the past. In other words, the same things are being done only more quickly. Several years ago people were talking about the possibility of creating a paperless office with computers talking directly to other companies' computers, and all internal reports being made available on VDU screens. For most businesses the opposite has been the case; there has been an explosion in the generation of paper outputs from these increasingly powerful computer systems, with consequently adverse environmental consequences and a significantly missed opportunity for businesses.

At present, it is fair to say that the critical constraint on the value adding capabilities of information technology is management's ability to understand and utilize the full potential of the software and hardware at their disposal. Applications are lagging far behind the increasing scale of technological sophistication. In many cases, managers have not worked out how to use one system properly before it is declared obsolete and replaced by something even more powerful and even faster, the capabilities of which they obviously do ..ot and will not fully understand. A simplistic example of this can be taken from the very large banks which have invested massively in high technology systems over the past years. One large US based bank has publicly stated that it has invested over $1 billion per year in information technology in each of the past five years. During the same period its profitability and, perhaps more importantly, its share price have consistently declined. Of course, it is possible to argue that without the huge investment in new information and processing systems the situation would have been even worse. More validly, it can be argued that the faster processing and notionally better information which has been generated by this investment has not helped the organization either to avoid several major strategic mistakes or even to respond to these mistakes more quickly and hence minimize their impact. A major factor has been that much of the investment has been spent in speeding up the operational side of the business and the value added to the management information process, i.e. supporting major decision-making, has been regarded as of secondary importance.

Even in this operational area of activity, many companies have not yet reaped the major advantages which are available but which can only be achieved by some large 'step type' changes in the way the business is carried out. The accounts payable area of the organization is a classic example of this. The technology has made it perfectly possible for companies to operate now what is effectively a 'peopleless payables' system. Such a system involves the use of an integrated computer system which links together the physical goods receiving areas with the ordering or purchasing department through the use of master files containing information on the suppliers and all outstanding orders. A master file is set up containing all the necessary information on all suppliers, and this must include details of their bank accounts into which the eventual payments are to be made. Another master file has to be established which holds the latest price data for all goods, materials and services, which are to be supplied by each external vendor. There is then a transaction file which holds all the orders which have been raised on these suppliers and are awaiting execution or physical delivery.

When the goods are delivered, the physical receipt by the goods inward department enters the items into the company's stock system. The same entry instruction, which can ideally be made using a bar scanning system, can also be used to match the actual goods delivered against the outstanding order file. This clearly validates that, as long as only properly authorized orders are entered onto this outstanding order file, the delivery should be accepted but, more importantly, this physical acceptance can also be the trigger for initiating the payment cycle. Normally the supplier has to send in an invoice which includes all the goods just delivered but also values them using the agrees order price. This document has to be checked by the customer's staff against the physical delivery documentation and against the original order which was raised. Once all these documents have been matched, the invoice can be passed through so that the payment can be made to the supplier. The payment routine often involves further clerical input because the customer has to request that a cheque and remittance advice are printed but, before signing, these are normally married to the relevant invoices so that the cheque signatory can ensure that the payment is in order and relates to goods actually supplied to the company. All these various pieces of paper are, of course, re-sorted, filed and have to be retained for several years.

The alternative is to use the physical acceptance of previously ordered goods as the basis for payment, which is not unreasonable as this is also the legal position. Instead of requiring an invoice from the supplier, the actual goods are valued by reference to the master file containing the latest agreed prices from this supplier. The agreed payment terms are accessed by reference to the supplier master file and the appropriate value is held in a pending payments file until the due date. When due for payment, the correct sum of money is automatically transferred to the supplier's bank account, details of which are also held on the master computer file. If desired, although it should be unnecessary, a remittance advice can be printed automatically and posted to the supplier; a better method of notification is for the customer's computer to send a direct electronic message to the supplier's computer telling it to expect the money. Even this should be unnecessary because the supplier should have a matching system for accounts receivable, so that it should already be expecting this remittance on the due date for the goods supplied.

This is not a scenario from Aldous Huxleys *A Brave New World* as the technology to run and control such a system has been available for several years. Yet very few companies have even partially implemented such a breakthrough which can have immense clerical savings for both suppliers and customers. Some companies have, however, gone even further because they allow suppliers to debit directly their bank accounts on the due date for goods supplied under an approved order. This extra stage starts to highlight some of the reasons for the slow introduction of these types of systems in many companies. Allowing suppliers to take money from the company's bank account requires a degree of trust in the suppliers and in the financial controls which have been instituted in the integrated computerized accounting and ordering system. However, these issues are often less important than the other internal management questions which are raised by such an automated system.

A key element in such a peopleless payables practice is that the order price file must be kept fully up-to-date or suppliers will be unhappy and complain if they are paid too little due to using the wrong prices; if they are paid too much, they will not be unhappy, but they may forget to tell the company about the overpayment! This should not be a problem if the buying department is given the responsibility for maintaining this updated price file and knows that any errors may cost the company money. Amazingly in several companies which have tried to implement this type of system, there have been major objections from the financial managers who have argued that it is their responsibility to input changes to the order price file because it is a prime accounting record and should, therefore, be under their control. The fact that their role would consist only of receiving information from the buyers when a price changes and then literally making the amendment does not seem to alter the view that they should have control. What is logical is that if financial managers do not have *control* over the input, they should not be held *responsible* for any errors caused by the file not being correctly updated. This responsibility must be shouldered by the buying department but in companies using the system this has not created any lasting problems.

Another argument put forward against the viability of such a system is that there will be no clerical support staff to investigate the inevitable differences and queries which will still arise. This is incorrect on two counts. First, most of the queries in accounts payables systems are caused by clerical errors, such as input transcription mistakes. By eliminating all the duplicated entries and validating each entry which is made, particularly to the master file data, this level of error and hence query will decrease significantly. Second, the role of the accounts payable clerical staff with regard to queries and differences has been misunderstood. If orders and invoices do not agree, the accounts payable staff members cannot resolve the queries, they can only refer them to the appropriate person in the buying department or goods inward department, who must then check the base data. Thus accounts payable staff are only acting as coordinators for resolving disputes, because they do not have the information to decide which party to the dispute is correct. This role normally serves mainly to delay the process and divert resources away from running the business; it, often, also means that all payments on the accounts are delayed while the query is resolved. The peopleless payable system forces the responsible departments in each business to communicate directly in order to resolve the query but payment for any items not in dispute should proceed normally, thus minimizing the impact on good supplier-customer relations.

This last point raises the most contentious area of such a system for many companies. Many of the cost reductions generated by such automation of the accounts payable functions are created by the removal of the need to trigger payment after matching accounting documents. However, setting up a procedure which will automatically pay suppliers when the payment falls due removes any discretion on the part of the customer to delay payment due to problems in processing these same accounting documents. The days of claiming that 'the cheque is in the post', or that 'we've lost your invoice, can you send us a copy?' in order to hang on to the suppliers' money for a few more days will be over. Without debating the immorality involved or the unethical nature of such behaviour, it should be obvious that it inevitably builds up an adversarial relationship which is normally counter-productive in the long run. It also encourages the supplier to build its financing costs into its selling prices and thus forces up costs over time, or it may make the supplier reduce its quality or become less reliable in terms of delivery. Trying to implement a 'just-in-time' inventory system, under which suppliers are required to deliver within 4 or 6 hours of receiving an order, may be difficult if the same supplier has to wait 60 or 90 days for payment for the goods delivered at such short notice.

The promise of guaranteed regular payments in line with agreed trading terms, when allied with significant potential clerical and administrative savings to the supplier, should enable the buying department to negotiate a very attractive, mutually beneficial supply agreement. Such an agreement is driven by a concept of partnership rather than one of trying to win at the supplier's expense. Consequently, for many businesses, there has to be a substantial change in business strategy and corporate culture before such a fundamental change in accounting systems could be successfully implemented.

This example further highlights the strategic problems which can be created if management accounting systems focus attention on the wrong issues, as was mentioned in Chapter 5 in the discussion on economic order quantity techniques The EOQ technique concentrated management attention on managing inventory levels rather than eliminating this problem by doing away with inventories. Similarly many companies, which are now at long last implementing just-in-time inventory management programmes, are finding this strategy is unsuccessful because it has not been properly implemented throughout all the affected areas of the business, particularly including the accounts payable area.

In this discussion we have dealt with the issues involved with operating such a system for supplies of goods, i.e. items requiring physical delivery, but there is no reason why it cannot be applied to accounting for the purchase of services. When the order is raised, the accounting system needs to be provided with an expected date by which the service should have been carried out and the name of the responsible manager who has been given the authority to trigger the payment process. At the appropriate time, the computerized system can send this manager a message requesting confirmation that the authorized services have been provided and, if this is received, the payment will once again be made automatically on the terms specified on the supplier's master file. Alternatively, the manager using the outside service can be made responsible for informing the accounts payable system that the work has now been carried out and that payment is in order. If this manager fails to provide this information the supplier will chase the company for payment and the first point of contact should logically be with the manager for whom the work was done. Introducing an accounts payable department as an intermediary only causes delays since, as before, an accounts payable employee can only refer the supplier's query to the manager involved, to seek authority to make the payment requested by the supplier.

It is very interesting that even those few leading companies which are implementing this type of advanced management accounting are concentrating on their physical purchases. Several seem to be arguing that the purchase of services is somehow more nebulous and hence the same tight system of automated financial controls cannot be implemented. As long as the disciplines regarding the raising of orders at the point of financially committing the business are rigorously applied in all areas and clear authority levels are established covering both commitment and subsequent authorization for payment, there should be no difference in the effective financial control process for these different types of purchases. In fact, this kind of analysis should highlight yet again that companies can only exercise true financial control over expenditure at the point of commitment. Thus the critical area on which the business should concentrate is on the raising of orders as this commits the organization to pay for any activities carried out in accordance with that order. In many organizations it is still much easier to raise such an order than it is to get approval for payment of the subsequently submitted supplier's invoice or statement. This kind of retrospective financial control is ineffective and its only value is in indicating the weaknesses in the company's existing authorization process.

This contrasting example of much slower implementation of the newer systems in the area of services also shows another opportunity to improve the effectiveness of the contribution of management accounting because it is common that financial techniques are less well applied in the services area of business. The classic illustration of this is the application of standard costs, the usefulness of which were demonstrated in Chapter 12. Standard costs are very widely applied in the production and engineering areas of businesses but very few companies have adopted the technique for a wider role covering all costs which demonstrate a predictable input to output relationship. An easy example is the control over salesforce costs which was mentioned earlier but the same can be achieved for other types of marketing expenditures, including television advertising. The technique can even be applied in the clerical area where the wide range of repetitive functions lend themselves readily to control via the use of standard costs and variance analysis. Thus in the sales invoicing area it should be possible to break-down the tasks into discrete areas so that a standard time allowance could be computed. This would enable the relative efficiency of the operation to be analysed more objectively but, more importantly, the changes in resources required as a result of any forecast changes in the level of sales activities could be predicted and evaluated more accurately. Such an analysis should result in the indirect consequences of managerial decisions being included in the financial analysis prior to implementing the decision. For example a decision to attempt to double sales volumes would have very different impacts on the resources needed in the sales invoicing department depending on whether the plan was to double the number of customers or to double the average order size to existing customers.

If management accounting techniques were applied more uniformly across the whole of the business there is little doubt that the quality of business decisions would be improved. This would also be achieved if management accounting systems concentrated more clearly on the critical success factors for the existing business strategy, rather than providing a uniform coverage of all financial items as if the management accountants were acting as some sort of disinterested, objective, external arbitrator.

Use of time as a competitive variable

Some companies now regard time as a key success factor and their business strategy puts great emphasis on being quicker than their competitors. This can take several forms ranging from shortening the operational cycle of the business through to trying to take business decisions faster than competitors, which demands better, quicker financial information.

If the key element in the strategy is saving time in the operational, selling and distribution chain, there are a number of issues for the way in which management accounting can add value to their strategy. Time should be regarded as a key limiting factor in the financial analysis process and the duration of each area of operations should be measured. Clearly any strategic initiative which reduces the elapsed time for any particular function should be financially evaluated against this critical success factor. This requires the business to attempt to put a value on the time saved so that the financial justification can be properly carried out. Valuing something nebulous may appear difficult but it is important to attempt to do this, as it may challenge the basic tenet of the corporate strategy. The strategy is driven by the desire to deliver the goods or services faster than the competition because, presumably, it is believed that this will create a sustainable competitive advantage for the business. This competitive advantage should itself result in a higher financial return over time which justifies the incremental investment needed to achieve a faster delivery time. Thus it should be possible to evaluate the financial benefit of this improved service to customers and the evaluation may indicate that there is a critical time gap which has to be achieved before any value is created.

An obvious example of this is in the area of fresh produce, say fruit and vegetables. If a particular company can get its produce to its end customer more quickly, and hence in better condition, there should be an improved financial return. This may take the form of selling the produce at a higher price due to its better quality or the non-availability of competitive products; alternatively, the company could sell at the normal market price but significantly increase its market share because of the timing advantage. These companies will therefore put a high priority on decreasing the time lag between harvesting the fruit and vegetables and delivering them to the end customer (for them, this may mean the retailer or the food processing company). However, the timing advantage must be of a significant size and be regularly achievable to have any financial value; arguing that today our company's apples are five minutes fresher than our competitors' is unlikely to be perceived by the customer as a good reason for paying a premium price for the product. Thus the financial value may need to be expressed in chunks of time, but even these blocks may not have the same value. In many cases there is a competitive advantage in being faster but there is a finite limit to the value created and hence the law of diminishing returns sets in quite quickly. There may be potential to obtain a premium price for fresh produce if the delay between harvesting and delivery to the retailer's store is reduced from five days to three days, by for example eliminating the wholesale marketing process and delivering direct from the grower to the retailer on a regional basis. However, the heavy incremental investment needed to reduce this timescale by a further one or two days may generate very little additional premium price advantage, because the retailer cannot recover any extra cost from the consumer for offering 'even fresher' produce. When the competition has caught up with this existing position, it may once again become financially attractive to invest in improving the relative position so as to maintain or restore the previous competitive advantage.

This indicates that, yet again, the analysis needs to be done on a relative basis, i.e. being fast is not the issue, it is a matter of being significantly faster. This analysis must also be regularly updated so as to ensure that the relative advantage is being maintained. What constitutes significant depends totally on the specific competitive environment. In the extremely competitive and time critical world of financial services, such as foreign exchange trading, a significant advantage can be obtained from having information available to the dealers literally seconds faster than the competition; hence the previously mentioned vast investments in operationally biased computer systems. Unfortunately, competitors tend to catch up very quickly and so the technology race continues increasingly with the major winners appearing to be the suppliers of this sophisticated hardware and software.

Another way of using the timing of information as a competitive strategy can be to identify a previously missed critical success factor and concentrate on managing this area of the business without adversely impacting the operational areas of the organization. This can be regarded as a key element in the success of Martin Sorrell who has contributed significantly to a change in the financial control procedures operated within advertising agencies. Originally as financial director of Saatchi and Saatchi plc in the early 1980s and subsequently as Chief Executive Officer of WPP Group plc, he has instituted very tight financial controls, which include centralized management of cash balances and outstanding receivables and payables. Not only does this free the senior management of the operating agencies to concentrate on what they should be good at, namely solving the creative marketing problems of their clients, but it places enhanced and continuous emphasis on a critical financial area of the business which, in many cases, had previously been largely ignored. Advertising agencies have very substantial cash flows passing through their bank accounts because they normally pay the media companies, e.g. television stations, for the advertising booked for their clients and are themselves paid by the clients. Their operating profitability is largely based on their commission, which is deducted from the advertising billings placed, but the management of the timing of these relative cash flows is also a critical success factor. If monies have to be paid out to the television companies before they have been received from the client, the agencies can face liquidity pressures and the consequent financing costs can severely impair their profitability levels. When the position can be reversed, even for a few days, the opportunity to generate an improved return and ease the overall financing pressures can be substantial. Hence a major advantage can be created by instituting a fast, comprehensive and accurate financial information system which is monitored constantly and professionally.

This concentration on time as a critical success factor has been used in a new way of spreading costs across the organization, which can serve to concentrate line managers' attention on the time taken to carry out their financial responsibilities. If reducing time is seen as a key strategic objective, there is an argument for using the time spent by the products in each department as a basis for apportioning indirect costs to the operational areas of the business. Thus instead of using sales revenues, product volumes or some other arbitrary method of apportionment, department managers find themselves charged for the total elapsed time spent by products within their departments. An increase in their throughput levels consequently reduces the per unit charge made to their areas of responsibility; the concept is, not surprisingly, known as 'throughput accounting'. It does not remove the fundamental reservations regarding the relevance of apportioned costs to financial decisions which have been expressed throughout the book, but it has the significant benefits of focusing the managers on an area which may well be critical to the business strategy of their company. As stated at the beginning of the section, it represents an attempt to regard time as the limiting factor for the business and, as discussed in Chapter 4, the business should always maximize the contribution per unit of limiting factor.

Link of management accounting to business strategy

This innovative idea illustrates one way in which management accounting techniques can be adapted and developed to fit into modern business strategies. As discussed in Chapter 10, most management accounting systems are not well designed to cope with the 'one-off' type of strategic decision which faces all businesses. Even more fundamentally, many such systems do not even have clear linkages to the strategic objectives of the business so that the regular management reporting does not indicate whether or not the business is progressing satisfactorily towards its objectives. In many companies, it is quite possible for all the separate subdivisions to have achieved their individual targets but for the overall organization to fall well short of the stated strategic objectives, due to the lack of proper integration of the plan within the business. This gap is not only caused by the difference between economic and managerial performance indicators, which was discussed in Chapter 11 and under which managers cannot be held responsible for issues over which they have no control, but which can, nevertheless, adversely affect the economic performance of the overall business. A more significant reason can be changing external relationships which have not been reflected adequately in the financial monitoring process so that the required modifications to the business objectives and/or the strategy have not been made.

A common reason for this can be changes in the balance of the value chain, which shows where the value is added in the total business process. Thus the value chain includes suppliers, channels of distribution and the end user of the goods or service, plus the internal operations of the specific business. Strategic moves by any element of this value chain can significantly alter the position of the company and yet most traditional management accounting systems, with their predominantly internal focus, would not pick up and reflect these changes. Consequently, the company may miss the opportunity to alter its strategy sufficiently quickly to affect the adverse impact or to take full advantage of the opportunity created, or it may continue to implement its original strategy, which is now either unattainable or substantially sub-optimal. Unless the internal departmental and functional objectives are carefully established to reflect the original strategy, there may be no specific reason for any area of the business to alter its mode of operations even if the strategy is subsequently modified.

The changes that have happened in UK retailing over the last few years provide a good illustration of such a change in the value chain. Grocery product manufacturers have experienced substantial changes in their negotiating power with some of their direct customers, i.e. the large supermarket chains, due to the consolidation and consequent concentration which has taken place at the top end of this industry over this period. For many companies this has led to a decline in their profit margins, which has been matched by an increase in the profitability of the retailers. The key success factors which are required to compete successfully in this new competitive environment have altered dramatically and yet many of these suppliers are still using virtually the same type of management accounting information which they were producing several years ago.

The historic emphasis on product costs from a manufacturing viewpoint may still be important if the company is producing a commodity style product but, even then, there are other issues which need to be highlighted by the accounting system. Many retailers now place great emphasis on the ability of their suppliers to meet stringent targets regarding delivery time-scales. This enables the retailers to minimize their stock levels and still avoid running out of the product, which would result in lost sales, lower contributions and disaffected customers. To cope with these demands, the manufacturer needs a sophisticated logistics system to plan its distribution and production scheduling requirements and the relative associated costs must be carefully evaluated. Supermarket retailers also now operate comprehensive financial information systems which provide their managers with very rapid details of the rate of sale of all products, normally directly linked to the electronic bar scanning systems at the check-out tills. This information is often allied to a product profitability system which generates a comparative analysis of the net contribution produced by all products bought from competing suppliers. Shelf space allocations are decided on the basis of this relative contribution per cubic metre of space occupied, and suppliers can suddenly find that their products have a reduced allocation with a consequent sharp reduction in sales levels. The supplier needs to be able to justify financially why it should be given an increased or maintained allocation by preparing its own version of this type of direct product profitability analysis for its major customers. The management accounting system needs to be developed to generate this information, where the external marketing advantage is the key element rather than the internal focus on manufacturing costing. Interestingly much of the initial development work on this concept of direct product profitability analysis was done by a major consumer goods manufacturer, Procter and Gamble, who used it as a major element in their marketing strategy with key retailers to justify or improve the space allocations and methods of distribution for their product range.

It is also interesting that at least part of the declining margin problem facing these manufacturers has been relatively self-inflicted due to the poor design of their financial control systems. Most manufacturing companies used to, and still do, emphasize accounting ROI as their major tool of assessing financial performance. As explained in Chapter 2 and 7, ROI is a ratio of some measure of profit divided by some measure of investment.

If ROI is used as the principal measure of both economic and managerial performance for the business, it is not surprising that line managers will place considerable emphasis on improving their perceived performance by trying to improve the value of the measure. This can, in a manufacturing business, often be done by ensuring that there is no unutilized or 'spare' capacity. It is normally possible to increase the probability of completely filling this existing productive capacity by reducing effective selling prices and, in the short term, this may be economically justified by ignoring fixed and committed costs when carrying out the financial evaluation. However, even using this short-term concept of contribution or 'marginal' pricing can present severe problems if they are applied to existing products, such as branded goods or services. It may be difficult to reduce the selling price of only incremental volumes of the existing products as it may be impossible to differentiate these lower priced products or to segment the market sufficiently clearly so as to attract specific new customers for these incremental sales.

However, many grocery manufacturers did manage to find a way of selling incremental volumes without appearing to affect adversely the existing sales levels of their higher priced branded products. The differentiation was achieved by supplying a similar product to these newly concentrated retailer groups, but which was sold under the retailer's name rather than the brand name of the manufacturing company. These private 'own' labels or 'retailer brands' were very successful as they tended to be sold to the end consumer at prices significantly below those charged for the original branded product. In the short term the strategy also achieved its objective of improving the accounting ROI by utilizing productive capacity and increasing the total contribution achieved by the business. Unfortunately, in many cases, the impact in the longer term has been less beneficial as the 'retailer brands' have developed a strong market position which has reduced the marketing strength, and hence financial value, of the existing manufacturers' brands.

By concentrating on a short-term accounting measure which was based only on tangible assets, managers did not necessarily consider the financial impact of their profit enhancing decision on the critically important long-term, but intangible, asset known as the brand. If the impact on the brand value had been considered, many companies may have made very different decisions when offered the opportunity to manufacture other 'non-competing' products which would improve short-term profitability by generating better utilization of fixed assets and committed costs. As has been argued throughout the book, the longer-term impact of apparently short-term decisions must always be properly considered in financial evaluations. If this had been done, the potential adverse long-term sales impact on branded products should have been highlighted and incorporated in the future cash flow forecasts used in the financial evaluation as to whether to produce the private label products.

Brands versus products

It is also very interesting that several major brand-led companies (such as Nestlé, Kelloggs and Heinz) have spent considerable sums of money on advertising that they do not produce private label products and that all their output is sold under their own branded formats. These companies have very clearly selected a business strategy which emphasizes the brand over the product and they should, consequently, have adjusted their management accounting systems to reflect this emphasis.

Historically, management accounting systems have tended to be internally orientated and to be based around manufacturing technologies and processes, rather than reflecting the externally based market environment in which these products are sold. Thus one marketing brand may cover a number of production technologies such as where related products are sold in different packaging formats or where generic branding is used to cover a wide product range (e.g. Heinz baby foods). It is vitally important that senior managers receive financial information which is organized to reflect this strategic emphasis on brands rather than on the other more tangible assets employed in the business. Unfortunately, even in many of the companies which do attempt to produce this essential brand based financial information, these specific reports are created by a restatement of the existing fundamental financial analysis which is based around products and not brands. Consequently, the supposedly tailored reports will already contain a considerable number of apportioned costs which are now being reapportioned on a different basis. If meaningful, useful financial information on brands is to be supplied, the management accounting information system must be redesigned so that the basic sales and cost data are recorded by brand wherever possible. This would enable much more accurate financial analysis to be carried out with regard to a potentially key asset of the business.

There is potentially another significant impact caused by a strategic change which emphasizes brands rather than products. Earlier in the book we discussed the relevance of the product life-cycle and its significance in terms of using the specifically appropriate financial control measure for each stage of the product's life. It is inevitable that any particular product will eventually cease growing and mature before finally declining and dying; thus it is important that the business identifies these stages and financially monitors and controls the product accordingly. However, it is not inevitable that a well-managed brand will wither and die, because it is possible to transfer the attributes of the brand to new products which are still in the embryonic or growth phases of their life-cycles. This transfer process is particularly visible where the brand name and the company name are the same, so that new products which are launched under the corporate 'umbrella' brand can immediately be identified by existing customers as sharing in certain values and attributes (e.g. value and price relationships). In the electrical field Sony has transferred its brand name from the now dead product of large spool tape recorders through televisions, video recorders, compact disc players, cam-corders to digital audio tape, without apparently confusing its customers or damaging its image even though many of its early products are now obsolete. Automobile companies such as Porsche, BMW, and Mercedes-Benz also transfer their brand names to new models which directly replace the existing but now outdated design. While there are clear potential benefits of this continued brand identity, there is also a risk that the total brand franchise of the business could be severely damaged by direct, close association with even one bad new product, which did not live up to customer expectations.

In many companies these strategic issues are debated intensely but without any analytical input from their financial manager, which, once again, is a sad condemnation of the current role of management accounting. Indeed, in some companies the role of financial accounting in this area has overtaken that of management accounting, because the values of some of these major brands have been incorporated in the published balance sheets of the company. Most examples include only those brands which have been acquired in the recent past but, as noted in Chapter 2, Ranks Hovis MacDougall plc have also capitalized, on their balance sheet, financial values for internally developed brands. The logical development from such a process is to use changes in these brand values as a way of evaluating the managerial performance of the relevant marketing managers as it would focus their attention on the longer-term impact of their decisions, rather than forcing them to concentrate almost exclusively on the short-term profit impact of most marketing decisions. As yet no companies have fully implemented such a financial control system.

However, several of these companies have explicitly recognized the major life-cycle difference between products and brands because, in their published financial statements, they are making no allowance for amortization of the brand values incorporated in their balance sheets. The stated rationale for such action is that a well-maintained brand does not decrease in value and thus there is no need to provide for amortization of the brand. However, this adds in the complication of defining 'well-maintained' and how should a change in value be calculated. If companies are prepared, in their prudently based financial accounts, to include brand values and to justify not reducing them, surely such companies can calculate the level of maintenance type marketing expenditure which is required each year to keep the 'well-maintained' brand at its previous level of performance. This acceptable level of performance could, itself, be clearly defined in terms of market share, customer attitude surveys, etc., so that it also became capable of regular monitoring and evaluation. Only then can the internal financial managers be seen as contributing positively to some of the most strategically significant decisions being taken by marketing led businesses.

Globalization of brands and markets

Even within these marketing led businesses, there are significantly different strategies being developed and implemented. In some industries, there are now global markets and most of the major competitors believe that, in order to be successful, a company has to possess global brands to compete in these global markets. This is true for the drinks industry in general where at the soft-drinks end Coca-Cola and Pepsi-Cola compete head to head globally. It is also becoming true in brewing through a series of mega-acquisitions and mergers during the 1980s which established relatively new companies like Elders IXL (with its Fosters lager brand) as a potential global player. On the wines and spirits side of the industry it is also true with a few very large companies dominating the branded sector. This has been achieved by a series of major acquisitions, particularly of brands where the values placed on the goodwill involved were enormous. For example, in 1987 when Grand Metropolitan plc bought Heublein from RJR Nabisco Inc, they were, to all intents and purposes, acquiring Smirnoff. The total price of $1.2 billion involved approximately $400 million of tangible net assets, leaving $800 million (or two-thirds of the total) as the price paid for the brand and its associated goodwill.

Very clearly the role of management accounting in supporting such momentous decisions, and then in evaluating the post-acquisition development of the new business, must include consideration of the brand values involved and the relevance of the subsequent marketing strategy proposed to develop the asset acquired. Also the global nature of these strategies and, in particular, the marketing decisions involved (e.g. sponsorship of a global sporting event such as The Olympics) mean that the normal management accounting techniques of apportioning costs and preparing local product and market reports are completely irrelevant. A whole new way of providing the supporting financial information must be developed and yet most companies have not yet started to tackle this problem.

New manufacturing systems

These rapid and extreme strategic changes do not affect only the marketing area of a business and, for many companies, recent revolutions in manufacturing practices have, once again, dramatically outstripped the development of their associated financial control systems. Many quite sophisticated businesses are still using production costing systems which concentrate on labour as the key controllable variable cost and calculate standard costs based on economic production runs of thousands of units at a time. By applying this type of costing system, businesses have been able, for the last forty or so years, to produce detailed regular management accounts which analyse the relative performance of all the various production areas. For most of this period, this management information has been relevant and useful and has helped managers to pinpoint problems quickly so as to reallocate labour resources to more productive areas of the business.

However, for many businesses today, skilled production labour is in reality a fixed cost which cannot be easily varied due to changes in output requirements. These changes in scheduling are becoming ever more frequent with the mutual trends towards 'just-in-time' inventory levels and individually tailored end products for increasingly segmented markets. Fortunately, the relative proportion of total manufactured costs which is represented by labour is declining substantially, due to the increasing use of sophisticated automation techniques which can cope with the current need for continually changing products.

Flexible manufacturing systems (FMS) enable companies to tailor their output to the needs of the market without dramatic decreases in operating efficiencies. In most cases this is achieved by computer controlled tool changes and process variations, which are transmitted to a whole array of interlinked machines (or robots) by a centralized controller. Not surprisingly these sophisticated engineering installations tend to be very expensive and can only be justified if the business really needs the flexibility which is incorporated into the system. Thus an automobile engine plant which is required to produce 500,000 of the same 1.6 litre OHC engine per year does not need this kind of automated flexibility. The management accounting system has to be capable of financially evaluating the benefits of building in added flexibility to any production facility relative to the incremental cost incurred for this flexibility.

Even more importantly, once installed, the critical success factor for an FMS layout is completely different to a traditional, more labour intensive, single product process production line. The major cost is now represented by the increased investment in plant and facilities and these costs cannot be regarded as variable, indeed they are committed, sunk costs. This means that if the expensive, automated plant is turned off, the business saves very little and generates no financial return on the massive fixed asset investment. Hence there is inevitable pressure to keep these automated plants working – the phrase 'lights out production' actually means what it says!

Earlier in this chapter, the problem caused by this over-emphasis on tangible assets was discussed in the context of reducing the value of brand assets. Many companies have implemented this type of FMS production process because of increasingly competitive markets which are demanding an ever more differentiated product but at a reduced price. The vital importance of the role of management accounting in helping to achieve the right balance among these conflicting pressures cannot be over-emphasized. However, the techniques of several decades ago may not be adequate to today's problems.

Communication gaps

We consider these challenges discussed above to be exciting and intellectually stimulating but our new breed of management accountants must remember not to overstep their role as decision supporters providing the right information to the right people at the right time. Identifying the appropriate manager and understanding the time pressure involved in the particular decision are difficult enough, but many management accounting systems still manage to make the task even harder by producing the report in a format which is either completely unintelligible to the recipient or forces the decision-makers to take time out to reformat or reprocess the relevant data. Far too many management information systems are still designed by accountants for accountants, i.e. they produce reports in the way accountants like to see them which may not be appropriate for the receiving decision-maker. Now, this problem should be relatively easy to solve as a start towards the 'new management accounting'.

Questions

1   Management accounting systems need to be focused on the critical success factors of the business, and these tend to change over time. How can the accounting system be designed to cope with this problem?

2   If the management accounting system is to contribute to the overall business strategy, it must take account of the external environment. What type of factors should be included in such an externally focused analysis?

3   The implementation of flexible manufacturing systems has meant that traditional product-based costing systems are no longer relevant to these companies. How can accounting systems be changed to cope with the needs of FMS?

4   'Management accountants should fulfil a key role as part of the management team of any business and should be actively involved in all financially based decisions, including strategic decisions.' Discuss.

Recommended further reading

Part Two   Analysis

Chapter 2

Reid W P and Myddelton D R (1988) *Meaning of Company Accounts*, Gower

Chapters 3–5

Anthony R N and Dearden J (1980) *Management Control Systems: Texts and Cases*, Irwin
Arnold J and Hope A (1983) *Accounting for Management Decisions*, Prentice-Hall
Horngren C T and Foster G (1987) *Cost Accounting: A Managerial Emphasis*, Prentice-Hall
Sizer J (ed) (1980) *Reading in Management Accounting*, Penguin

Readers may also wish to read the following specific chapters:
Chapters 17 and 18 of Davy C (1986 *Management and Cost Accounting*, Van Nostrand Rheinhold
Chapters 13-16 and 23 of Batty J (1978) *Advanced Cost Accountancy*, Macdonald & Evans

Part Three   Planning

Chapter 6

Anthony R N and Dearden J (1980) *Management Control Systems: Texts and Cases*, Irwin
Horngren C T and Foster G (1987) *Cost Accounting: A Managerial Emphasis* Prentice-Hall
Sizer J (ed) (1980) *Readings in Management Accounting*, Penguin

Also recommended:
Chapter 7 of Ezzamel M and Hart H (1987) *Advanced Management Accounting*, Cassell

Chapters 7–8

Franks J R and Broyles J E (1979) *Modern Managerial Finance*, J Wiley
Brealey R and Myers S (1984) *Principles of Corporate Finance*, McGraw-Hill

Chapter 9

Anthony R N and Dearden J (1980) *Management Control Systems: Texts and Cases*, Irwin
Rahman M and Halladay M (1988) *Accounting Information Systems: Principles, Applications and Future Directions*, Prentice-Hall

Also recommended:
Chapter 9 of Sizer J (1989) *An Insight into Management Accounting*, Penguin

Chapter 10

Ward K (1989) *Financial Aspects of Marketing*, Butterworth-Heinemann

Part Four Control

Chapters 11–12

Horngren C T (1974) *Accounting for Management Control*, Prentice-Hall

Part Five The Way Ahead

Chapter 13

Johnson H T and Kaplan R S (1987) *Relevance Lost: The Rise and Fall of Management Accounting*, HBS Press

Index